William Goodman
Civil War Horsesoldier

Larry Buege

Gastropod Publishing
Marquette, Michigaan

Other books by Larry Buege

Bear Creek (Humorous)
Miracle In Cade County (Mystery/Love Story)
Cold Turkey (Political Satire)
Super Mensa (Techno-Thriller)
Growing Up In Sparta and Other Adventures

Chogan and the Gray Wolf (Native American)
Chogan and the White Feather (Native American)
Chogan and the Sioux Warrior (Native American)
Chogan and the Vision Quest (Native American)

Published by Gastropod Publishing, Marquette, Michigan
Copyright © 2024 by Larry Buege

Library of Congress Control Number: 2016919905
ISBN: 979-8-9872588-3-5

DEDICATION

To the men and women who went off to war and never returned. May their souls rest in peace.

ACKNOWLEDGMENTS

It is often postulated that steeling ideas from one person is plagiarism, but steeling from many is research. With no firsthand knowledge of the Civil War, I have relied on individuals who survived the conflict and, with pen in hand, documented their experiences for the edification of future generations. The number of people from whom I have "borrowed" information is too extensive to give them proper recognition. There are some individuals whose works were indispensable in the writing of this historical novel.

Personal Recollections of a Cavalryman by James Kidd (1840–1913) written over a twenty-year span following the war provides a detailed account of life in the saddle. Although an officer with the 6th Michigan Cavalry, his unit fought beside Goodman's 5th Michigan Cavalry Regiment. The Michigan 5th was included in many of Kidd's detailed battle descriptions.

No one provides a more detailed account of Belle Isle and Andersonville POW camps than John Ransom does in his *Andersonville Diary*. Ransom penned almost daily entries into journals, which spanned several volumes by the time of his liberation. These historic notes would have been lost if it were not for an unknown Minnesota Indian nicknamed Battese. Battese took a liking to Ransom and nursed him to health on more than one occasion using wild herbs and Indian folk medicine. Ransom credits Battese for his surviving imprisonment. There is no known Civil War historical record of a Minnesota Indian named Battese. He is one of many Civil War heroes who will never receive proper recognition.

Other works worthy of reading include: *Oh Has Thou Forgotten* by Richard Hamilton; *Under Custer's Command* by James Henry Avery; *One Continuous Fight* by Eric J. Wittenberg; *Andersonville—A Story of Rebel Military Prisons* by John McElroy.

CHAPTER ONE

"This one's mine." George Thompson leveled his muzzle loader, fixing his aim on the large tom strutting across the open field. I had clear-cut the timber the previous fall, and knee-high grass now carpeted the field. It was perfect cover for the flock of turkeys. If not for their heads protruding above the green foliage, they would have been invisible.

"Wait until he gets closer," I suggested—not that George ever listened to my advice.

The tom turkey attracting George's attention was less than twenty yards away. Still, it remained a difficult shot. Moving targets always were.

"Shoot in front of the turkey. The turkey will walk into your musket ball." The large turkey lying at my side would feed my small family. It was George's turn to bag a turkey.

Black smoke belched from Thompson's gun as flint ignited gunpowder. Grass and dirt exploded two feet behind the turkey, hardly close enough to ruffle its tail feathers. The ball from Thompson's gun inflicted little more than insult, but it was enough to encourage the turkey to take off running. The turkey would be in the next county before Thompson reloaded his musket. I lowered the barrel of my gun, aiming ten feet in front of the running turkey, and pulled the trigger. The turkey jumped into the air and then flopped to the ground.

"Damn!" I said. "I missed him by a mile, but your shot sure hit a vital spot. He didn't run far."

"William Goodman, does Mary know you swear like that?"

"Damn doesn't qualify as swearing when used appropriately. I only use such language when I miss a fat turkey like that," I replied. "My shot hit three feet behind him."

We walked over to the turkey. It was obviously dead by the time we arrived, a single lead ball lodged in its breast. "I was right," I said. "You hit a vital organ." I pointed to the hole in the bird's breast.

"Will, you make a better marksman than you do a liar. Someday I'll have to teach you the finer points of lying. Your ball made that hole—and on a turkey at full run. The Union Army needs sharpshooters with your skill."

"The Army has men far better with a long gun than I am," I replied.

"Will, this war isn't going well. Lincoln needs men like us. It's time we defended our country...stand for what we believe. The Governor's recruiting men for a new cavalry regiment. If they have a slot available, I 'spect I'll enlist."

George was young and impulsive. His decision did not surprise me. He harbored no shyness when it came to political opinions. I shared many of those views, but George was nineteen and single. I was twenty-four with a wife and three small children. That made a difference.

"I wish I could join you," I said, "but I have family. You're talking about a three-year enlistment. Who would care for my family while I am gone?"

"This war can't last long, Will. Not if Lincoln gets the men he's requesting. We'll be home in time to plant spring wheat. Your brothers can care for Mary and the kids while we're gone. It won't be the same without you at my side. There's talk of a draft. You could still end up in the army."

I felt a yearning to enlist with George. He was a good friend. If I had to go to war, there would be no better comrade in arms. The cavalry suggested majesty. Riding was better than walking, and I was good with animals.

"Your offer's enticing, but I can't desert Mary and the kids."

"A recruiter's speaking at the school tonight. It won't hurt to hear what he has to say. You can watch me enlist."

"I suppose there's no harm in that," I replied. To be honest, I yearned to hear the man speak. Watching George scribble his name on the enlistment form provided a proper excuse. We gathered our turkeys and headed for home. We walked in silence, lost in our own thoughts.

∗ ∗ ∗

Mary had boiled turnips, sausage, and turnip greens waiting for me when I arrived home. I hung the dead turkey on a hook just outside the back door, while the two boys watched in fascination; the dead turkey would be tomorrow's supper. The smell of boiled turnips and sausage suggested an adequate meal for tonight. I plucked Mary Elisabeth from her cradle and tossed her into the air. She giggled with delight when I caught her.

"Don't you drop that child," Mary admonished.

"I don't know," I replied. "She's getting mighty heavy. She might just slip through my hands." I tossed her up again and she rewarded me with more giggles. This war was important, but not as important as family. Mary and the kids were what I lived for. I couldn't imagine leaving them even for a short war. I returned Mary Elisabeth to her cradle and sat down at the dinner table. The food looked even better than it smelled. The military couldn't offer a quality meal such as the meal Mary had placed before us. I offered a blessing for the meal the Lord had provided and then reached for a piece of sausage.

"George Thompson is enlisting," I said.

"That doesn't surprise me," Mary replied. "He's a nice boy, but he's impulsive."

"He's nineteen, hardly a boy."

"What that man needs is a good woman. I've a mind to find him one if he can't find one on his own."

"I hear Casper Raab and Gottlieb Miller are joining." I added another turnip and some greens to my plate.

"That Casper Raab must be pushing fifty if he's a day old. He should know better."

"He knows what he's doing. He served nine years in the Prussian military before coming to America, and then he fought in the Mexican War. He knows about war. People are talking about this new cavalry unit being organized. Casper probably got caught up in the emotion."

"William Goodman, you aren't thinking of enlisting, are you?" From the tone of Mary's voice the correct answer was obvious.

"Enlist in the military and give up all this great cooking?" I asked. "Don't be ridiculous. I did promise George I would go with him to the meeting and watch him sign his papers."

Mary changed the subject, making it clear any further discussion concerning war or enlistment would not be tolerated at the dinner table. Mary was open-minded on most subjects and willingly agreed with my viewpoints. On those rare occasions when she did voice an opposing opinion, I knew better than argue the point. Running off to war was one of them.

Following supper we sat silently in front of the fireplace. Neither of us mentioned the war, but thoughts of the war hung over us like the ominous clouds of a pending thunderstorm. It was a common conversation around Salem Township. Few households escaped the debate. I was torn between devotion to family and love for my country. I couldn't placate both passions. I played with Mary Elizabeth and the two boys, but my thoughts kept returning to George signing his enlistment papers. I would miss him after he joined the cavalry. He was my closest friend outside of family. At seven o'clock I bid goodnight to the kids, kissed Mary on the cheek, and slipped out the back door. It was an hour walk to the school house and too dark to make hitching our horse up to the wagon worthwhile. I walked no more than fifteen minutes when I met Casper Raab heading toward our mutual destination. He provided welcome conversation for the remainder of the walk. Casper struggled with English, as many German immigrants were inclined to do. My parents grew up in Germany, and I felt comfortable in either language. As a courtesy, we conversed in German. Needless to say, the war was the topic of our discussion. Casper recounted tales of his nine years in the Prussian army as well as his experience in the Mexican War. His adventures and worldly exploits filled me with envy. The occasional stubborn mule was the greatest adversary I had encountered to date.

The school house had filled to capacity by the time we arrived. All the seats were filled. It was standing room only.

"Over here, Will!"

I scanned the audience searching for the source of the voice until I saw George Thompson waving us down. He must have arrived early; he had seats secured for us in the front row. I was eager to attend the meeting, but I would have preferred a less conspicuous location. I sat beside him and waited anxiously for the meeting to begin. No women were in attendance. That came as no surprise; few wives or mothers were eager to see their men march off to war no matter how patriotic the cause.

"You sure you want to go through with this?" I asked George. "Three years is a long time."

"Give us a year and we'll have those Rebs begging for mercy. You join with me and we'll have them licked in six months tops."

I wished I shared his optimism. Newspaper reports were not painting a rosy picture. The Union Army was facing stiff resistance everywhere except in the west. The Rebels had strong beliefs and the courage to defend them.

"Who's that sitting at the desk?" I pointed to the tall, lanky man sitting at what was normally the teacher's desk. He was wearing a suit with vest and tie, not the normal attire of a local farmer.

"That's William Williams," George replied. "He'll be the company commander if he can recruit a hundred people. It won't be hard getting that many recruits. I just hope he has a slot for me."

Williams' attire and demeanor suggested a family with money and the advanced education to keep that money flowing. He was obviously in charge of tonight's meeting. The absence of military uniform was disconcerting. "What's his rank?" I asked. One would hope a man commanding a cavalry company possessed military experience.

"He'll be a captain once he signs up a hundred men. He's an attorney from Allegan—a pretty good one, I hear."

"He may be good at summing up a court case to a reluctant jury, but in war the jury will respond with ball and shot." George ignored my sarcasm. Williams was standing up to speak.

I had to admit, Williams was an eloquent speaker. He began by explaining the commitment: three years at thirteen dollars a month. "They also provide room and board and uniforms," George whispered. Williams then went on to explain the critical need for soldiers and how important they were to the survival of our nation. He had everyone sitting on the edge of his seat.

"Are we going to let a bunch of southern hooligans destroy our nation?" he asked.

"NO!" the crowd replied.

"Are we going to let a few rich plantation owners tell us how to run our country?"

"NO!"

"Are you going to stand idly by while other men fight for what we all believe in?"

"NO!" The crowd was getting more vociferous with each challenge. I found myself joining the throng; Williams definitely had a way of words. I could easily see him swaying a reluctant jury.

"Where do we sign up?" someone asked.

Williams pointed to a sheet of paper on his desk. The man eagerly worked his way to the desk. Two other men got in line behind him.

"I best get in line before the slots are filled." George stood up. Since we were in the front row, that automatically placed him in line to sign the paper.

I stood next to him. "Are you sure you want to do this?" I asked. George was too caught up in the fever to offer a response. His attention was focused on the man signing the sheet of paper on the desk.

"HIP, HIP, HOORAY!" the crowd shouted when the man finished signing his name. The man raised both fists over his head as if he had just won a prize fight.

"HIP, HIP, HOORAY!" the crowd the crowd repeated when the second man added his signature.

George signed his name and received the same acclamation. Then he turned and passed the pen to me. "Go ahead and sign it, Will. We need you."

The crowd grew silent when they noticed my hesitation. Every eye in the school house focused on me. It wasn't right to enlist and leave my family, but if I walked away with everyone watching, I'd be leaving as a coward. Was a cowardly father the proper legacy to leave my children? I hesitated for another moment, and then I dipped the pen in the ink well and scratched my name on the parchment. The room erupted in applause. I didn't feel like rejoicing. I quietly slipped out the side door and began the long walk home.

It was late and I knew the kids would be in bed. I wouldn't have been surprised if Mary were also in bed, but I could see a light in the window. Perhaps she had left the lamp on for me. I opened the door and stepped into the room. Mary was sitting at the table in her nightgown reading the Bible. She often turned to the Bible during periods of stress. Light from our kerosene lamp outlined her facial features. She was a wonderful woman, far more than I deserved. She closed the Bible and looked up at me. There were tears in her eyes. I returned her gaze but didn't say anything.

"You enlisted, didn't you?"

I nodded. There wasn't much I could say.

"I knew you would," she said.

"I'm sorry."

"It is late. Come to bed." Mary turned down the lantern wick to reduce the light and carried the lamp into the bedroom. I followed behind like an admonished puppy. She set the lamp on the dresser and climbed into bed. I quietly exchanged my clothes for pajamas, turn off the lamp, and crawled into my side of the bed, but I didn't think I could sleep. I lay in silence trying to think of something to say, but no words of wisdom came to mind.

"It's not a legal document," I finally said. "It's only a letter of intent. No one swore me into the army. I don't have to go." I waited for a reply, but none was forthcoming. Then I felt Mary's head resting on my shoulder. She wrapped her arm around my waist.

"Your signature is as good as your word, Will Goodman," she said. "You must go."

"What about you and the children?"

"In a few days we'll have the crops harvested. Our root cellar is filled with potatoes, turnips, and onions. We'll survive."

"The army will provide food and clothing," I said. "I won't need the thirteen dollars a month. I can send it home."

"No, you'll need the money for coffee and postage stamps; I expect you to write frequently." Mary snuggled closer to me and tightened her grip about my waist. "I'll have egg money and our two milk cows provide more milk than we need. I can sell milk and butter in town. John will soon be five. He can feed the chickens and help watch the other two children."

"I'll talk to my parents tomorrow. Perhaps you can live with them until I return," I said.

"No, Will. I'm staying here. This is our home. I want to keep it ready for when you return."

"I will return," I said. "I promise."

Mary slipped her hand under my nightshirt, and her fingers gently explored the skin on my chest. "I need you to love me tonight," she whispered.

I worked my hand under her nightgown and caressed her left breast while kissing her neck. Then I pulled her toward me and pressed her body against mine. She offered no resistance.

CHAPTER TWO

"It's going be hot today," Mary said. "Don't forget your hat and water jug."

"I won't." I grabbed my straw hat and the brown ceramic jug Mary had filled with water. We talked about the weather. We talked about the high price of sugar. We talked about the chickens that were no longer laying eggs. We talked about everything except the war. Mary would hear nothing of it—as if denial would make the war disappear. "I'll have the last of the wheat in the barn before the heat of the day," I said. I was being optimistic. It would require the better part of the day. I gave Mary a perfunctory kiss on the forehead. Mary was suffering. It grieved me knowing I was causing her pain. There was little I could do to mitigate her anguish. I couldn't erase my name from that piece of paper. Too many people had watched me affix my signature. In a few days I would be leaving Salem, not knowing when I would return. I suggested reneging on my vow. Mary hated the war, but a written commitment was a matter of honor, and honor was important to Mary. If I reneged on my vow she could no longer hold her head high.

"If you return for lunch, there's ham in the icebox and bread in the cupboard. You can make yourself a sandwich. The kids and I will be in town selling eggs and milk. Supper may be late."

Taking eggs to town on a Monday was unusual. Mary normally went on Thursdays. Perhaps she needed the escape. I couldn't blame her.

"Want me harness Prince to the buggy?" Prince was our gelding. He was too old for the plow, but he could pull our two-wheeled buggy, if we weren't in a hurry. I used a pair of oxen for plowing. I wouldn't be plowing fields in the spring. To be truthful, I didn't know when I would plow our fields. I hated to part with the oxen, but they were extra mouths to feed and money would be tight. Mary's cousin made a fair offer. He would treat them well. We had exchanged money, but he said I could keep the oxen until I completed the harvest. The extra money would see Mary through the winter.

"I can harness Prince," Mary replied. "I must learn to do such things for myself."

I left the house and headed for the barn. I had cut the wheat the previous week and bundled the stalks into sheaves to dry. Wet grain would rot. Now the grain was dry and I needed to store the sheaves in the barn where they would remain dry. Thrashing the sheaves to separate the wheat from the straw could be done at our leisure. I tied the double yoke to the two oxen and then hitched up the wagon. It would be an easy day for the oxen. Once we reached the field, they could stand in place or lie on the ground while I filled the wagon.

I looked at the cloudless sky. It was early morning, but the August sun was already revealing its warmth. Mary was right as usual; it would be a hot day. All the more reason to gather the sheaves before noon. I removed my shirt and set about my task.

I have never carried a pocket watch, but from the position of the sun, I judged it past noon when I loaded the last sheaf of wheat onto the wagon. Pocket watches were an expensive luxury for a farmer. A farmer's day began with the first crow of the rooster and ended when the sun set in the west.

The oxen were relaxing on the ground and chewing their cud. With encouragement from a small switch, they reluctantly stood up and headed toward the barn. Once I removed their yoke, their work would be done for the day. Had they known that, they would have been less reluctant. Prince and the buggy were absent when we reached the farmhouse—Mary was gone.

I unloaded the wagon and turned the oxen loose in the fenced-in pasture. I considered thrashing some of the wheat, but decided against it. Thrashing was easy. Even our four-year-old could stomp on the wheat sheaves placed in a half-barrow. The farm had numerous small repair jobs that required my attention before I left for the army. I replaced a broken hinge on the barn door, patched a hole in the fence around the pigsty, and replaced some torn shingles on the roof of the farm house.

When the sun was resting low in the sky and Mary had not yet returned, I began to worry. She could have broken an axle or Prince could have thrown a shoe. Numerous scenarios came to mind; none of them pleasant. I was about to harness the oxen to the wagon and set out for town when I saw a buggy kicking up dust on the road to our house.

"Where have you been?" I asked when Mary pulled into the barnyard.

"Wouldn't you like to know?" she replied with a smile. It was not a sarcastic smile or a mocking smile. It was a playful, impish smile with no sign of depression; the girl I loved and married had returned.

"Be a dear and brush down Prince while I fix dinner. I'm starving."

I unhooked Prince and brushed him down. Then I turned him loose in the pasture with the oxen. When I returned to the house, Mary was using a small-mouth Mason jar to cut dough into biscuit-size circles. A pan of sausage gravy was heating on the stove. She was humming one of her favorite hymns. I don't know what happened in town, but I found the transformation pleasing.

That evening Mary retired early. She had had a long day. I was also exhausted and decided to do likewise. I went to the dresser to retrieve my pajamas. I stored my night clothes in the top drawer. Mary claimed the drawer beneath mine. Her drawer was partially open. Even in the dim light I could see a small box tied with a bow. I had never seen the box before. Perhaps it contained some of Mary's jewelry, although she seldom wore jewelry. It was her property in her drawer and it should be left alone, but if I could have untied the bow and then retied it to look undisturbed, I would have done so. Curiosity was my downfall. I took my pajamas from the top drawer and headed for the bed.

"Are you through with the light?" I asked after I had slipped into my pajamas. It was a pointless question as she was already snuggled under the covers.

"Let there be darkness," she replied in a playful twist of scripture.

I lay quietly in bed. I was exhausted but not sleepy. I had worked hard during the day and the evening was pleasant but confusing. It would take more than the Wisdom of Solomon to understand women. There was little hope for lesser men.

"You goin' tell me what you did in town today?" I asked. I thought she had decided to ignore my question; then I felt her head resting on my shoulder. Her arm encircled my waist.

"There are better things to do in bed than discuss the price of eggs. No, Will Goodman, I do not want to discuss what I did in town today." In a moment, she was all over me. "I want you to love me!"

Mary awoke just as cheerful as when she went to bed. She apparently had accepted the inevitable. By the time I was dressed, she had eggs frying in one pan while she stirred sliced potatoes frying in a second pan. The children were still asleep; apparently she was preparing most of the food for me.

"Smells good," I said. I had planned to limit our conversation to small talk. I had no desire to destroy her congenial mood.

"I have to fatten you up. There's no telling what that army chow will do to you. Men should never be allowed in the kitchen. They need women cooks if they expect to win this war."

"Can't argue with that," I said. I sat down at the table, and Mary piled the eggs and potatoes on my plate. It was more than I could eat. "I need to deliver the oxen today. Then I should drop by and bid farewell to the kinfolk." I eagerly attacked the potatoes; I also questioned the quality of army chow. No army cook could fry up a batch of potatoes like Mary.

"We're going with you. Let me get the children up."

From the tone of her voice I knew it was not a request—it was a statement. I finished eating while Mary dressed Mary Elizabeth. John and Henry were capable of dressing themselves if provided proper supervision.

"I'll hitch Prince up to the buggy," I said.

"Take your time," Mary replied. "I still have to feed the children."

If Mary Elizabeth sat on Mary's lap and the two boys scrunched together behind the bench seat, we all fit in the buggy. We did it every Sunday on our way to church. I found Prince munching grass near the gate. Even though the fenced-in pasture provided room to roam, he preferred a spot near the barn. "How's breakfast?" I asked. Prince ignored my question and reached for additional grass. I slipped the harness around his neck between bites. My family would not be the only ones I would miss. Prince had been a faithful servant for many years. I wished I could take him with me although I knew he was too old to be of service. I walked Prince over to the buggy and attached his harness. "Prince, tomorrow I must leave you. It may be a long time. I want you to take good care of Mary and the kids." I knew he would. Prince was kind and gentle with the kids. He no longer had the strength of younger horses, but he still provided maximum effort.

The two oxen were not as accommodating. They assumed my arrival meant work. I secured a rope around the neck of the first ox and then tied him to the rear of the cart. I had to chase the second ox around the paddock before he too was secured to the rear of the cart.

"We're ready," Mary said. She and the children were dressed in their Sunday clothes. I felt out of place in my everyday work clothes. Our two-wheeled buggy had a bench for the driver and one passenger. There was just enough room behind the bench for groceries or two small boys sitting cross-legged. That was all

Prince could pull. I hoisted the two boys onto the buggy and then held Mary Elizabeth while Mary climbed onto the bench.

"You ready to go for a ride, Mary E.?" I picked her up and gave her a short toss to Mary's waiting arms.

"Will Goodman, one of these days you are going to drop her!" Mary Elizabeth just giggled.

"That's okay," I said. "After last night, maybe we'll have another one on the way." I ignored Mary's scowl and climbed onto my seat. "Let's go, Prince." I gave a flip of the reins and Prince plodded down the driveway. I decided to deliver the oxen to Mary's cousin before we visited the other kinfolk; spending the day tied to our buggy would have been unfair to them.

I had expected a short tour with brief visits to the local relatives, but that was not to be. At each visit Mary paraded the children into the farmhouse where the host felt obliged to offer tea and whatever eatables happened to be available. The topic of discussion at each visit was my departure in the morning. Several individuals offered to take in Mary and the children, but she would not hear of such talk; she had a home. Her cousin offered to plow the fields in the spring with the oxen and perhaps even plant the fields for her if time permitted. At the end of the day I felt much better, knowing the kinfolk would care for my family.

It was late in the evening when we returned home. We were so filled with cookies, cake, and other treats that no one was hungry. I tucked the boys into bed while Mary fed Mary Elizabeth. At eight months, Mary E. could not reap the benefits of the abundant sweets the rest of us had consumed. Once the children were secure in their respective beds, Mary took it upon herself to help me pack. She was disappointed when I told her the clothes I wore on my back would be given away. I would be wearing a uniform. There would be little room for personal possessions. As a compromise Mary packed lunches for the trip to the train station in Kalamazoo. She needed to stay busy; I didn't discourage her. Kalamazoo was fifty miles south of Salem, and a lunch would be welcome before the day's end. George's brother consented to drive us there in his buckboard, but Mary packed food for twice as many people.

Mary was in a romantic mood again that night and very clingy. She eventually fell asleep with her head resting on my shoulder. Sleep did not come easy for me. I lay awake, my mind consumed by thoughts of the coming morning. I still felt a patriotic need to defend our nation, but leaving the woman whose head was resting on my shoulder was a high price to pay; I couldn't have both. Perhaps it would be a quick war as George had suggested, but the newspaper accounts were not encouraging.

After a fitful night I fell asleep. Dawn seemed to appear only moments later. Mary was frying bacon and eggs. To ensure I was up in time, she sicced the boys on me. They attacked from both sides of the bed. I wrestled with them for a bit, pretending to let them get the best of me. I had to formally surrender before they allowed me to get dressed.

"It smells good," I said. I gave Mary a hug, but it felt awkward.

"Sit down and start eating. George and his brother will be here before you know it." Mary sat opposite me at the table and watched me eat.

"Aren't you going to eat?" I asked. Eating under her watchful stare made me feel self-conscious.

"I'll eat when I feed the boys."

I ate in silence. Outwardly, Mary appeared cheerful, but her moist eyes conveyed a different story. I feared any conversation would trigger a deluge of pent-up tears. Neither of us wanted that.

"That must be George." Mary went to the window to confirm what we already knew. The groaning of a buckboard under strain and the stomping of horse hooves were unmistakable.

I ate the last of my eggs and headed for the door. George jumped down from the wagon. So much energy this early in the morning made me jealous. His brother remained in the driver's seat. Kalamazoo was a long drive; we had little time to dally. Large sacks of corn filled the back of the wagon.

"As long as we're going to Kalamazoo, my brother thought he'd haul the corn to market," George said when he saw me eyeing the sacks. I nodded.

"Boys, come say good-by to your father," Mary said. "He may be gone for a long time."

I wondered how much they understood at age three and four even though we had discussed my departure on several occasions. I gave each one a hug. "I want you boys to take care of your mother while I'm gone. Help her out as much as you can." At their age they could offer little help, but it seemed the proper thing to say. The boys assured me they would.

Mary stepped out from the house with Mary Elizabeth in one arm and a large sack in the other. She placed the sack on the bags of corn. "I packed lunches for the three of you," she told George.

I took Mary Elizabeth from Mary's arms and gave her a toss in the air. I needed to hear her giggle one last time. She didn't disappoint me. Mary pulled me toward the house where we could say our good-byes in private. George and his brother pretended to be busy. I gave Mary and Mary E. a group hug and then kissed Mary on the lips.

"Promise me you'll come back," Mary begged. The pent-up tears gushed forth. She did not bother wiping them from her cheek. "I don't care how many limbs you have. Please tell me you will come home."

"I wiped away her tears with strands of her long hair. " That's a promise," I said.

Mary reached into her apron pocket and retrieved a small bag. "This is for you," she said. "Don't open it until you are on the train."

"I love you," I said. I gave her another quick kiss and then climbed onto the wagon. There was only room for two people on the bench seat, so I made a comfortable nest from the bags of corn. I hadn't slept well during the night and looked forward to some shut-eye on the trip to Kalamazoo. A flip of the reins sent the team of horses plodding down the long driveway. I watched my wife and children grow smaller and smaller until they were out of sight. I wondered when I would see their faces again. I had no doubt Mary Elizabeth would be walking by then. My eyes began to water and I had to force back the tears.

The swaying of the wagon quickly rocked me to sleep. I dreamed of Mary. She was sitting in the grass near a crystal-blue lake. She was calling out to me, but my legs wouldn't move. It wasn't a nightmare, but neither was it a pleasant dream. The sun was high in the sky when I awoke. George and his brother had eaten their lunches, but enough food remained to feed two more hungry men. I ate a sandwich and then took a drink from the water jug. George and his brother were discussing the best time to sell corn. I had no desire to join the conversation, so I kept my own council. I had other thoughts on my mind.

Soon the packed clay on the road turned to cobblestone; we were approaching Kalamazoo. I don't often visit big cities. I sat up to take notice. Many of the houses rose up three or more stories and were gaily painted. Their lawns looked like someone trimmed them with scissors. I could only imagine such wealth. The residential district gave way to factories and warehouses, as we approached the train station. I had seen pictures of trains, but I had never ridden on one. Any residual melancholy gave way to excitement. We passed two flat-bed cars loaded eight feet high with logs. From the small diameter of the logs, I assumed it was pulp wood. Three wagons the size of our buckboard could easily fit on any one of those flat-beds. Farther down the tracks we came to a string of passenger cars. I assumed they were for us. A crowd of men gathered on the platform next to the tracks.

"Pull over here," George said. The wagon came to a halt and I jumped down.

"This must be where we're supposed to meet," I said. I looked around, but I didn't see anyone who appeared to be in charge.

George said his good-byes to his brother and climbed down from the wagon. "I think we're early," he said. I never carried a pocket watch, so I didn't know.

"GEORGE, WILL, OVER HERE!" I scanned the crowd to see who was shouting at us. Then I saw Gottlieb Miller waving us down from the edge of the crowd.

"There's Gottlieb," I said. George and I worked our way through the crowd. We found Casper Raab standing next to Gottlieb. The four of us shook hands and slapped backs like long lost friends, something we would not have done had we met at the feed mill in Salem. Although we were eager to defend our country, a modicum of fear and self-doubt resided deep inside our souls. There was strength in numbers, and we desperately needed that strength. No one said anything, but we assumed the four of us would be a team.

"Where do we go from here?" I asked. I was hoping Casper or Gottlieb had additional information.

"I saw Captain Williams earlier," Gottlieb replied. "He said we'd be boarding soon."

I looked around the crowd for Williams. I assumed he would be in uniform. I only found one person in a uniform. It wasn't Williams, but he did look official. He was checking off names from a chart and the men were boarding one of the train cars.

"They're boarding over there." I pointed toward the man in uniform. "We better get in line if we want to sit together."

We worked our way toward the man in uniform where the line was forming to board the train. By unanimous consent we let Casper lead the way. At fifty-one he provided a father image, and he had previous military experience. That was sufficient credentials for the rest of us.

"Casper Raab, sergeant." The sergeant checked the name off his list and Casper climbed the steps leading into train car. I assumed Casper could tell the man's rank by something on his uniform. The uniforms looked the same to me.

"Next!" I gave the sergeant my name and followed Casper up the steps.

I peered inside a train for the first time. A long corridor ran the entire length of the car. Soldiers sat on padded bench seats on either side of the aisle. There was room for two men on each bench. Opposing the bench was another bench allowing four persons to converse; the car was no doubt built for the social needs of civilian traffic. All the benches were occupied. Casper continued down the aisle until he reached the end of the train car. I was wondering where we were to sit, when Casper opened two back-to-back doors and entered another passenger car. This one was half full. He found two opposing empty benches and sat down. The rest of us followed suit. I was quick to claim a window seat.

"How long will it take us to get to Detroit?" It was a rhetorical question. I didn't expect anyone would know. Detroit was on the far side of the state, almost into Canada.

"Best guess is late morning or early afternoon," Casper replied. "Depending on the number of stops."

"Why do we have to stop?" Gottlieb asked.

"Steam engines need water to make steam and coal or wood to feed the boiler."

Casper was an experienced traveler and our curiosity was insatiable. We peppered him with questions until the man in uniform passed through our car counting heads. Minutes later a blast from the locomotive's whistle rattled the windows. The train began pulling away from the station. The three of us clung to the windows to watch the houses and trees pass by. We were traveling faster than a man could run, maybe even fifteen miles per hour—and the steam engine was pulling five cars. Casper leaned back in his chair and closed his eyes. I didn't see how anyone could sleep with so much to see.

After an hour the novelty began to diminish; one can only watch so many trees fly past the window. Then I remember the small package Mary had given me before we left. I was not to open it until we were on the train. I retrieved it from my knapsack. The package was wrapped in paper and tied with string, nothing elegant. I untied the string and peeled away the paper wrapping, revealing a small box tied with a ribbon. It was the same box I had seen in Mary's drawer. I untied the ribbon and removed the lid. A folded sheet of paper lay on top of a small Bible. I unfolded the paper.

Dear Will,

There are many things I wished to tell you before you left, but I feared I would only cry and make our parting more painful. Defending your country is something you truly believe in. Deep inside I knew you would enlist when you left for the meeting. One must do what he must. I want you to know I am proud of you. You may soon be in battle. I will pray for your safety every night. Prayers from your side will also help. I hear tales of heavy drinking and wickedness in the military. Please do not forsake your faith. I know German comes easier for you when you read. I bought you a small Bible. It only has the New Testament and the Psalms, but I wanted it small enough to fit in your breast pocket. Carry it with you always. The Bible is so you never forget the Lord. The other gift is so you never forget your wife and family. I love you and wait anxiously for your speedy return.

Love Mary

I removed the Bible from the box and flipped through the pages; it was written in German. I discovered an inscription on the first page. I held it up to the window for additional light. *To Daddy from John, Henry, and Mary E.* Most of the words were in Mary's handwriting, but I could tell the boys and printed their own names. Mary Elizabeth's name was very sloppy and difficult to read. I had no doubt Mary had guided her hand across the page. There was a blank page in the back of the Bible. Mary had written suggested verses under various topics such as fear, loneliness, and sorrow. I hoped I would never experience such feelings, but I knew I would. I placed the New Testament in my shirt pocket; it fit perfectly.

The second object in the box was wrapped in tissue. I carefully unwrapped it. It was a silver pocket watch with attached chain. I had never owned a pocket watch; farmers only acknowledge sunrise and sunset. Such a watch would not come cheap. Mary must have used some of the money from selling the oxen. We love you, Will Goodman was inscribed on the cover. Below it was Mary's name, but I knew she wished to represent our family. I opened the cover. On the inside of the cover was a small picture of Mary smiling back at me. It was a new picture of her that I had never seen. She had the photograph taken while in town and then had to wait until the photographer developed the picture. That was why she was so late returning. My eyes began to water. I wiped away the tears with my handkerchief while pretending to blow my nose.

I attached the chain to my suspender button and then clutched the watch against my chest. The gift was too precious to remain hidden in my pocket. I opened the cover several times that evening to check the time, but it was not the time I wished to see; I needed to see Mary's beautiful eyes looking up at me. I whispered "I love you" each time I closed the lid. Darkness came swiftly once the sun had set. Idle conversation ceased as we became captivated with personal thoughts. I wondered if my three comrades were as homesick as I was.

CHAPTER THREE

The sun was streaming through the window when I awoke. It felt warm against my face, suggesting our car could become unbearably hot before the day was out. It was mid-August and we were heading south. Hot days were to be expected. I considered opening a window. The cool air would be welcome, but it would include the soot and sulfurous stench from the steam engine. The fumes were already giving me a headache. I decided to pass.

George was sitting across from me, quietly staring at the passing trees, lost in thoughts known only to him. I couldn't remember ever seeing him in such a pensive mood. Gottlieb's hat partially sheltered his eyes from the sun, but his rhythmic breathing suggested deep sleep. Coarse snoring left little doubt concerning Casper's current condition. I vaguely remembered stopping several times during the night to take on coal and water; but, otherwise, I had slept well.

"Anything interesting out there?" I quietly asked. I did not wish to wake the others.

"Only if you find trees exciting," George replied. "The conductor came by while you were sleeping. He said we're approaching Detroit."

I looked at my new pocket watch: It was twenty past eight. We would arrive in Detroit sooner than Casper had predicted. I joined George at the window and together we watched the trees, swamps, and cultivated fields pass before us. Each hour took us farther from our homes and family. Neither of us felt like talking. The train passed over a wooden trestle bridge spanning a small ravine. Below, a river swollen from a recent rain worked its way through the ravine. The tracks then curved south, allowing the morning sun to briefly suffuse Gottlieb's and Casper's faces with sunlight. Both men began to stir.

Gottlieb looked out the window but saw nothing that looked familiar. "Where are we?" he asked.

"We're approaching Detroit," I replied, offering the same information George had provided moments ago. Gottlieb nodded and then joined us at the window to monitor the ever-changing scenery.

Crossroads became more frequent and virgin timber gave way to cultivated fields. The train ambled through small villages. The early rising inhabitants waved at us. We waved back. Some old veterans gave us a salute. They must have known we were fresh recruits. We entered a never-ending residential district that gradually gave way to factories and warehouses. This had to be Detroit. The train slowed and then rumbled to a stop next to a long wooden platform.

"Rise and shine, gentleman." The sergeant walked through the train car to ensure everyone was awake. "Line up on the platform outside." The aisle quickly filled as everyone tried to exit at once. George and I stood up to join the group.

"Sit down and relax," Casper said. "The first rule you boys need to learn about the army is hurry up and wait. Those eager lads will be waiting for us on the platform when we debark, and they won't arrive at Camp Banks any sooner than us."

Over the coming weeks and months I discovered there was much truth to Casper's admonition. We waited in our seats until the aisle was clear and then casually departed the train. As Casper had predicted, everyone was waiting for us on the platform. The sergeant was trying to arrange them into a column of four. He was having minimal luck. Captain Williams, the only other person in uniform, appeared as confused as the rest of us.

"GENTLEMEN, WE ARE NOW GOING TO MARCH TO CAMP BANKS. LEFT—FACE!"

Some people turned to the left, some looked to the left, and a few turned to the right. Most of the recruits remained in place with bewildered looks. It was not the outcome the sergeant desired. Instantaneously knowing right from left was not a common virtue among farmers, and even fewer had any concept of a military command. The sergeant finally capitulated, realizing it was unlikely he could convert us into soldiers in one day. He walked to the front of the line.

"GENTLEMEN, PLEASE FOLLOW ME."

The sergeant stiffly marched toward what had to be Camp Banks. The rest of us followed him like inquisitive goslings following a mother goose. We walked a good three miles before arriving at the camp. After sixteen hours on the train, the walk was a welcome diversion.

Other than a very long single-story wooden structure, I could find little to qualify as a military camp. The structure had glass windows and multiple doors. I assumed this would be our barracks. I was disappointed. I had been expecting a cannon or two or perhaps a wooden palisade with guard towers surrounding the camp. There was nothing to suggest a military establishment. Captain Williams climbed upon some wooden crates that were conveniently stacked in front of the building.

"Gather around, men."

We formed a semicircle around the company commander. I could tell the sergeant was not pleased with the manner in which Captain Williams was addressing his troops. I am sure he would have preferred men neatly lined up like rows of corn—that was not about to happen. At least, not today.

"We have a busy day ahead of us," Williams said. "After you are sworn in, we will feed you breakfast. Then we have paper work for you to fill out. That's to ensure you get paid."

The captain's last comment was greeted with applause. The sergeant found this behavior annoying. I feared he would be a difficult person to placate. The captain took no offense; he appeared pleased.

"After breakfast we will be issuing bedding and fitting you for uniforms. We will be bunking in the barracks behind me. You are members of Company I of Michigan's fifth Cavalry Regiment, and we will bunk on the east section of the barracks. Tomorrow with the help of our First Sergeant" Williams pointed toward the sergeant, "we will begin training."

"I don't think I'm going to like that First Sergeant," I said. Gottlieb and George echoed my sentiments. Farm boys grew up expecting to be in charge—even if their subjects were farm animals.

"He's only doing his job," Casper replied. I was beginning to resent Casper's previous military experience.

I had assumed our entry into the military was a foregone conclusion, but before we were given our oath, we were lined up before a surly horse. We each had a turn riding bareback around a circle, first at a walk and then at a trot. Unless we fell off the horse which few did, the mustering officer sent us to the surgeon's tent for a quick exam. The surgeon had us hop on each foot and then swing our arms around like a windmill. As long as all four extremities functioned properly, we were sworn into the U.S. Army for three years. It was August 30th, 1862. Many people assumed the war would be over quickly, now that the Union had additional troops. Perhaps we would be home in time for spring planting. I was already missing Mary and the kids.

After taking our oath the First Sergeant ushered us to the mess hall behind the barracks for a breakfast of biscuits and sausage gravy. Several men prepared the food under sheds, without sides or front. Steam or smoke, there was no telling which, billowed out of the limited enclosure. The mess hall, if you could call it that, consisted of long wooden tables. No protection was provided for inclement weather. I bit into one of the biscuits;

they were hard and dry—and the gravy was too salty. Mary was right; men shouldn't be allowed in the kitchen.

"I think I broke a tooth on the biscuit," George announced. I wasn't sure if he was joking or serious. With those biscuits, it could go either way.

After breakfast the First Sergeant sent us to the supply room to get "fitted" for uniforms. Fitted was a very loose term. We discovered military clothing comes in two sizes: too large and too small. Twenty-two minutes later (according to my new pocket watch) we returned to our bunks with a cavalry jacket, reinforced trousers, forage cap, and boots which came to the knee. They even issued sabers. They were exceedingly dull, and we had no whetstones to sharpen them. Casper said that was for our own safety. I could see his point. At the far end of the barracks two individuals were engaged in a mock saber fight, three musketeer style.

Real training would not begin until the following morning, leaving our afternoon free. George, Gottlieb, and I were eager to explore Detroit. Casper, proclaiming all cities are the same, preferred to remain in the barracks. He had discovered several military manuals and was eager to discover what had changed since his last war. Military manuals could wait for another day in my opinion. We donned our uniforms, attached our sabers to our belts, and headed out to see Detroit. According to rumor, we would not receive firearms until later in our training. Even so, we felt invincible with our dull sabers at our sides.

We discovered we were a stone's throw from the Detroit River. On the far side was Canada. I had never seen another country before—even from a distance. Fort Wayne, which did look like a fort, secured the river. We discovered our uniforms offered free passage into the fort. We entered through an arched passage that traversed the thick masonry walls and led to an open court yard where new recruits were drilling. We assumed they were infantry and inherently inferior to cavalry. I had to admit, they marched better than we did.

After a few minutes of observation, boredom set in; one can only watch ants march across a field for so long. We climbed to the top of the east wall where heavy cannons fortified the two wedge-shaped bastions facing the Detroit River. A smaller semicircular fortification between the two bastions extended outward from the fort. This appendage was also heavily fortified. No vessels could traverse the Detroit River without the blessing of Fort Wayne. I assumed the cannons were sufficient to defend the fort; if not, we were prepared to defend the fortification with our three dull sabers.

A row of large dwellings extended south of the walled fort. This was where the officers resided, according to one of the artillery men we met. The regular army men were friendly, although several individuals acted as if we should salute them. Being new to the military, I think they cut us some slack.

We returned to our barracks late in the evening. Casper was still perusing military manuals; he was taking this war too seriously. The outcome of any battle would depend on the courage of the participants, not on a military manual. I assumed the outcome of any battle would be in our favor.

Our barracks was one large open bay with rows of bunk beds. The bunk beds had four tiers with two men to a bunk. The four of us commandeered two lower bunks. The only light in the evenings came from widely separated oil lamps. Casper had the foresight to choose bunks next to the oil lamp. I would never have considered that advantage while the morning sunlight was streaming through the windows. Finding the light from the lamp insufficient for older eyes, Casper closed his manual and prepared for bed.

"You goin' to bed already?" I asked. "The evening is yet young."

"Someday you will appreciate a good night's sleep," he replied. "And I fear that day is not far off."

We ignored Casper's words of wisdom. There was too much to discuss. We were now military men—cavalry men, even if we didn't have horses. We talked late into the night.

* * *

"I WANT EVERYONE DRESSED AND STANDING IN FORMATION IN FRONT OF THE BARRACKS IN TWENTY MINUTES." The two oil lamps were burning brightly. I looked to see who was yelling at us—it was the First Sergeant.

"What time is it?" Gottlieb asked.

"It's the middle of the night," George replied.

Apparently, I was the only one with a pocket watch. I held it up to the light of the lamp: It was four-thirty. George was right; it was the middle of the night. Four-thirty didn't qualify for morning even by farm-boy standards. Casper was half dressed before the rest of us had cleared the sleep from our eyes. It was closer to thirty minutes by the time everyone was standing in front of the barracks. We drifted around in the dark until the First Sergeant arrived. He was accompanied by several henchmen who proceeded to line us up in four rows. Except for the men in the first row, we stood directly behind the man in front of us.

"WHEN I GIVE THE COMMAND RIGHT...FACE, EVERYONE IS TO TURN NINETY DEGREES TO THE RIGHT."

The First Sergeant and his henchmen demonstrated the maneuver. It looked easy enough; but when we tried it, several individuals tripped over their feet and fell to the ground. A few troopers turned to the left, but most of us faced ninety degrees to the right, give or take fifteen degrees. We practiced right and left face until most of us felt competent with those maneuvers.

"WE WILL NOW MARCH TO THE MESS HALL FOR BREAKFAST. WHEN I GIVE THE COMMAND FORWARD...MARCH, STEP OFF WITH YOUR LEFT FOOT."

The First Sergeant turned us to the right and gave the march command. Individuals in the front row stepped out smartly. Those behind them waited their turn. The company stretched out like a giant night crawler. By the time men in the rear began to march, the front of the company was half way to the mess hall. When the First Sergeant gave the command to stop, the tail of the night crawler contracted until we were again in formation.

"That was a silly way of walking from point A to point B," George said as he sat down at the table to eat breakfast. "And why does he call it a mess hall? It is nothing more than some tables under the stars. Eat...Chow would have been a more appropriate command."

I had to agree with George. Marching to the tables behind the barracks was not the most efficient way of getting to breakfast.

"Sometimes we won't know where point B is," Casper said. "Marching as a unit ensures everyone gets to point B. No one is left behind."

There was logic to what Casper was saying, but logic should be reserved for situations when point B was unknown. The mess hall was less than forty yards away. It would have been even closer if the First Sergeant would have let us cut through the barracks. At least this breakfast was not bad; the biscuits were eatable. I took another bite of scrambled eggs.

"FALL OUT...ON THE DOUBLE!"

The First Sergeant marched up and down the tables to ensure his order was carried out. I grabbed my toast and ran with the others. Apparently, the army did consider meals a social event. The First Sergeant's henchmen were waiting for us in front of the barracks—they must have eaten earlier. They lined us up according to their specifications, but at least now we had some understanding of the desired formation.

"I thought we joined the cavalry," George said. "This is more of a prelude to a marching band."

"This was your idea," I reminded him.

"NO TALKING IN THE RANKS."

Farm boys were accustomed to speaking their piece. I assumed it was guaranteed by the constitution. The First Sergeant had obviously not read that document. I discovered I could converse in a low volume as long as my lips didn't move. The First Sergeant couldn't properly identify the offender although he would look at me in a suspicious manner.

The First Sergeant divided us into platoons of thirty people for smaller classes. The two henchmen each took command of a platoon and marched them off to locations unknown, leaving our platoon standing in front of the First Sergeant—we had been selected for the First Sergeant's personal attention.

He marched us over to a large burr oak for our first lesson. The First Sergeant stood in the shade of the tree while we remained in the sun at parade rest. I don't know why they call it parade rest; it was almost as rigid as standing at attention. When my nose itched, I liked to scratch it. The First Sergeant didn't believe an itchy nose warranted such attention.

Our first class was identification of rank and how to salute officers. At least we were allowed to break ranks long enough to practice saluting.

"Good afternoon, Sir George." I gave George a crisp salute and then gradually lowered all my fingers except the middle digit. It was a well-known gesture even among Roman soldiers, so I assumed it would be appropriate in this setting. George accepted the salute in good humor; the First Sergeant did not. I made sure he could not see my one-fingered salute, but he must have heard the verbal exchange. My lips didn't quiver, and he was now hopelessly trying to ascertain the guilty party. He returned us to parade rest.

"You will salute all officers and maintain that salute until the officer has returned the gesture," the First Sergeant said. "The only exception is during combat. Never salute an officer during combat. That marks him as an officer and could cause his death."

"If we go into battle, the First Sergeant will be the first person I salute," Gottlieb mumbled with slightly parted lips. George and I acknowledged the wisdom of Gottlieb's statement. The First Sergeant glared at us. He knew the remark came from one of us; we stood there with slightly parted lips. He was quick to label us trouble makers.

The First Sergeant marched us to the second class of the day. There was another shady tree for the First Sergeant and hot sun for the rest of us. We were hoping our class would incorporate horses. Instead, we were staring at a saddle securely strapped to an old wine barrel. I had as much experience with riding horses as the next farm boy, but I had never seen a saddle like that. It was small and appeared light. That much I could understand. What I couldn't understand was the three-inch wide slit running from front to back.

"This is the M1859 military saddle," the First Sergeant said. "Some of you are wondering about the hole running lengthwise across the saddle. That is to relieve the pressure against the horse's spine. The health of your horse is your primary concern."

George raised his hand. I knew no good could come from this.

"I have a different concern," George said. "What happens when my personal equipment gets lodged in that crevice? I may have to sing soprano."

The entire platoon erupted in laughter. Even Casper chuckled at George's jest. George was quite pleased with himself; the First Sergeant was not.

By suppertime we were hungry, tired, and some of us sunburned. Gottlieb and I filled our plates and sat down next to Casper. We were hoping the First Sergeant would let us at least finish the evening meal.

"Where's George?" Casper asked.

"The First Sergeant has him working on a special assignment," I replied.

"He's going to miss supper if he doesn't hurry."

"I don't think he's going make it to supper," Gottlieb said. "Will and I thought we'd bring him something to eat." Casper nodded. There was no way we could carry the mashed potatoes and gravy but we did procure some extra biscuits and cheese. I wrapped them in my handkerchief. We finished our meal and set off to find George.

After considerable searching we found him behind the cooking sheds. He was marching back and forth in front of the garbage cans. A three-inch diameter pole was slung across his shoulder to simulate a rifle. He was greeting any rat who chose to dine at the garbage cans with a, "Halt! Who goes there?"

"How's it going?" I asked.

"Some of those rats are bigger than alley cats," he replied.

"We brought you some food." I opened my handkerchief and showed him the biscuits and cheese.

"Thanks; I was getting hungry. Another hour without food and I'd be fighting the rats for the more appealing kitchen waste. Judging from the size of some of those rodents, the outcome could be in doubt." George looked around to ensure no one noticed he was no longer pacing in front of the garbage cans, and then attacked the biscuits and cheese with vigor.

"How much longer do you have to guard the garbage," I asked.

"I don't know, but if I don't return to the barracks, tell my family I died in the service of my country."

"George, if it makes you feel any better, I thought your comment was funny."

"Thanks."

Fort Wayne Photos

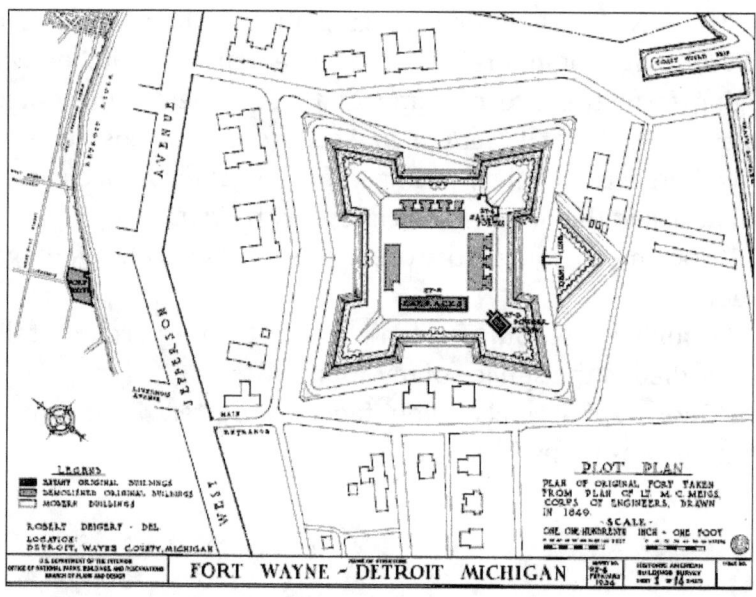

In 1840 the U.S. Army began surveying land for construction of Fort Wayne. This was to be a five-point star artillery fort overlooking the Detroit River. Its top of the line cannons would control all shipping along the river. The biggest concern was possible hostilities with British Canada. Before the cannons were installed, the U.S. and British Canada signed a treaty certifying their borders. An artillery fort was no longer needed. Since the fort was nearly completed, it was converted to an infantry fort.

Fort Wayne saw little usage until the Civil War when it became an induction center and training ground for Michigan troops. The U.S. Army continued using the fort as an induction and training center throughout World War I, World War II, and the Vietnam War. The author visited Fort Wayne in 1966 when he was inducted into service during the Vietnam War.

Beginning in 1948, the Fort was slowly turned over to the City of Detroit and is now run by the Detroit Recreation Department with the help of Historic Fort Wayne Coalition.

1848 Limestone Barracks

In 1848 a four-story limestone barracks was constructed inside the walls of the fort. It is possible that William Goodman stayed in these barracks, but it is more likely that he was housed in Camp Banks just outside Fort Wayne. Fort Wayne was overwhelmed by new enlistees. The limestone barracks would have been a logical choice for Infantrymen since they required little room. A cavalry regiment needed barns for the horses and storage for hay and oats. Camp Banks is now gone and little is known of its history.

During the summer, the Historic Fort Wayne Coalition hoists many events with reenactors creating Civil War period foods and real life skirmishes. Check their website before you arrive to see what is available.

CHAPTER FOUR

Sept.14, 1862

Dear Mary,

It has been two weeks since I left you, but it seems like an eternity. I miss your head resting on my shoulder as I fall asleep. I now share my bed with George, who is a restless sleeper and takes up far more bed space than you ever did. My current bedroom is the size of a warehouse. Casper and Gottlieb are above us, which is nice except for Casper's incessant snoring. I dare say he can generate more noise than that steam engine that brought us here. There are four more people above them. Each bunk has four layers which is enough to sleep an entire squad.

They promoted Casper to corporal last week. He is now in charge of our eight-man squad. Much as I would have liked that promotion, it is best that Casper received the honor. I doubt if George or Gottlieb would take orders from me. Casper is older and has military experience. All the men respect him. I think his calm nature will keep us out of trouble.

I assumed we had joined the cavalry, but we have yet to see a horse. We march everywhere on foot. Today they are planning a forced march with the entire regiment. I fear it will be a long day.

The cooks in the mess hall are devoid of imagination. Their meals never change. We eat lots of potatoes and biscuits and gravy. One can drive a tent stake with those biscuits. I fear your superb cooking has spoiled me to the point that I shall never appreciate military fare.

Last Sunday a parson from town arrived at camp to conduct a service. He was accompanied by many women of the community dressed in their finest clothes, but none of them could compare with you. The parson preached a fine sermon. It is unclear if he will return. If he doesn't, I will make use of the Bible you have so thoughtfully provided. Once we are off to war, I trust it will deliver the strength to see me through difficult times.

I am becoming more appreciative of the pocket watch you gave me with each passing day. Time had little meaning on the farm, but here reveille, guard duty, and meals are scheduled by the clock. Gottlieb, Casper, and George are constantly pestering me for the time of day. I suppose coordinating a company or regiment without a time piece is nearly impossible. What I enjoy most is your picture on the inside cover. As I write this letter, the watch is lying on the table, so I can see your sweet face.

"Reveille! Let's hustle, men." Casper grabbed his cap and headed for the door.

I signed my name to the bottom of my letter and slipped it into an envelope. Then I placed it under my pillow. I would have to mail it later in the day. The First Sergeant discovered a musician capable of playing the bugle. He now had us jumping and dancing to a variety of bugle calls.

Reveille was the longest bugle call. According to my pocket watch, it took the bugler two minutes to play it, give or take five seconds. When the bugler finished the last note, the First Sergeant expected to see us standing in formation. Two minutes was sufficient time if you were up and dressed. I grabbed my cap and followed Casper out the door.

Darkness obscured the normal landmarks, but brilliant colors in the east suggested the sun was preparing to make an appearance. I slipped into my position next to Gottlieb and came to attention just as the bugler sounded his final note. The vacant spot behind me would have been obvious if the sun were higher in the sky. George quietly filled the void while the First Sergeant had his back turned to converse with Captain Williams.

"You lucked out again," I whispered. In the semi-darkness there was little need to fret about moving lips. George tucked in his shirt and pretended he had been there all along.

We hadn't seen much of Captain Williams since our arrival. Casper said the captain and the other officers were taking classes on military strategy. I hoped he received good grades. Our lives could depend on it. Today the twelve companies of the 5th Michigan Cavalry Regiment would be maneuvering as a unit under the command of Colonel Joseph T. Copeland. I hadn't heard of Copeland, but Casper said he had military experience and was a Michigan Supreme Court Judge before the war. The military experience sounded good, but I was leery of politicians and attorneys.

The First Sergeant concluded his conversation with the company commander and called the company to attention. Most of us were already standing at attention. I assumed it was a requirement at the end of reveille. Captain Williams stepped forward to address the company.

"Gentlemen, today the 5th Cavalry regiment will be defending a strategic river crossing." Williams could have been addressing a jury. The First Sergeant never called us gentlemen. "The 20th and 21st Michigan Infantry regiments will attack our positions in an attempt to seize the bridge. I needn't point out we will be outnumbered two to one, but defenders traditionally have the advantage. This is a training maneuver on rapid deployment of troops. All twelve companies must arrive in sufficient time to set up our defense before the infantry can organize an attack. You will not draw your sabers or engage the attackers. We don't want injuries. Do I make myself clear?" There were many nods of agreement.

"I also have good news to share," Williams continued. "Tomorrow you will be issued horses. We will be cavalry."

"Hip, hip, hooray!" The outburst was spontaneous and almost unanimous. The Captain seemed pleased with the response, but the First Sergeant did not share his pleasure. That was not proper military behavior for troops standing at attention. Due to the multitude of people requiring discipline, the First Sergeant chose to overlook the indiscretion.

"COMPANY—RIGHT FACE." We turned to the right in unison.

"The company commander is calling out the marching orders," I whispered to Gottlieb.

"I'll take him over that First Sergeant any day." George assumed he was safely hidden behind me and didn't bother to whisper.

"FORWARD—MARCH."

Everyone simultaneously stepped out on his left foot, and the company moved forward as a unit. The quality of our marching had improved considerably during the prior two weeks. Captain Williams marched us in a column of fours alongside the road leading west. We must have marched two or three miles before we reached the outskirts of the city.

"COLUMN RIGHT—MARCH." The four columns turned ninety degrees to the right and headed across a field.

"ROUT-STEP—MARCH."

Rout-step allowed us to walk normally as long as we stayed close to our regular formation. It would have been impossible to march in step across the fields.

"Do you think the Captain knows what he is doing?" George asked.

"You were the one who bestowed high praise when we left the fort," I reminded him.

"I merely suggested he was more humane than the First Sergeant."

"I want to know how he expects us to defend a bridge if we have no firearms and can't use our sabers." Gottlieb asked. The Company Commander must have entertained similar thoughts.

"COMPANY HALT!"

"Gentlemen, we will take a fifteen-minute break. See that patch of tag elders? I want everyone to cut a three and a half foot section and remove the branches. They will be our rifles for today's exercise."

"FALL—OUT."

Fifteen minutes later we were back in marching formation with tag elder poles at right-shoulder-arms.

"You happy now, Gottlieb?" I asked. "We are now sufficiently armed."

Gottlieb was sulking and ignored my statement. The tag elders were one more item to carry. It was not that they were heavy, but they did occupy an arm that previously had been free to scratch itches should they develop.

We must have walked another two miles across fields, meadows, and the occasional woods. Many of the men were grumbling, but I personally enjoyed the exercise and fresh air, and the walking wasn't difficult.

"Will, see that split rail fence up yonder?"

I looked where George was pointing. No farther than one hundred yards ahead of us was a split rail fence blocking our path.

"You know the military marching command for scaling a fence?" George asked."

"Climb-fence—march?" I asked.

"I don't think that command is in the military vocabulary," George replied. "I'm betting the Company Commander won't know what to do."

"I say we march right into the fence like lemmings leaping off a cliff," Gottlieb suggested.

Gottlieb was in the front row and fully capable of pulling off such a stunt. A monstrous pile up of one hundred men did offer possibilities. I was in favor of anything humorous that would break the monotony of the long march. I could tell from the Company Commander's worried expression he was cognizant of our plans. Gottlieb and his three companions in the front row were marching toward their destiny with renewed vigor. The Company

Commander was facing a no-win situation: Asking the First Sergeant for help, would suggest he was incompetent. Letting one hundred men pile up on a split rail fence would prove he was incompetent.

The fence was fast approaching. Gottlieb increased his pace and the other three men in the front row did likewise. I was thinking Gottlieb deserved a promotion; he was exhibiting leadership. Gottlieb was within three paces of his moment in glory!

"Company—halt!" Captain Williams pulled out a map as if the fence was not an issue.

"Gentlemen, I need a moment or two to study my map. Take a five-minute break and then reform on the other side of the fence." Williams returned to his map while his disheartened troops climbed over the fence. I could tell Gottlieb was particularly disappointed. Victory had been within his grasp and then the Company Commander checkmated him with an unorthodox command. He had been cheated. Never trust a lawyer.

We reformed on the other side of the fence and continued marching in the same direction as before, proving what everyone had suspected—reading the map had been a deceitful ploy. Twenty-six minutes later—according to my pocket watch—we arrived at a small farm.

The owner of the farm—a Mr. Adam Brickly—was not pleased to see one hundred men armed with tag alder branches descend upon his premises. He was even less joyful to hear that eleven additional companies were converging on his farm. Captain Williams explained we had arrived to protect his bridge from two infantry regiments. Adam Brickly turned out to be a patriotic fellow, and after the training exercise was fully explained gave us his blessing. He gathered his wife and children into his house where they could observe the engagement from the safety of their farmhouse.

Within minutes other companies marched in from the surrounding fields and forests. It was impressive that twelve companies could converge on a single location within minutes of each other. Perhaps marching in formation had its virtues. One would think twelve hundred men would have little difficulty defending Brickly's Bridge against mere infantry soldiers. The bridge was little more than a few timbers over a small creek, hardly worth the effort, but that was a decision for officers.

Once all the companies were present, Col. Copeland set about organizing the defense of Brickly's Bridge. A large stone wall ran along the south side of the Regiment's perimeter. He assigned our company and two other companies to defend the wall. A drainage ditch flowing into the creek provided a natural moat on the north side of our perimeter. Anyone attacking from the north would have to descend into the ditch, wade across the water, and then crawl up the other side. Col. Copeland assigned three companies to ensure no attackers made it up the ditch.

The east side of our perimeter would be the most difficult to defend; there was no natural barrier, but that didn't deter the three companies assigned to its defense. They carefully turned several wagons onto their sides before Mr. Brickly could articulate his displeasure. The stack of firewood beside the Brickly farmhouse was relocated to form a three-foot high wall between the wagons. Old packing barrels and water troughs plugged what gaping holes remained. The regiment commander kept three companies in reserve in case they were needed to reinforce a weakened position. This was a common strategy.

"That should hold them even if they do outnumber us two to one," I said.

"They're only infantry," George replied.

"One glimpse at our fortifications and they'll turn tail and run for their mommas," Gottlieb suggested.

It was our first battle and, needless to say, we were exuding confidence. No foot soldiers would gain the best of us. The fact that we lacked horses was a trivial circumstance beyond our immediate control; we were still cavalry. We would defend Brickly's bridge to the last man. We would take on all comers— and we would be victorious.

It wasn't long before our adversaries appeared on the battlefield. Row after row of infantrymen marched to the cadence dictated by ten drummers and two fife players. Their officers deployed the troops in a semicircle around our defensive positions. I was relieved to note they also lacked weapons. It appeared they didn't even possess tag elder branches.

"You ever see a prettier marching band?" I asked George.

"They might look good in a Fourth of July parade, but this isn't Main Street," George replied.

"Their drummers have to be better than our bugler," Gottlieb said. "That bugler of ours couldn't carry a tune with a tote pole."

We watched as company after company of infantrymen filed into their fighting positions, all to the beat of the drummers. The two full infantry regiments provided an impressive gathering of men. There must have been close to three thousand soldiers lining up in front of us. We had at most twelve hundred men. We were all that stood between our adversaries and the Brickly Bridge. We waited, standing shoulder to shoulder with our tag alder guns resting on the stone wall we were determined to defend.

"Gentlemen, listen up." Captain Williams was making the rounds to exhort his men. "When the infantry gets close to the stone wall fall back to the Brickly Bridge, where we will surrender. But wait until they almost reach the wall. We want to make this look good." Williams hurried on to explain the drill to the rest of his company.

"Did you hear that?" I asked.

"Don't expect me to be the first to surrender," George replied. "I'm here to defend this real estate."

"I'll still be here defending the Brickly Bridge long after the regimental commander has lowered his colors." Gottlieb took up a defiant stance, tag elder rifle at the ready.

I heard similar sentiments mumbled along the ranks; the majority of the troops shared our distain for surrender. If the infantry wanted the Brickly Bridge, they would have to come and take it. And it appeared they were about to do that. The line of skirmishers began advancing toward us. Drums continued to roll. A large wheat field was all that stood before us. Adam Brickly was fortunate to have harvested the wheat, otherwise it would have been trampled to the ground; there were that many soldiers. Officers on horseback rode behind the assemblage.

"Here they come!"

I had no more than said that when the officers on horseback yelled, "Charge!" The men broke into a run, yelling at the limits of their voices as they traversed the last hundred yards. The attackers looked silly running across the field without so much as a tag elder rifle. They must have heard we would surrender, because they momentarily stopped in bewilderment several yards in front of the wall when we failed to yield. Then they attacked in vigor.

I swatted my tag elder at the first man to reach my defensive position. He grabbed the branch and tried to wrestle if from me but quickly released his grip when I punched him in the throat. George had his adversary in a headlock while Gottlieb gave him a severe tag elder thrashing. I looked over at Casper—he was holding his own. Not bad for a man of fifty-one. No one had yet breached our perimeter.

"Fall back, men!" Col. Copeland was doing his best to follow the script, which did not include hand to hand combat. I doubt if any of the men would have followed his order even if they could have heard it above the whooping and hollering of the contestants from both sides. He ordered the bugler to play the bugle call for CEASE FIRE followed by RETREAT. Neither bugle call swayed the course of battle. Sheer numbers did exert an influence. Several attackers breached our wall, and we were in danger of being overrun. I thought all was lost, and it would have been if not for one of the companies held in reserve. The men in the reserve company decided it was time for deployment with or without the blessing of the regiment commander. They charged into our ranks and forced the aggressors back across the stone wall. The other two companies held in reserve reinforced the left flank and the perimeter front.

I didn't have time to consult my pocket watch, but the *Battle of Brickly's Bridge* must have lasted well over twenty minutes. It didn't end until the infantry commanders ordered a retreat. Fortunately, their men were better at following orders.

We had won our first battle, but it was not without cost. George had a split lip. My knuckles were bleeding, and my right eye was beginning to swell shut. Casper and Gottlieb also sported an assortment of battle injuries.

The officers were verbalizing their displeasure with our behavior, but they were not the ones I feared most. I scanned the wounded warriors searching for the First Sergeant. Then I found him standing defiantly before Brickly's Bridge. He had the beginning of a shiner—and he was smiling!

CHAPTER FIVE

As I had feared, my pain intensified on the day following the *Battle of Brickly's Bridge*. Swelling during the night severely compromised my right eye, and muscles I previously hadn't believed existed bitterly complained with every movement. Despite my misfortune, I fared better than some individuals: Three people shattered bones during the melee and now sported short-arm casts. It was doubtful if the military would retain their services.

There were benefits to our recent scuffle. Yesterday we were individuals. We restricted our friendships to those we knew prior to enlisting. The *Battle of Brickly's Bridge* changed that forever. Now we were battle hardened veterans who wore their bruises proudly. Now we had pride in our unit. We were no longer just members of the 5th Michigan Cavalry Regiment—we were members of the Fightin' Fifth!

Although we had our aches and pains, not all was unpleasant; we were assigned horses as the company commander had promised. The First Sergeant introduced us to a new bugle command called *Stable Duty*. After the bugler gave this new ditty his best shot, the First Sergeant marched us down to the stables and introduced us to our horses. My horse was a three-year-old gelding with a chestnut coat and big floppy ears. I was thinking of a relaxing horseback ride through the countryside. The First Sergeant was thinking otherwise. He issued pitchforks instead of saddles. It had been several weeks since anyone had last mucked out the stables. Apparently, the First Sergeant expected us to learn horsemanship from the ground up. This was business as usual for a farmer, but you should have heard the city boys complain.

"You think we'll ever ride these nags?" George scooped a pitchfork full of manure and tossed it into a waiting wheelbarrow. Enough manure remained to fill the wheelbarrow several times.

"If you can find a couple of saddles, I'm willing," I replied.

I had every intention of mucking out my stall, but I felt introductions were in order. Horses can be apprehensive about strangers in their stalls. They fear the unknown just like people. With fear comes anxiety and that is when people get hurt.

"Hi, there, big fellow."

The chestnut gelding studied me for a moment trying to decide if I were friend or foe. I knew first impressions were important, and I came prepared. I had filled my pockets with apples from an apple tree I had discovered just outside the camp. My Prince could never resist a fresh apple. I was hoping this horse had similar tastes.

"Would you like a juicy apple?"

I held the apple in my open palm, but waited a respectable distance from the horse. I assumed the horse would feel less threatened if it came to me. I remained motionless and talked softly. I was in no hurry, but neither was the horse. It looked at the apple in my hand and then looked at me. It was a difficult choice. In the end, the horse declined my offer.

"Have you eaten an apple?"

Not all horses have had that pleasure. I gently placed the apple on some clean straw and stepped back. The horse reassessed the situation, and then after a moment or two stepped forward and bit into the apple.

"I have more where that came from." I retrieved a second apple from my pocket and held it out. He must have liked the first apple, because I now had his undivided attention.

"If you want this one you have to come and get it." I held the apple at arm's length. The horse stepped forward to grab the apple and then stepped backward into the safety of its stall. All the horses were saddle trained, but some were wary of new masters. After the third apple, I knew we would be friends.

"I have a horse at home just like you," I said, "but maybe a tad older than you. His name is Prince." I scratched the horse behind the ear, something my Prince thoroughly enjoyed. "I think I will also call you Prince. Is that okay?" Prince ignored my comment and worked his head toward the one remaining bulge in my pocket. "Okay, but this is the last apple. I'll bring some more tomorrow."

I cleaned out Prince's stall and spread down fresh straw. Then I brushed him down and checked his hooves. I picked loose several stone chips embedded under his shoe. Prince seemed appreciative. It was close to noon when I finished grooming Prince. I fed him some oats and then hunted up George. He was brushing down the dun colored gelding assigned to him.

"You ready for chow?"

"Let me give Sam some oats first," George replied.

Casper and Gottlieb had already been through the serving line when George and I arrived at the makeshift mess hall. We filled our trays and sat down beside them. They were rehashing yesterday's battle. It was Gottlieb's opinion we could have defended the bridge against three infantry regiments if necessary. Casper was more rational in his assessment; we were armed with tag alders, our opponents were defenseless.

"Will, you got a letter from home today." As squad leader, Casper was responsible for delivering letters to his men. "I placed it under your pillow."

"Thanks."

That had to be a letter from Mary. I gulped down my food and then almost ran to the barracks. This would be my first letter from Mary. I found the letter under my pillow as Casper had said.

Sept. 17, 1862

Dear Will,

We are doing fine, but we miss you. Several times the boys have asked for their daddy. I have told them you may be gone a long time. They don't seem to fully understand, and will ask again the next day. Mary Elizabeth is too young to verbalize her thoughts, but she knows something is not right.

I am keeping busy thrashing the wheat you left in the barn. In another two or three days I will take some to town and have it ground into flour. The vegetables from the garden will soon be ready for canning, and I have already dug up the potatoes and stored them in our root-cellar. With the money from our eggs and milk, we should make it through the winter.

We did have some excitement the other day. The pigs broke through that fence you built and immediately converged on the garden. I was able to shoo them away before they created much damage. My cousin came over and helped me round them up. Pigs look lazy, but they sure can run. We patched the fence such that I doubt they will escape again.

The folks at church ask about you. I tell them how proud I am, and I promised to share your letters, at least the parts that aren't too personal. Please write frequently. I need to hear from you to know you are safe. I think I miss you the most at night when I lie in the bed I had shared with you. That is when we shared the small talk. I know small talk means little to a man, but a woman needs small talk. I pray every night for your safety and that this war will end quickly so you can return home to your family. I love you, Will.
Love,

Mary

I returned the letter to its envelope and placed it inside my pillow case. I knew I would want to read it again.

That afternoon we rode our horses for the first time. Prince had the potential to make a fine mount. He was full of energy. I bribed Prince with an apple before cinching on his saddle. As long as I had apples, we bonded well, and he offered no complaints when I climbed onto the saddle. I think he was as eager to get out of the stable as I was.

The First Sergeant tried to get us into formation on the parade grounds outside the barracks. We were to advance in a column of fours. Prince and I had no difficulties, but some of the city boys had never ridden a horse. They had their horses so confused they were spinning in circles. By late afternoon we had mastered a few limited maneuvers. The First Sergeant must have been impressed with our progress, because he lined us up in a parade formation for the company commander's review. Captain Williams appeared pleased with our new skills.

"Gentlemen, how about a ride in the countryside?" We had been in the military long enough to know an officer's suggestion was the same as an order.

"COMPANY—RIGHT FACE."

Prince responded to my command and turned ninety degrees to the right. I gave him an atta-boy and patted him on the neck. Other horses were not so accommodating, mostly because their riders did not properly relay the command. Some horses stepped forward and others reared up in place. After a few moments of confusion everyone faced the same direction.

"FORWARD MARCH." Captain Williams led us west in a column of fours. It wasn't a pretty sight, but most of the company achieved the required formation. Individuals with limited equestrian skills quickly learned to give the horse free rein. The horse then dutifully followed the horse in front of it.

"This is more like it," I said. "Let the infantry do the walking."

Gottlieb, George, and I rode in the front rank with Casper as squad leader on our right. Being in the lead rank we didn't ingest the dust generated by the hooves of a hundred horses, nor did we have to stare at the posterior of the horse in front of us. We were able to enjoy the scenery.

"This is okay, but I would like to gallop our horses," Gottlieb replied. "I'd like to know how fast I can retreat if I had to."

I knew Gottlieb was jesting, but I also hankered to know my horse's limitations. It was unlikely we would get such a chance while walking our horses in formation. After an hour and ten minutes by my pocket watch we arrived at a meadow bounded by a small stream.

"Gentlemen, we will take a twenty-minute break to rest and water the horses." Captain Williams dismounted and led his horse toward the stream. George and Casper did likewise.

"Will, Ya think the water on the far side of the stream is sweater?" Gottlieb asked.

"Only one way to find out," I replied.

We both shortened our reins and leaned forward. A slap on Prince's rump sent him forward at full gallop. I had thought Prince could outrun Gottlieb's nag, but we were galloping side by side as we approached the stream. I aimed for an opening along the stream where no one was watering horses. As we reached the edge of the stream I went into a two-point stance and gave Prince his head. I grabbed a fistful of mane to maintain my balance. Prince gave the jump his best but the mud under his hind feet was soft and gave way, severely limiting his jump. Prince and I came down short of the far bank. Gottlieb didn't fare much better. The resultant splash sprayed water over some troopers watering their horses. I didn't find out until later that one of them was the First Sergeant.

✳✳✳

"You guys want something to eat?" George asked.

I looked around to assure that no one was watching. The sergeant monitoring our guard duty was nowhere in sight. He must have responded to nature's call. George had chosen his time wisely.

"Thanks," I said. "I was starving." George gave each of us a sandwich.

"You were lucky," Gottlieb said. "You only had to march back and forth in front of the garbage cans. Now that we know close-order drill, the First Sergeant expects us to smartly execute an about face at the end of our walk and then do a right-shoulder-arm or a left-shoulder-arm to keep our simulated rifles on the outside shoulder."

"And he expects us to pass each other in the center of our walk," I added.

"In the future check the stability of the riverbank before jumping. No horse could have made that jump without wings," George suggested. "I have to go. The sergeant of the guard will be back soon."

Gottlieb and I returned to our guard duty: Fifteen paces, about face, right shoulder arms and repeat. No rat would sneak past while Gottlieb and I were on guard.

CHAPTER SIX

My enthusiasm for the war began to wane as the weeks passed. Training was long and demanding. I returned every evening exhausted from the effort. Even farming was not this arduous. I longed to see Mary and the kids one more time before deploying to the front, but that was not to be. We now trained with a renewed sense of urgency. Every day we rode into the countryside, where we charged imaginary foes with our sabers and slew sawdust bags hanging from trees. We had yet to receive the new Spencer rifles we had been promised, and that was disconcerting. Sabers are nice, but they can't reach out and touch someone like a rifle bullet.

The war was not going well in the east; General McClellan was bogged down, Confederate troops were threatening Washington, and Mosby's Raiders were disrupting federal supply lines. The more proficient we became, the closer we came to deployment. Rumors of our departure for Washington floated about like leaves on a windy autumn day. We were not surprised when Casper gathered the men of our squad one afternoon for a short meeting.

"We have orders," he said. "We leave for Washington on December 4th."

We knew the orders would be coming, but we had expected more time to prepare. A week's furlough to say good bye to our families would have been nice.

"What about our rifles? Won't do much good sending us to Washington without rifles."

"Will's right," George added. "Sabers are no match against rifles and artillery."

No one wanted to shirk his duty, but marching into combat without rifles was foolhardy. I had little doubt we could whip the Rebels in a fair fight with appropriate hardware.

"The Spencers are waiting for us in Washington," Casper said. I hoped he was right.

"The fourth is two days away," Casper continued. "Training is over; use your time wisely. Pack your personal gear and horse tack. We'll ride in passenger cars at the front of the train. The horses will travel in special cars attached to the rear. Any questions?"

Before it had been an abstract concept; now it was a reality. We were going to war. I wrote a quick letter to Mary and packed my gear. Prince and I had become close companions, and I hated the thought of being separated even for a few days. Perhaps they would allow us access to our horses during stop-overs. I tried to explain our new plans to Prince, but I knew he couldn't understand. Two days later we were boarding a Michigan Central railcar heading for Washington.

George, Gottlieb, Casper, and I grabbed adjoining seats and stuffed our personal gear in the racks above our benches. Detroit was the farthest I had been from Salem. Now we would be traveling half way across the continent. Mary seemed so distant. A portion of me wondered if I would see her again. I opened my watch to push those thoughts from my mind. Mary stared up at me with her beautiful blue eyes as if to say it would be all right.

We stared out the window as we watched the last remnants of Michigan pass before us. The reality of what was happening did not strike me until they transferred our cars to the Chesapeake and Ohio Railroad—we were no longer in Michigan.

"How long do you think it'll take us to get to Washington?" I asked no one in particular.

Casper was the only one willing to venture a guess. "Two days, maybe three days at most," he replied. We continued staring out the window, looking at nothing in particular. No one had much to say. After several hours the train stopped to take on coal and water for the steam engine.

"How long will it take to load the coal?" I asked.

"Maybe half an hour," Casper replied. "What do you have in mind?"

"I'm going to check on Prince."

"The engineers will blow the whistle just before they start up. Make sure you're on board. They shoot deserters."

I ran for the exit. Horses are easily spooked, and they don't understand trains or close confinement. Horses died during such transits. That would not happen to Prince if I could prevent it. I found Prince in the third boxcar. As I suspected Prince was agitated; all the horses were. Prince saw me coming and extended his head beyond the converted cattle car's chest-high side walls. His boxcar was not enclosed, which helped. I couldn't imagine the anxiety Prince would have experienced had he been confined to a dark box for two or three days. I climbed onto the car until I stood level with Prince.

"Hello, Prince." I rubbed his muzzle. He pushed his head against me like a scared puppy. Animals were like humans—they sought comfort when terrified. "I brought you an apple." I filled my pockets and rucksack with apples prior to leaving. I assumed they would come in handy.

All the horses were confined to small boxes to prevent them from running when spooked. It was an accident waiting to happen should the train make a sudden stop. I felt along Prince's shoulders but discovered no cuts or bruises.

When I heard the blast from the train whistle, I gave Prince one more apple and ran for my car. I grabbed the handrail and pulled myself up as the train began to gather speed.

"How's Prince?" George asked when I had returned to my seat.

"Terrified," I replied. "Some of those horses won't make it to Washington."

"They're the lucky ones," Casper said. "Horses don't fare well in war. Their survival rate is worse than the men who ride them into battle. Some horses are killed by rifle or artillery, but the majority are worked to death."

I never considered the danger horses faced in combat, but what Casper was saying made sense; horses provided a larger target. I couldn't prevent him from being shot, but as long as he remained my horse he would not be worked to death.

We watched the passing trees and the occasional village until evening approached and the view outside our window faded into darkness. I closed my eyes and leaned my head against the glass. I fantasized that I was lying in bed with Mary's head resting on my shoulder. I could smell the sweetness of her shampoo. I pulled her tightly against me. The rhythmic rocking motion of the train soothed my muscles and I began to relax. I was quickly overcome by sleep. When I awoke the sun was shining through the window. My three companions were awake and staring vacantly at the passing scenery. Mary was gone. No one had much to say. They were lost in their own fantasies.

"Anyone know where we are?" I asked.

"The conductor came through while you slept," Gottlieb replied. "He thought we were somewhere in central Ohio."

I nodded. Ohio was a big state. I assumed it would be late in the day before we crossed into the foothills of Pennsylvania. Our train pulled many cars, which profoundly stressed the engine, forcing frequent stops to satisfy the engine's hunger and thirst. Each time we stopped, I ran back to check on Prince and offer an apple. Prince began anticipating these visits, and as soon as the train stopped he would poke his head over the rail and look toward the passenger cars. I don't know if he was excited to see me or just wanted my apples. Either way, I think the visits helped both of us endure the train ride.

Horse Photo

Farm boys like William Goodman knew how to properly care for farm animals such as horses, but for the U.S. Army, they were just another commodity to be used or abused. The military needed to transport hundreds of horses from Fort Wayne to Washington D.C. by train. The most economical method was to overload them into cattle cars. It is questionable how often they were fed or provided water during the three day trip. The unfamiliar noise, smoke, and motion of the train must have terrified the horses. Many horses were injured by the time they arrived in Washington. Any horse that died was replaced. They were only a commodity.

William Goodman and his fellow horsesoldiers endured numerous hardships on long forced marches, but they always rode horses. Senior officers often pushed the horses and men just for a few complimentary headlines in the newspapers. Horses were only a commodity.

***

By late evening we crossed into Pennsylvania. We would never have known from looking out the window, if the conductor hadn't walked by and confirmed it. Twenty minutes into Pennsylvania the engineer diverted our train to a side track. We had an extensive layover while railway workers transferred our cars to the Pennsylvania R.R. I made use of the time to stretch my legs. A patina of white snow covered the ground, not unexpected for this time of year. I checked on Prince and then got a bite to eat at a local cantina. It was late in the evening, and few locals noticed the arrival of twelve hundred men in uniform. Those that did notice gave us little thought. We were approaching the war zone where men in uniform were a common sight.

I climbed onboard when the whistle blew. The train pulled out from the station, heading east. We were hugging northern Pennsylvania. I found that odd since Washington was much farther south.

"Casper, are we still going to Washington?" I asked. "The train is going too far north for Washington."

"I think the army is sending us to New York," George added. "Army information isn't noted for its accuracy. It's just like the army to tell us we are going to Washington and then send us to New York City."

"Going to New York City wouldn't hurt my feelings. I got kinfolk there," Gottlieb offered. I had thought he was sleeping.

"The last three months we've been training for war. You think we'll find any battles to fight in New York City?" Casper loosened the cravat around his neck. It was just like him to offer a teaser and then leave us hanging in suspense. "Have you heard of Mosby's raiders?" He asked. I had heard the name before, but I couldn't remember the context.

"It's a renegade cavalry unit," he continued. "They work behind Union lines cutting telegraph wires and destroying railroad tracks. They have us traveling through northern Pennsylvania to avoid contact with Mosby's raiders. We'll probably turn south at Reading, Pennsylvania and then continue into Washington."

That was a sobering revelation. If what Casper was saying was correct, we were already at the front lines. If Mosby's raiders were to attack us, we would be totally helpless. Sabers were useless against rifles. We stared out the window. If Mosby were out there, we would not have seen him in the darkness. The train continued eastward with its steady rocking motion.

I awoke when the train lurched forward. It must have stopped momentarily. It was now slowly creeping forward again. The overcast sky suggested a gloomy morning. My three companions were still sleeping. I flagged down a conductor who was passing through our car.

"Do you know where we are?" I asked.

"We just pulled into Reading," he replied. "We'll change cars to the Reading and Philadelphia R.R. Then we'll head south to Washington. We should arrive before evening."

"Thank you," I said. Our journey was almost finished. I was beginning to feel claustrophobic in the confines of our train car. Farm boys need open spaces. I was sure the journey's end would please Prince. He had weathered the trip well. That was more than I could say for many of the horses. At least three horses in Prince's car had gone lame. I saw another horse with a large gash on its shoulder. It must have been thrown against the railing. Not much could be done for any of them until we arrived at our destination.

Towns and villages were more closely spaced on the east coast, but we didn't stop at any of them unless the engine was in need of water or coal. Our cars were filled to capacity. We had no room for additional passengers even if travelers were to seek accommodations.

We skirted the west side of Baltimore without stopping for coal and water. I questioned the conductor about this oddity and was told Baltimore had too many southern sympathizers. They had experienced ugly confrontations in the past and had no desire to risk further violence. As long as coal and water were available in smaller towns, stopping at Baltimore wasn't worth the risk. We had entered the buffer zone between north and south. Several hours later we crossed the Anacostia River and ambled into Washington.

The train stopped on a short side spur. I looked out the windows on both sides of the train and saw nothing to indicate a train station, but the unfinished capitol dome in the distance left little doubt we had arrived in the nation's capital. Droplets of water from a light mist dripped down our windows. It must have rained harder in the recent past, since the road paralleling the tracks was covered with mud. That didn't deter the numerous military supply wagons rushing toward their destinations. Men in uniform filled the streets. We had reached the war zone.

"GRAB YOUR GEAR. FORMATION IN FRONT OF THE TRAIN FOR HEAD COUNT." The First Sergeant walked from car to car to ensure everyone heard his order. The few individuals who managed to sleep through our arrival into Washington were rudely shaken awake. I was now a firm believer in Casper's hurry up and wait philosophy. I was not excited about standing in the rain any longer than need be. I grabbed my gear and waited for the aisle to clear before walking toward the exit.

The light drizzle had momentarily ceased, but the overcast sky suggested a downpour could erupt any moment. December was cold, even in Washington, and we had no raingear. If we were to get drenched, it wouldn't take long for hypothermia to set in. We needed shelter. I wondered where the city would find accommodations for an additional twelve hundred men.

The First Sergeant lined us up in a column of fours while his platoon sergeants took roll call. After everyone was accounted for, the First Sergeant marched us down the mud-caked street. Fortunately, he allowed route-step, which permitted us to walk freely. No one could march in step through that deep mud. Even walking provided a challenge. Our feet sank up to our ankles and we had to fight the suction when we extracted a foot for the next step.

Despite the momentary hardship, it felt good to escape the confines of the coach. The train cars had been warm and dry and the bench seats soft. I knew we would soon long for such luxuries, but we did not enlist for lavish comfort. We hiked about a mile and then turned east. Gossip passed down the ranks suggested we were heading for Capitol Hill east of the Capital dome. They called it a hill, but one would find sledding down such a gentle slope challenging, assuming they acquired sufficient winter snow. I would have preferred snow to the on and off light drizzle. Snow does not penetrate clothing as efficiently as rain.

The First Sergeant marched us onto an open field, where thick sod eagerly soaked up the water; we were out of the mud, which met everyone's approval. He brought us to a halt in front of a medium-sized, walled tent. I assumed the tent somehow justified our standing in the rain. The First Sergeant slipped into the tent and exited moments later with our company commander. We hadn't seen him during the trip. He must have arrived on an earlier train to coordinate our arrival.

"Gentlemen, welcome to Washington. We have a lot of work to do today, so I will defer my boring speech till a later day." This statement produced laughter from the men. The First Sergeant was not impressed. Apparently, levity enjoys no role while standing at attention.

"Each squad leader will draw a Sibley tent from the quartermaster. This field will be our base camp for the coming months. The tent was designed for twelve people. An eight-man squad should have plenty of room for gear."

"What about our rifles?" someone shouted from the back. This further elevated the First Sergeant's displeasure. He vainly tried to identify the culprit, but with over a hundred men in our company, the task was hopeless.

"The Spencer rifles were mistakenly shipped to Detroit. I have been assured by the army that upon arrival in Detroit the rifles will be returned to Washington on the next available train." This confession was greeted by mixture of groans and laughter.

"Perhaps we should return to Detroit and wait until the army decides where it wishes to fight this war," I suggested without moving my lips.

"I think we should declare war on Allegan County," George replied. "We could battle it out with wild turkeys in the afternoon and be home in time for dinner. Roast turkey with dressing and cranberry sauce would make a nice dinner."

Captain Williams continued explaining minor details concerning our deployment in Washington, but few people were listening. The rain was beginning to penetrate our clothing. We were more concerned with finding shelter from the elements. He finally ran out of trivia to discuss and concluded his briefing. He returned to the warmth of his tent, while the First Sergeant dismissed us.

Casper volunteered Gottlieb to help him procure our Sibley tent. They returned with a folded pile of canvas and a fancy wooden pole with three metal side-spokes at one end. They dropped them in a pile in front of us. We stared at the equipment for a moment until we decided that wasn't productive.

"Ever put one of these up?" I asked Casper.

"Nope, they didn't have 'em during the Spanish American War."

We stared at the canvas some more, as if that would somehow motivate the tent to erect itself.

"I propose we ask Mr. Sibley to show us how to operate this apparatus," George suggested.

"You'll need permission from his commanding officer," Casper said.

"And who might that be?"

"Robert E. Lee. Major Henry Sibley joined the Rebels over a year ago."

That revelation didn't sit well with me. We would be sleeping in a tent designed by the enemy. The rain was coming down with increased intensity, and the dense cloud cover suggested no immediate relief. I decided to put political differences aside; we needed shelter from the rain.

I picked up the wooden pole. It was about eight feet long. Three metal spokes on hinges separated from the pole forming a tripod of sorts. The wooden pole telescoped upward through the apex of the tripod.

"I think the canvas goes over this pole," I suggested.

We stretched out the canvas. In the center we found a hole circumscribed by a metal hoop. Chains extended inward toward a metal cup.

"I think the tip of the pole fits into this cup," I said. No one offered an opposing opinion.

Up to this point the other four men in our squad had been watching our efforts with mild curiosity. Corporal Raab assigned each one a task. The squad members grabbed an edge of the tent while I guided the pole under the canvas and inserted the tip into the metal cup. I heaved up on the pole, but the tent was too heavy.

"I need some help," I said. Two men came to my aid, and we raised the pole to an upright position. Once we spread the legs of the tripod, the pole stood by itself. Then we raised the pole up through the apex of the tripod until only a hook at the bottom of the pole remained between the legs of the tripod. I assumed the hook was for hanging a kettle over a fire pit under the tripod.

"Everyone grab a stake and the edge of the canvas." Casper worked his way around the circumference, pounding in the stakes with a stone. When the tent was finished it measured twelve feet tall at the center and eighteen feet in diameter. It would provide plenty of room for the eight squad members and our gear. Once we had a roaring fire in the fire pit, our canvas dwelling became quite cozy—almost too hot.

"Listen up, men," Casper said. "We're free for the rest of the day, but make sure you stop by the quartermaster. He'll issue you a cot, blanket, and oil skin. There will be a roll call at dusk. Be back before then.

Sibley Tent Photos

Interior of Sibley Tent

The Sibley tent was invented and patented in 1856 by West point Graduate Henry Sibley who resigned his commission to become a Confederate general. The tent has many similarities to the Native American teepee except that the tent is held up by a single pole mounted on a tripod. It was 12 feet high and 18 feet in diameter and could house a dozen soldiers. The above sketch is by Herbert Eugene Valentine (1841–1917) of Company F, 23rd Regiment, Massachusetts Volunteers.

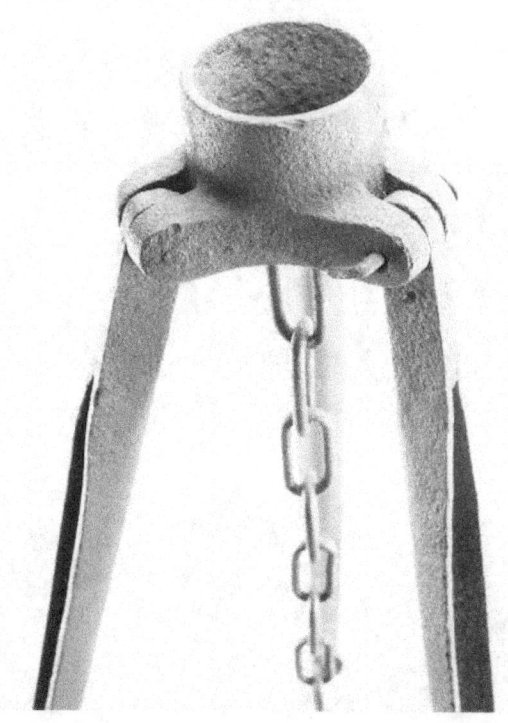

The key design feature of the Sibley tent was the unique tripod with a cup at the apex. The cup held the center pole, which telescoped up twelve feet. The canvas was fixed in place by twenty-four tent pegs. The telescoping center pole made the tents easy to store or transport. At the apex of the tent was a smoke hole, so soldiers could create a cooking fire under the tripod and hang a pot from the dangling chain. If the soldiers were lucky, they might have had a Sibley stove as shown in the first drawing. This worked like a potbellied stove.

The Union Army produced nearly 44,000 Sibley tents during the war, but Sibley received no royalties from his patent. His relatives tried to obtain royalties after the war but they were unsuccessful.

***

Dear Mary,

We have safely arrived in Washington after a tedious seventy-five hour train ride. I do believe we stopped at every village and town along the way to take on water and coal. The train ride terrified Prince, but he suffered no physical harm, unlike many horses. A large bay has a nasty gash on its shoulder from being thrown against the wall, and several horses are lame. I expect they will all recover with time.

It appears we will be living in tents for the foreseeable future, but it is not as bad as it sounds. The tent is eighteen feet in diameter, which provides plenty of room for our squad of eight people. We have a fire pit in the center for warmth and brewing coffee. The military provides a generous ration of coal.

The regiment still hasn't issued rifles. They said our Spencer rifles were sent to Detroit and would be sent back to Washington on return train. If that were so, we should have them by now. We are of little use to the country without guns. The army can be so disorganized at times. It is little wonder the war is lingering as long as it has.

This will be my first Christmas without you since we were married. I will miss your honey-glazed ham and your sweet potatoes and your pumpkin pie. But most of all I miss you and the children. I look at your picture on the inside cover of my pocket watch several times a day. You are the last image I see before I retire. It is the only thing that makes this war tolerable.

Mary Elizabeth should soon be walking if she isn't already doing so. Children grow so quickly. I fear she will not remember me upon my return. I will save my money and purchase a photograph of me for you and the children. Perhaps you can show the picture to them, so they will not forget me.

We have much idle time and many of the men suffer boredom. I will use such time to write to you weekly, although notable events are infrequent, leaving little information to convey.

I read scriptures from the German Bible daily. The pocket watch with your picture and the Bible are the best gifts you could have given me. I do hope this war ends soon. I can't wait to hold you in my arms.
Your loving husband,
Will

CHAPTER SEVEN

We spent December and January hunkered down in our tents on East Capitol Hill. The army had issued breach-loading Spencer rifles capable of firing seven rounds without reloading. Now that we were armed with Spencers and .44 caliber Colt Army Revolvers, we felt invincible—not that we had need of such weaponry. War was seasonal. Supply wagons can't travel in deep snow and without supply wagons armies cannot function.

I felt a chill and rose to add coal to the dwindling flame in the fire pit. The day was cold with little evidence the weather was inclined to improve before morning. We would need a larger fire to see us through the night.

"You're wasting coal," Casper said when he saw me adding the coal. "We won't need it tonight."

Casper strapped down the canvas flap to the tent door. He had just returned from a meeting with our platoon leader. Either he was predicting balmy weather and sunshine or he was bearing significant information from higher up. Needless to say, he had everyone's attention.

"So, what's up?" George asked.

"At one a.m. the regiment will be moving out. Each man will carry three days' cooked rations and forty rounds of ammunition. You'll need a bag of oats for your horse. Any questions?"

"What about the rest of our belongings?" Gottlieb asked.

"Personal gear and tent stay behind; it looks like we're returning."

"Who's in charge?" I asked.

"The regimental commander...but the XO and Major Ferry are coming with us," Casper added when he sensed my reservation.

Colonel Norvell had a justly-acquired reputation for drunkenness. I didn't know how many accusations were true, but if a tenth of them had merit, it provided grounds for concern. A trooper from Company D said Norvell had him search a house and barn for alcohol. Another trooper claimed Norvell interrupted a forced march, so he could nap at a convenient farmhouse. Several variations of that story had Norvell passed out and carried to the bed. This was not the competency of a commander I wanted to follow into battle.

I looked at my pocket watch; we would be leaving in less than three hours. Casper escorted the squad to the supply tent where we obtained three days' supply of hard bread and meat. We stabbed the meat with our sabers and then roasted the meat over the fire-pit flame; the extra coal I added came in handy. We only browned the outside of the meat. Any fat drizzling off our meat was lost nourishment. Some men ate their meat raw to avoid wasting fat; I preferred my meat, at minimum, brown on the outside. After cooling, we added the meat and hard bread to our haversacks. Spoilage was not a concern in Washington's cold, February weather.

We fed the horses and then ate a midnight meal. Departing with full stomachs reduced the food we needed to carry. With our preparations complete, we sat around the fire pit debating the significance of our new orders. We had never ventured forth as a complete regiment, and training exercises never commenced at midnight. Officers are creatures of comfort. They enjoyed their sleep. Something beyond their control was brewing and it filled me with excitement and trepidation. There were always rumors of Rebels approaching Washington. Sometimes rumors become fact. I hoped this was not the case.

At precisely one a.m. the bugler sounded *Boots and Saddles*. Moments later, he played *To Horse*. We slipped into our boots and grabbed our saddles. A steady drizzle had drenched everything exposed to the elements. At the current temperature, it could turn into snow. I would have preferred snow. You can brush snow off your clothing. I looked up at the sky hoping to see an occasional star shining through the cloud cover—I saw none. The weather offered no indication of improvement, further suggesting this was not a drill; officers don't train in the rain. I slipped my oil-skin poncho over my head. They were designed to keep us dry, but I could feel cold water dripping down my neck.

We had tethered our horses to a stake beside our tent. They stood motionless, oblivious to the rain. With horses it was difficult to tell when they were sleeping. I gave Prince the benefit of the doubt; I did not wish to throw a saddle on a sleeping horse.

"Wake up, Prince," I said from a distance. "We have work to do."

Prince wiggled his ears, but he otherwise ignored me. He assumed night was for sleeping. I agreed with him. Unfortunately, some officers thought otherwise. I placed the saddle blanket on his back and then strapped on the saddle. I disliked placing a saddle on a wet horse, as it often creates skin sores. I hoped the dry saddle blanket would provide some protection. I strapped my bedroll and shelter half to the back of the saddle and mounted up. The First Sergeant did a quick roll call. Once everyone was accounted for, the bugler sounded *Forward*. We marched out in a column of fours.

Twelve hundred men and horses paraded through the deserted streets of Washington. Those fortunate enough to sleep in warm beds had been exposed to the cacophony of war too long to fret about hundreds of horses splashing through the puddles below. We passed the uncompleted dome of the Capital. At one time we would have paid notice, but tonight it was little more than a shadow in the rain.

We continued west, confirming our suspicions; we were heading toward Virginia. Column of fours was the standard formation for cavalry marches. Casper, George, Gottlieb, and I made sure we were in the same row. The four men behind us completed our squad. I gave Prince the reins as did the others. The horses dutifully followed the horse plodding ahead of it. We could almost sleep in the saddle. I wasn't sure if the horses were also sleeping.

I reclaimed the reins as we approached Long Bridge, which spanned the Potomac and connected Washington with Virginia. The Washington Alexandria Railroad owned the bridge, but it no longer had the structural strength to support locomotives. Horses pulled the train cars across the bridge.

"Ya think this contraption can support twelve hundred men on horses?" George asked.

"We'll soon find out," I replied. By army standards each horse had to be fifteen hands high and weigh at least nine hundred and fifty pounds. With rider, that was over half a ton per horse, and we had four in a row. I tried to imagine the weight of a locomotive and arrived at an impressive number. It would have been more prudent to spread the convoy over the bridge. Instead, our horses marched nose to tail. I assumed the officers had already cleared the bridge.

"Company A is leading this parade," I said. "They'll test the bridge before we commit our men and horses." That was reassuring although the span had no doubt accommodated entire divisions in the recent past. The greatest threat to the bridge was not cavalry regiments, but Rebel saboteurs. Infantrymen guarded both sides of the bridge to prevent such mischief.

"Don't look down, Prince."

Prince was reluctant to step onto the bridge once he saw the river far below us. I had to admit, it would have been a long fall. I nudged him with my heels and he moved forward. The width of the bridge was sufficient to allow four horses traveling abreast. Large wooden beams crisscrossed on the sides to lend support, but there was no railing. If a horse were to spook and run to the side, both horse and rider would perish. I was hoping Prince had enough horse-sense to avoid that scenario.

The bridge spanned more than a mile and at one time our entire regiment was at the mercy of the bridge. We plodded forward. We had been in the military too long to question orders. The transit seemed to take forever. I never thought a mile could be so long. I was relieved when Prince placed his front hooves on Virginia terra firma. He also appeared pleased and quickened his pace. We had not traveled far into Virginia when the column came to a stop.

"Anyone know why we are stopping?" I was hoping Col. Norvell hadn't stopped to search farmhouses for alcohol. No information concerning the length of the break was forthcoming. It had been a long night and the sun would soon be sneaking up on us from the east. I dismounted.

"I'm going grab a few winks." The others dismounted to do likewise. The ground was saturated with water, but then so was I. I found a tree to lean against and was quickly overcome by sleep.

When I awoke from my brief nap, the reason for the layover became obvious; we were joining the 6th Michigan Cavalry Regiment. Our convoy was now over two thousand men strong. I hunted up an acquaintance of mine from the 6th Michigan. He was as bewildered about our mission as I was. We had a good chat, but our conversation was cut short when the bugler sounded *To Horse*. We found our mounts and continued our march toward Alexandria. The rain was not heavy, but it was persistent. Our clothing was drenched and the chill it produced penetrated to the bone. The oilskins provided minimal relief. Water leaked down our necks. We might have fared better as infantrymen. Walking heated the body. Riding a horse only warms the horse. We rode through Alexandria. It was a city ravished by war. Much of its former splendor had been transformed into boarded up buildings and rubble. I was sure each boarded building and destroyed home had a story to tell. They could tell of the quenched aspirations and dreams of families caught up in this endless and senseless war. We rode on through and did not linger to hear the tragic tales.

We reached Centerville as the sun was setting in the west. We only knew it was setting by the dimming of the daylight. The rain that had persisted throughout the day had decreased to a drizzle, but the damage had been done. Mud and large puddles covered the ground. I searched in vain for dry wood to brew a cup of coffee but found none. A hot cup of coffee would have dissipated the deep chill I had endured throughout the day.

"We're spending the night here. Get some sleep."

Casper didn't have to tell us twice. I was exhausted. The short nap earlier in the day was just that—a short nap. I searched for a suitable location that didn't contain standing water. There weren't many to choose from. Most of the men found trees to lean against; it had worked for me before. I claimed a large oak and wrapped the oilskin around my torso. Sleep came quickly.

In the morning three more regiments, the Fifth New York, the First Virginia, and the Eighteenth Pennsylvania, joined our force. According to a rumor, an Englishman by the name of Col. Sir Percy Wyndham was now in charge of the combined force. I assumed this arrangement was preferable to a drunken commanding officer, but I discovered I was mistaken. He immediately pushed toward Warrenton at a pace few horses could endure.

"The man's crazy. He's hell-bent on killing both man and horse." George was the first to voice his complaint, but others maintained similar thoughts. George was not shy when it came to expressing displeasure.

"This is for the benefit of newspapers," Casper replied. We all looked at Casper in disbelief.

"How will killing horses benefit newspapers?" Gottlieb asked.

"Newspapers don't give a damn about horses. They like to print that Colonel so and so marched so many miles in so many days. We are killing horses so an arrogant colonel can get a favorable review in a newspaper."

Casper's observation left a bitter taste in my throat. There was no need for such haste. We were secure behind the lines of Hooker's army. The only Rebels we encountered were scouts and spies, and they were seen in good supply by vigilant observers. We continued our forced march through the town of Warrenton. Warrenton would have been a good location for a short break.

We could have watered the horses in the small stream. The horses could have grazed in the open fields on the outskirts of town. Sir Percy had more important priorities. We continued our forced march.

"Will, see those two men on the hill?"

I followed George's gaze to a small hill about a half mile from our right flank. Two men on horseback were looking down at us. One appeared to have binoculars. Their gray uniforms left no doubt as to whom they were or what they were doing. We pointed them out to Casper. He rode ahead and informed our company commander. We had visions of giving chase and no doubt returning with prisoners in tow.

"What did the Captain say?" I asked when Casper returned.

"Sir Percy is aware of the Confederate scouts," Casper replied. "Capturing the scouts apparently holds no military significance."

I looked back at the Confederate scouts brazenly watching us from the hilltop. They did not fear capture; their arrogance was justified. I began to wonder if we really were at war.

That night we camped past Warrenton. The light drizzle changed to a steady downpour making sleep impossible. Lying on the ground was little different from sleeping in a shallow river. Many men had consumed their three days' rations and were now feeling the pangs of hunger. To say we were miserable understated our misfortune. I had yet to appreciate any achievements during the previous three days to justify our suffering. I didn't believe our situation could be any worse; I was wrong.

"We have picket duty," Casper said.

"Why doesn't Col. Wyndham shoot us now and be done with it?" George was already in a foul mood; adding picket duty to our list of burdens did not improve his disposition.

"Why waste bullet and powder when Johnny Reb can do the chore for him," Gottlieb replied.

Picket duty was the most dangerous job in the military, at least according to conventional wisdom. The sentry on picket duty defended a guard post several hundred yards in front of the unit's perimeter—that was enemy territory. In theory the sentry would provide advance notice of an attack by firing a warning shot into the air. In reality the warning shot was as likely the sound of a sniper's bullet striking the sentry's forehead. If for some unforeseen reason the sniper missed his mark, the sentry's own troops finished the job when the sentry ran toward the safety of the unit's perimeter.

"We are well behind our own lines," Casper said. "It is not like there are Confederate troops out there."

"Who were those men in gray uniforms watching us with binoculars?" Casper ignored George's sarcasm.

"How long do we have to be out there?" I asked.

"Our squad has two outposts to man. With eight men in the squad, I was thinking of two-hour shifts. You'll still get six hours of sleep."

"In this weather?" It was a senseless question. I didn't expect an answer and none was given. "Give me the first shift. Maybe a Rebel sniper will put me out of my misery."

I gathered extra rounds from my haversack while Casper doled out the remaining assignments. The sergeant of the guard came by to escort me to my post. George shook my hand and said it was nice knowing me. He was trying to add some levity, but it did little to cheer me up. I was too wet and too cold to appreciate his humor.

I followed the sergeant of the guard past the perimeter manned by men wielding Spencer rifles and itchy trigger fingers. I reminded them there would be friendly troops in front of their position. They replied that I better not be whistling Dixie when I came running to them for protection. Everyone wanted to be a comedian.

The sergeant led me through the woods. With the rain and overcast sky, I wasn't sure I could find my way back to the perimeter even if I had to. He came to a stop at the edge of a clearing. In daylight it might have been a farmer's field. Tonight it was only blackness.

"Anyone coming across that field will not be your friend," he said. "Shoot off a round and then make your way back to the perimeter. Someone will relieve you in two hours. Any questions?"

I shook my head, but the sergeant of the guard was already gone. He obviously had places to go. Perhaps he had a place with overhead shelter, where he could build a fire and heat a cup of coffee. I would have given a month's salary for a hot cup of coffee, anything to bring warmth to my insides. I found a log under a tree upon which to sit. It didn't protect me from the rain dripping down from the leaves, but it kept me out of the mud.

I retrieved the last of the cooked salt pork from my haversack. That also would have tasted better hot, but I was famished. Hunger improved the taste of any food. Unless Col. Wyndham was able to produce miracles, there would be no food tomorrow.

I stood up and marched in place to reduce the chill. It only provided marginal relief. I wondered if the Confederate scouts we had seen earlier were as miserable. They probably had a small dog tent hidden in the brush on high ground. They were probably sleeping under warm, dry blankets. They surely weren't preparing to attack five regiments of cavalry, not that I could stop them.

They could stroll twenty feet in front of me and I wouldn't see them, such was the rain and darkness. Nor would I hear them. The rain on the leaves produced a steady murmur, hiding all but the most flagrant noise. Under such conditions, sentry duty was worthless. It only added misery to an already unpleasant assignment.

I was tempted to strike a match to consult my pocket watch. Military wisdom stipulated that two men could light cigarettes from the same match, but the third man on a single match was a dead man. It took that long for a sniper to line up his sights and fire a round. Surely I could check my watch in less time. I resisted the temptation. Checking my watch was like watching a pot boil; it wouldn't shorten my two hours.

It might have been my imagination, but I thought I heard noise in front of me. I grabbed my rifle—it had been leaning against the log. The rain had tapered to a drizzle, allowing me to see maybe thirty yards in front of me. I saw shadows. I stared at them; they appeared to be moving...or were they small fir trees waving in the gentle breeze. I looked at the leaves in the tree above me. There was no breeze!

I considered firing off a round and running toward the security of our perimeter, but the movement, if there was any, was subtle. I continued watching. Whatever I was seeing was not getting any closer. My imagination was transcending common sense. I saw Rebels behind every bush and tree. Any noise, ever so soft, was confirmation of my fears. Thus I spent my two hours immersed in panic. My fear was not without benefits; I was pleasantly warmed by the adrenaline rush.

I heard footsteps behind me. This time I was sure the footsteps were real. I spun around and leveled my rifle. Two men were approaching.

"Is that you, Will?" It was George and the sergeant of the guard.

"Over here," I whispered.

"Your two hours are up," the sergeant of the guard said. "Pvt. Thompson is replacing you."

George looked cold and miserable. He hadn't had the adrenaline rush to keep him warm. I lowered my rifle and tried to look relaxed. That was much easier now that I was no longer alone. Companionship always augmented one's courage.

"See anything out there?" George pointed to the open field in front of me.

"Been pretty quiet," I said. "Your two hours will go fast."

The sergeant of the guard was giving George final instructions, but I assumed I was dismissed. I headed for our perimeter. Getting any sleep in the cold drizzle was unlikely, but I felt more secure surrounded by friends.

"I'm coming in," I said as I approached the perimeter. I didn't wish to be shot by friendly forces. I needn't have worried.

Everyone was wrapped in oil skins and trying to sleep. No one paid notice as I walked past. I would have found that disconcerting if we weren't so far behind our own lines. We were green troops and had much to learn before we would be ready for true combat.

I searched in the dark and the rain until I found our squad. Like the men on the perimeter, they were wrapped in their oilskin ponchos and unsuccessfully trying to sleep. Most of them were propped against trees to keep as far above the puddles as possible. I wasn't optimistic about sleep, but I was exhausted. I found a vacant tree and leaned against it. I awoke hours later; it was dawn and no longer raining.

"*Boots and Saddles* in twenty minutes," Casper said. He had more energy than a man his age had a right to possess. He appeared as if he had been up for some time. I rubbed my eyes awake and looked around. I had momentarily forgotten where I was. The reality of our deplorable circumstance quickly emerged. I was cold, hungry, and exhausted despite my sleep. Today's prospects did not appear much improved.

Twenty minutes was sufficient time to prepare for departure when you lacked food for breakfast and had minimal gear to organize. I checked on Prince. He had likewise consumed his three days' rations, but he was happy munching on grass. I was envious. At least the sky had partially cleared, although the weather threatened to deteriorate at a moment's notice. My clothes had partially dried during the night. They were no longer dripping wet, but they remained cold and damp. I saddled up Prince and attached my oilskin poncho to the rear of the saddle as the bugler sounded *Boots and Saddles*. Prince was not happy when I disrupted his grazing with a bit and harness.

"Casper, you have any idea where we are going today?" I asked.

"Gossip among the squad leaders is we are heading for Falmouth. That's the closest supply depot where we can replenish our rations."

That was not what I wanted to hear. Falmouth was forty miles to the southeast and required a full day's forced march. I wasn't sure our horses could tolerate another such march. They were exhausted from the previous day. It also suggested no food until late in the evening; I was already famished. The bugler sounded *To Horse* and we mounted up.

The rain held off for most of the day and the ground began to dry. We were now able to scavenge dry wood to brew coffee. Whenever the commander authorized a halt, dozens of small fires appeared under tin cups. I have never tasted coffee as good as what we brewed in those little tin cups. The heat it generated in our stomachs revitalized us and made the day again worth living. It was an inadequate replacement for a meal, but it did fill our stomachs.

Late that evening we arrived at Falmouth. The rain that had mercifully withheld its fury during the day returned with a vengeance. We were without shelter and the ground was again covered with water. Campfires of the men from Hooker's army were all about us. They had dry wood and dog tents to protect them from the rain. Some of them strung their shelter halves from trees to create a roof and sat in front of their campfires. And they had food! We had been without food for twenty-four hours, and our bellies ached. Rations were available in abundance in the Falmouth warehouses, but no one had the forethought to obtain them at the end of the day. Some of the men paid Hooker's men exorbitant prices for meager portions of salt port. I must admit, I was tempted when I saw men eating their rations at the end of the day, but I had promised to send my wages to Mary. Mary and the children needed it more than I.

George and I wandered about the many campfires, stopping whenever hospitality was offered. Hooker's men were battle-hardened infantry; we were green and had much to learn from them. We were able students.

After the fires had burned down, we returned to our unit, where several members of our squad were sitting in mud puddles and leaning against trees. If they were trying to sleep, they were unsuccessful. It would be another long night. I found a vacant tree and joined them. I dozed off for perhaps an hour and then awoke chilled to the bone. Only marching in place averted dying from the cold. I alternated napping and marching throughout the night. I thought of Mary and the children. They would be sleeping in warm beds. The thought of their well-being bolstered my spirits, but did little to diminish the cold. I still feared I would die before seeing combat. Mary and the children would receive little solace from my death knowing I had accomplished nothing. I prayed for daylight.

"Are we dead yet?" George was leaning against a tree next to me. He was visibly shivering. A faint hint of dawn was showing in the east.

"My best guess would be no," I replied. "I wouldn't call this heaven and it's too cold for hell."

"Will, I'd give a half-month's wages for ten minutes in hell. It'd take that long just to thaw out my bones."

Ten minutes in hell would sound pretty good if I had a guaranteed round-trip ticket. At least the rain had stopped during the night. It appeared the storm had passed. A sliver of sunlight was shining through the trees—another positive sign. I hadn't seen the sun in three days.

"Where's Casper?" I looked around. He was nowhere in sight.

"He's checking on rations," Gottlieb replied.

We had become dependent on Casper. His prior military experience was invaluable. He understood the ways of the army. I could make no sense of army logic—assuming there was logic in the military. I would have waited for the rations to come to us.

"Think we can find dry wood for a fire?" I asked. A warm fire wouldn't be as good as ten minutes in hell, but it still offered an improvement over our current situation.

Any wood lying on the ground was useless. I found some branches on a dead spruce that didn't have sense to fall to the ground. Gottlieb gathered dry Spanish moss for kindling. We soon had a small fire burning. Tin cups filled with ground coffee and water surrounded the fire.

"Listen up, men," Casper said upon his return. "At eight o'clock we'll be drawing our rations as well as forage for the horses. Rumor has it we will be spending the day here and leaving for Washington in the morning. Use the day wisely. Get some rest."

I looked at my pocket watch—we had twenty minutes of starvation. My coffee was now hot. I was hoping the hot coffee would tide me over until I had real food in my belly. I took a sip; it was too hot for anything more. I can't remember when coffee tasted so good. I closed my eyes while the hot fluid worked its way to my belly. The pleasant sensation momentarily made me forget my hunger. I hadn't felt this warm in several days. I took another sip. I was down to coffee grounds at the bottom of my cup when Casper returned with a sack of rations.

"Double rations for everyone," he said. Somehow he had finagled the quartermaster out of extra rations. I assumed Casper had offered something in trade. None of my possessions were missing, which made the exchange all the more worthy.

I warmed my piece of salt pork over the fire until the fat began to liquefy. The meat was still raw, but it was warm and raw. Any further cooking and the fat would have dripped off the pork. I wanted all the nourishment the salt pork could provide. I rubbed the fat on my hard biscuit. It softened the biscuit and provided flavor to an otherwise tasteless cracker. Breakfast couldn't compare to what Mary would have made, but hunger made the vilest food palatable. I was now warm with a full stomach. My curiosity turned to the Rappahannock River, which was all that separated us from Lee's Army of Northern Virginia; we were on the front lines. With Hooker's army bivouacked all around us, I assumed we had little to fear.

"Will, you up for a recon mission? I'm hankering to see how those foot soldiers survive."

George shared my curiosity, but he had a tendency toward impulsiveness. I feared the mischief he might generate if allowed to interact with infantrymen without adult supervision. I reached for my Spencer. We were secure in our current situation, but the weapon made me feel equal to the soldiers around us.

The foot soldiers had dog tents and were well rested after a dry night's sleep. A few were still sleeping; others were eating breakfast or brewing coffee. We stopped and made conversation at several campfires. The men were a miserable lot. We listened to their dreadful accounts of the battle of Fredericksburg. If there was any truth to half of what they said, their melancholy was more than justified. No more than two months earlier twelve thousand union soldiers died or were severely injured on the far side of the Rappahannock. Twelve thousand men were more than I could visualize. That was equivalent to ten regiments the size of the 5th. People died in war, but I had assumed it would be the result of a well-placed bullet. I hadn't considered the carnage produced when charging toward artillery. The foot soldiers told of men with arms and legs blown off littering the battlefield, screaming in pain sometimes for hours before dying. Many of them were crying for their mothers. The image of a man holding his own intestines nearly made me vomit.

"George, we need to leave," I said. I had to get out of there. I couldn't listen any further. War had lost whatever charm it once possessed. I no longer felt invincible. For the first time I realized I might not return home to Mary. By the time we left the hospitality of the numerous campfires, I shared their melancholy.

"Let's walk down by the river," I said.

George headed toward the river without comment. He was unusually quiet, which was not normal for George.

"George, if I don't make it back to Salem, will you look after Mary and the kids?" George stopped in his tracks.

"William Goodman, I don't want to hear of such talk. We are both going home once this war is over."

"Promise you will care for them," I pleaded. I hoped George couldn't see the tears in my eyes. I had always assumed we would fight a victorious battle and then return to Salem to tell the story. Now I realized people got killed in war. It was possible I would never see Mary again.

"Okay," he said. "But if you go and get yourself killed, I will personally kick your butt all the way back to Salem."

I don't know why George's promise provided satisfaction, but it did. We continued walking toward the river. The river was no more than one hundred yards across, but it adequately separated the two armies. Many of the houses and shops on the far side had been reduced to rubble. I wondered how many families lay beneath that debris. Armed sentries patrolled our side of the river bank. Rebel soldiers performed similar duties on the far side. They were within rifle range.

"Why don't you shoot those rebels?" I asked one of the sentries. He looked at me as if I were crazy.

"You must be new here," he replied. My silence confirmed his suspicions. "If I shoot him, his buddies will shoot me. Might as well shoot myself and call it a day. I have a wife and a child I have yet to see. I want to live to see my daughter. If you are smart you will do likewise."

By unspoken agreement the sentries fired no shots but that didn't discourage them from exchanging obscenities. We walked along the river until we came to a crew setting up an observation balloon. We watched in fascination as they added iron filings to dilute sulfuric acid, which produce hydrogen. I didn't believe the balloon could leave the ground, but two men in a basket thought otherwise. The balloon slowly filled with hydrogen until it rose over the men in the basket. The men untied several large sandbags tethered to the side of the basket. The balloon and men rose into the sky. Only a thin rope controlled their ascent. The men on the ground played out the rope like a child with a kite.

"See that black wire attached to the rope?" George pointed toward the tether rope. "That's a telegraph wire. The men in the basket telegraph their observations to the men below."

Normally I would have questioned George's assessment. He had a tendency to translate opinion into irrefutable fact. We didn't have such balloons in Salem. There was no way George could have gathered such knowledge, but what he said made sense. We watched the men play out the tether until the balloon rose over a thousand feet. They couldn't pay me enough to ride that balloon, but George was envious. The balloon drifted aimlessly within the limits of its tether. I saw nothing to suggest it was earning its keep. Too much of this war was failing to make sense. We quietly returned to our unit, neither of us speaking along the way. Our walk had generated much to think about. We were still spectators, but the war had become real.

Casper awoke us early the following morning. There was plenty of salt pork for breakfast. We roasted additional meat for the two day ride back to Washington. The sun was just rising in the east when the bugler played Boots and Saddles. We mounted our horses and headed for Washington.

We were pleased to be heading back to Washington, but that did not justify our haste or the suffering we inflicted on our mounts. Washington was a three-day journey, but Col. Wyndham was obsessed with accomplishing the transit in two days. Prince went lame half way through the second day, as did many other horses. He was favoring his right front leg. I examined his ankle and hoof, finding no injury to shoe or ankle. I hoped I had merely pushed him beyond his limits. He was a good horse and did not deserve the abuse I had inflicted upon him. I dismounted and we walked the last few miles side by side. I was filled with guilt.

Our tent on Capitol Hill was a welcome sight. I tethered Prince to the stake beside our tent and then checked his leg again; there was no change other than some mild swelling. It should heal with time, I tried to convince myself. I gave Prince some water and an extra helping of oats, before I retired to my cot in the tent. I was exhausted.

It was late in the evening and the sun hung low in the west. My cot with its soft pillow and warm blanket beckoned me. Instead I opened my pocket watch. I didn't need the watch to tell me it was late in the evening—I needed to see Mary's face again. Talking to the veterans of Fredericksburg made me realize how much I had to lose. I wondered if I would ever see my Mary again. I reached for quill and ink.

Dear Mary,

I cannot express on paper how much I miss you. My heart craves for the time when this war will be behind us and I can return home to find your smiling face greeting me at the door. I fear that time will not come soon.

This last week we have been on extended patrol. We traveled more than a hundred miles through Northern Virginia without hint of purpose or plan. I am beginning to question the wisdom of our senior officers. We saw several Rebel scouts, but our officers declined to authorize pursuit. The only wounds we inflicted were against our horses. I am too ashamed to express on paper how savagely we treated our horses. I dare say no more than twenty percent are currently fit for duty. My Prince has a bum front leg, but I believe with some well-deserved rest and good care he will fully recover.

The trip was also taxing for the men. We slept in the rain without shelter and ate cold food. There were days when we didn't eat at all. I now realize how fortunate we are to have a house to shelter us from the elements and hot food on the table. Despite the hardships we endured on the trip, I think it was worth it. We learned a lot and will be better prepared for our next adventure. We surely can do no worse.

I fear my lack of sleep is causing me to ramble. I must now close this letter and indulge in the comfort of my warm cot. I will leave my watch open, so I can fall asleep gazing at your lovely picture. I love you.

Your ever-faithful husband,

Will Goodman

CHAPTER EIGHT

"Pack up the tent. We're leaving Washington."

I assumed we would eventually vacate the comforts of Washington, but Casper's announcement caught me by surprise. It was March 11. Armies hibernate during the winter—not from any fondness toward civility, but owing to the immobility of supply wagons in deep mud. Roads were impassible until the ground had thawed and was capable of absorbing moisture; the ground had yet to thaw.

"Does that mean I'll miss my afternoon nap?" Casper ignored George's comment.

We had been an independent cavalry brigade assigned to the defense of Washington. Our only duty consisted of scouting patrols around the outskirts of the city. A recent restructuring now placed us in the 1st brigade of General Stahel's Cavalry Division. I should have known a change was imminent; cavalry divisions were designed for battle, not guard duty.

"Where are we going?" I asked.

"Don't rightly know," Casper replied. "Fairfax Court House will be the new division headquarters. I assume we'll be fixing up camp somewhere in that vicinity."

Fairfax Court House was twelve miles west of the Potomac. The new bivouac site would still be a stone's throw from

Washington, but any visiting rebels would have to knock on the door of the 5th Michigan Cavalry Regiment before saying "howdy-do" to Abe Lincoln.

We spent the morning loading our tent and personal gear onto the supply wagons. Colonel Norvell, our regiment commander, wandered by to assess our efforts. He was not a formidable man, but that opinion may have been colored by rumors of frequent drunkenness. I didn't know if there was any validity to those rumors, but if a fraction of those rumors held substance, we had reason to worry. A drunken commander was not a desirable asset going into battle.

"Will we need to draw rations?" For reasons understood only by God, Gottlieb had been fashioned in a likeness of a shriveled fence post—there was hardly an ounce of fat adherent to his frame—yet he consumed more food than any two men I knew. His major concern always fixated on his next meal.

"We eat lunch here and then draw rations for our evening meal at the bivouac site," Casper replied.

After a hasty lunch the regiment saddled up and headed west into Virginia. We had learned from our previous experience, and were better prepared to face the elements. Fortunately, it was a sunny day, although cool. We crossed Long Bridge without the fear we experienced on our previous foray into Virginia—we knew it could withstand our weight. Four hours later we dismounted at our new camp site. It was an open field with little protection from the wind, but offered the advantage of sunlight, if the sun was inclined to render an appearance. Our commander had picked high ground with good drainage. We set up housekeeping in our Sibley tent and fed our horses. The rest of the day was ours. Some of the men used their free time exploring their new surroundings. I assumed I would see plenty of the countryside in the next few days. I read several of my favorite psalms from the German Bible. Then I wrote a letter to Mary. I told her I was reading from her Bible. I knew that would provide satisfaction. I omitted any reference to the war, not that I was privy to any knowledge beyond gossip. There was no shortage of speculation, but such talk would only worry Mary.

With spring approaching, our departure generated many rumors. No one could vouch for their origin or authenticity. Fitzhugh Lee was approaching with a large force. Stonewall Jackson had started another raid through the Shenandoah Valley and would be attacking us at any moment. I even heard our regiment had been captured several times without our knowledge.

Frequently there was a scrap of truth to such rumors. Stonewall Jackson's troops could be marching up the Shenandoah Valley, shielded by the Blue Ridge Mountains. He would then be in a position to attack us from the west or even the north. General Stahel assigned the task of separating truth from fiction to the 5th and 6th Michigan Cavalry Regiments. We departed for Ashby's Gap three days after our arrival at our new base camp. Ashby's Gap was one of several passageways across the Blue Ridge Mountains and into the Shenandoah Valley. It was a logical portal for any army in the valley to attack Eastern Virginia. By luck of the draw, our troop was given the lead. We left before sunrise, which did not set well with George. He was not an early riser.

"Give you two to one odds this is another wild goose chase," George offered. "Won't find nothing more than an empty picnic basket discarded by Mosby's Raiders."

I was hoping George's assessment held merit. We had yet to experience a significant battle; I preferred to keep it that way. Rumors of large Rebel forces marching north had been just that— rumors. Mosby's Raiders, however, was a force to be reckoned with. They were small in number and no match for two cavalry regiments, but they excelled at hit and run ambushes.

"A fat goose roasting over our campfire can't be that bad," I replied.

"George, can you find a goose filled with cornbread stuffing?" Gottlieb asked.

The conversation was becoming silly, which occurred with regularity during long boring rides. We had been on the road for several hours during which we had multiple stops. We were not far from Ashby's Gap, which was our destination. I could see no purpose to the stops, but it appeared someone had ordered another halt. Men were beginning to dismount.

"Why are we stopping?" I asked no one in particular.

"Isn't that Colonel Norvell up ahead?" George asked.

I looked where George was pointing. A man in an officer's uniform was staggering toward a farm house. It could be none other than our commanding officer. Colonel Norvell apparently judged something within the farmhouse worthy of halting the column. I dismounted and stood patiently beside Prince, waiting with the other men. With nothing better to do I took out my pocket watch. I told myself I wanted to time the commander's foray into the farmhouse, but I knew I just wanted to see Mary's picture again.

After twenty minutes there still was no sign of our commander. The lieutenant at the front of our column was unleashing his frustration on some poor sergeant. The lieutenant was at a loss at how to rectify the current situation; lieutenants do not question the motives of regimental commanders.

"WHAT'S HOLDING US UP?" Major Noah Ferry came riding up from his position in the rear. He was expecting answers, and he wanted them now. I didn't know Ferry personally, but I have been told he was the son of Presbyterian missionaries and that he had been a wealthy timber baron before enlisting in the military. He was well respected by the men of the 5th Michigan.

We all watched with morbid curiosity as Major Ferry conferred with the lieutenant for a few minutes and then headed for the farmhouse. We knew something was about to happen; the Major did not look happy. Someone in the farmhouse would soon feel his wrath. He returned moments later and then sent a sergeant after an ambulance.

"I don't know what's happening, but my money is on the Major."

George had no takers. Even from a distance the anger on Major Ferry's face was unmistakable. We were witnessing the clash of pretty large egos. The ambulance wagon arrived moments later.

"You don't reckon someone is injured, do you?" I asked.

"That wouldn't surprise me," Gottlieb replied. "The Major looks mad enough to kill, and I don't think he's a hunting Rebels."

"Let's get closer," George said. "I want to hear what's going on."

I preferred maintaining a safe distance whenever officers displayed a difference of opinion, but prudence was not one of George's better virtues. He goosed his horse with his spurs and headed toward the farmhouse with Gottlieb in close pursuit. Casper and I reluctantly followed. George at least had enough sense to pull up ten yards behind the ambulance. I had feared he would ride up to the cabin door. George sometimes came up short when displaying common sense.

No sooner had we claimed our front row seats when the cabin door opened. Our commanding officer came out the door feet first with the assistance of a sergeant. Major Ferry carried the shoulders. I hadn't heard any gun shots, and I couldn't see any blood, so I assumed he was still alive.

"He's stone drunk!" George pronounced.

George was right. Colonel Norvell was passed out in a drunken stupor. Major Ferry and the sergeant carried the regimental commander toward the ambulance, but the sergeant dropped a foot, which aroused our drunken commander.

"Colonel, you are in no shape to lead the regiment. I'm placing you in the ambulance." The anger in Major Ferry's face had dissipated, but he still spoke firmly. Colonel Norvell begged to be allowed to return to the farmhouse to retrieve his boots and ride. Major Ferry reluctantly consented. Colonel Norvell managed to mount his horse and headed for the front of the column.

Our orders were to scout the vicinity around Ashby's Gap but stay clear of the Gap. No one had reconnoitered that area. It could be controlled by John Mosby's guerrillas. Mosby's guerrillas were no match for an entire cavalry regiment in a fair fight, but guerrillas do not fight fairly. They were noted for hit and run ambushes. The narrow gap with steep walls on either side offered a perfect location for an ambush.

"Where are you going with these men?" Major Ferry asked.

"Through the gap and down the Manassas Gap on the other side. Go back and tell Lt. Colonel Gould to bring his column."

"No sir, the Lt. Colonel will not come."

"Why not?" Colonel Norvell asked.

"Because the column is going the other way. Give the command to halt."

When it became obvious the Colonel would not issue the command, Major Ferry rode to the front of the column and gave the order to halt. Colonel Norvell rode up the other side of the column and ordered them to continue. The column froze in indecision.

Major Ferry pulled out his pistol and pressed the barrel against the ear of the lieutenant leading the column. "Turn around, Lieutenant." The lieutenant was quick to oblige.

"Can you believe that?" George asked once the excitement had faded.

"I hope you men appreciate what Major Ferry just did," Casper said. "He placed his career on the line for us. One of those two officers will be court marshalled, and majors don't fare well when they take on a colonel. I hope his fellow officers have the good sense to support him. We didn't see either officer for the next two days, but we did turn back and headed toward our base camp at Fairfax.

The weather turned cold and foul. We marched through the night while the snow continued to fall. Mud and slush made the going tough and arduous. At two o'clock in the morning the column halted for the night. We tried to build camp-fires, but the sticks and branches were so wet not even Abe Lincoln could convince them to burn. A cup of hot coffee was little more than a dream. We stood around in the snow, stamping our feet and swinging our arms, in a fruitless effort to keep warm. We felt relief when the bugler sounded *Boots and Saddles* in the morning. It was easier staying warm when in the saddle. We were above the mud and the horse added warmth to our thighs. It was impossible to sleep on the ground, but doable when snugly settled in the capacious McClellan saddles. I pulled the cape of my overcoat over my head and pressed my chin against Prince's neck. I gave him free rein and he dutifully followed the horse ahead of him. Sleep came quickly.

I don't know how long I had slept. It must have been a substantial time, because I now felt refreshed. I looked around. Prince was still following the horse in front of him, but I didn't recognize any of the men. I wondered if Prince also slept while he walked. We were lost.

"What troop are you men from?" I asked the man beside me.

"E Troop," he replied.

If the troops were marching in order, which was the normal case, I was four troops in front of my unit. I pulled out of formation and waited for familiar faces. The troopers and their mounts slowly plodded by. More than half the men were sleeping as I had been. Hopefully, someone at the head of the column was awake and directing us toward Fairfax. I took out my pocket watch to check the time. I needed an excuse to look at Mary. I think it was Sunday, but I wasn't sure. If it was Sunday, Mary would be hitching Prince up to the wagon and taking the kids to church. They would eat roasted chicken with cornbread stuffing when they returned. If I had listened to Mary, I would be sitting at that dinner table eating her chicken. I ate my remaining salt pork; it wasn't the same.

Eleven minutes later, according to my watch, men from I Troop rode into view. I pulled Prince in beside George. He was asleep on his horse. A layer of snow covered his back. He had not noticed my absent. We rode across a covered bridge spanning an unnamed river. I am sure the locals had a name for it, but to us it was just another river to cross on the way to Fairfax Courthouse. I remembered the bridge; our base camp was not far away. I had slept longer than I thought.

It was well past noon when we arrived at camp. I fed and brushed down Prince and then headed to the shelter of our Sibley tent. George had a fire crackling in the fire pit. I pulled up a stool to take advantage of the heat. Then I notice a letter lying on my bed. "I picked up the mail," Casper said when he noticed me looking at the envelope. "I think it's from your wife."

I opened the letter and lay back on my cot to read it; a letter from Mary provided more warmth than any campfire.

Dearest Will,

The newspapers in Michigan are full of reports predicting dreadful battles now that spring is approaching. They tell of men returning home with missing arms and legs. I fear for you day and night. The children and I pray for your safe return every night. John and Henry ask about you. I tell them you will be home shortly, but that is becoming old. Mary Elizabeth is adjusting better than the boys. She is walking and beginning to talk some.

We have some bad news. Prince died the other day. He just dropped over dead. I believe his time had come. He has been a faithful horse for many years. I will miss him. Your cousin loaned us a horse to pull our wagon. He says he won't need the horse until spring plowing. That is two months away. I don't know what we will do after that.

The people at church ask of you. I tell them how proud I am. They are praying for your safe return. The pastor made a bulletin board with the names of men who are off to the war. When no one was looking, I moved your name to the top of the list. Perhaps now you will get more prayers. I know that is selfish, but I can't help myself.

Will, I would still love you if you were to lose and arm or a leg, but I don't think I can survive if you do not return. I love you so. Please be careful.

Your loving wife,
Mary

Major Noah Ferry

Noah Ferry was born in 1831 on Mackinaw Island. He was the third son of Presbyterian missionaries who were serving at a church for Native Americans. The family moved to Grand Haven in 1834 where they started businesses in lumber, iron, ship building, and banking. Noah took over the Ferry and Sons Sawmill in White River Township when he was 23 years old. He became the township's wealthiest citizen, and largest employer.

During the Civil War, Noah and many of his employees enlisted in the "White River Guard." He was elected their commander. The guard combined with others to become the Michigan Cavalry Brigade.

Major Ferry was well respected by the men in the Michigan Cavalry Brigade. The same could not be said for the Colonel Freeman Norvell who was the brigade commander. He was noted for his constant drunkenness, and that could get horse soldiers killed. Most officers looked the other way (he was the brigade commander) but not Major Ferry.

While on a patrol to the entrance of Ashby's Gap, Colonel Norvell called a halt and entered a small cottage. Major Ferry rode up to find out why the column had stopped. He discovered Colonel Norvell drunk and passed out on a bed. As they were carrying Colonel Norvell to the ambulance, he insisted he was fit to ride. The brigade rode to the entrance of Ashby's Gap, which offered passage through the Blue Ridge Mountains and into the Shenandoah Valley. The gap had steep side, which offered a perfect site for an ambush by Mosley's Raiders. Colonel Norvell ordered the lieutenant leading the column to enter the gap. Major Ferry rode up and reminded Colonel Norvell that their orders were to avoid entering the gap. Colonel Norvell again ordered the lieutenant to enter the gap. The lieutenant faced conflicting orders from a drunken brigade commander and the sober and well respected Major Ferry.

Here historians diverge. They all agree that Major Ferry pulled out his pistol. Some say he pressed it against Colonel Norvell's temple and ordered him to relinquish his command. Others say he pressed the pistol against the lieutenant's temple. The results were the same. The column returned to base came.

Disobeying a superior officer's order is a form of mutiny. Major Ferry could have been in serious trouble. Major Ferry formally charged Norvell with drunkenness in the line of duty soon after they returned to base camp. Norvell discovered he had few friends. To avoid an ugly court martial, Norvell was allowed to resign his commission. Major Ferry was offered the position of Colonel of the Brigade, but he turned down the role insisting he had not yet earned this position. Major Ferry led 200 unmounted cavalrymen into battle at Gettysburg, famously saying, "Rally boys, Rally for the fence" He was shot in the head and died instantly. He is buried in Grand Haven, Michigan.

CHAPTER NINE

Casper needn't have worried about Major Ferry's future. Colonel Norvell's drunkenness had disturbed the moral values of more than one regimental officer. Despite appeals for compassion, Norvell received negligible support from his colleagues. Ferry formally charged Norvell with drunkenness in the line of duty soon after we returned to base camp. I would have preferred tar and feathers, but the Division Commander let Norvell resign in lieu of facing a hostile court martial. Russell Alger from the 6th Michigan Cavalry replaced Norvell as regimental commander. I had heard favorable reports about Alger from several friends in the 6th who could find no fault with the man. They were deeply saddened by his departure from their regiment. That was reassuring, since the summer offensive would soon commence.

The decision makers in Washington still had our division headquartered at Fairfax Courthouse. After nine months in the military, we had yet to experience combat. That created discontent among the more adventurous men, but I was willing to bide my time. War lost its enchantment after hearing the horrors of Fredericksburg. Death had become real and the fear of never returning to Salem produced more than one sleepless night. I had to consider Mary and my three children. They needed me.

We were still entrusted with the security of Washington, which until now had been a benign assignment, but persistent reports suggested Lee's army would be marching toward Washington—if not already on the way. If those rumors held any validity, we were destined to endure more combat than any man had a right to encounter. Our regiments formed an arc around Washington with the right and left flanks butting against the Potomac River. Each troop spent twenty-four hours on picket duty followed by forty-eight hours off. If Lee were to march on Washington, he must come through us, and a few cavalry regiments would do little more than annoy the Army of Northern Virginia.

Hooker's army clashed with Lee near Chancellorsville in late April while we sat idly by on the outskirts of Washington. It was an ignominious trouncing, and even though we did not participate in the engagement, we shared the shame of that defeat. The outcome would be little different if Lee were to strike Washington. Morale among the Union troops couldn't sink much lower. More than one member of our regiment questioned our ability to compete against Rebel soldiers.

Lee marching toward the nation's capital wasn't the only rumor emanating from Washington. Reliable informants suggested J.E.B. Stuart's cavalry had broken through our lines and was threatening Baltimore. Several rumors even included our capture. Truth was no one knew where Lee's army resided, but we all assumed Lee was on the prowl.

On Sunday, June 21, we awoke to heavy cannonading in the direction of the passes in the Blue Ridge Mountains. Some of Pleasanton's cavalry units had encountered Stuart and Fitzhugh Lee at Middleburg and a fierce engagement was raging.

"Pack what you can," Casper said. "We leave in half an hour, and I don't know when or if we'll be returning."

No one had to ask why. The cannonading to the west was sufficient reason. We were riding into battle. We knew it would come to pass. That was why we trained night and day; at least that was the reasoning according to the First Sergeant. The bugler played *Boots and Saddles* forty minutes later, and *To Horse* quickly followed. We mounted our horses and rode forth in a column of fours.

"Will, pardon my ignorance, but doesn't the sun back home arise in the east?"

"That has been my experience," I replied. I wasn't sure I understood George's point.

"The sun's on our left. Unless the sun behaves differently in Virginia, I believe we're heading south."

George was right. The sounds of battle were west of us, but we were heading south. I assumed we would soon turn west, but the column continued south toward Warrenton and then on to Fredericksburg. General Hooker must have suspected the fighting in the mountain passes was a diversion and that Lee's main army was marching toward Washington as the rumors had suggested. We rode hard for three days, pushing men and horses to their limits. Sometimes we outrode the wagon trains and were without food or forage. We scouted Kelly's Ford, Gainesville, and Bealton Station but encountered no enemy, not even Rebel scouts. Fortunately, a light rain had cleared the road of dust making it a pleasant trip.

A grove of old cherry trees lined one of the roads. In late summer the branches would be bowed beneath loads of ripe and luscious fruit. We could have broken off lower branches and ate cherries until we had consumed our fill. The fruit would have been a pleasing addition to our salt pork and hard tack. My imagination was getting the best of me. Our reconnaissance mission was pleasant, but the pace was fatiguing. We were grateful when we returned to our base camp.

I had expected a few days of rest and recuperation after such a hard ride, but Casper awakened us at two o'clock on the morning of June 25th.

"Pack everything; we're leaving basecamp."

Casper was dressed and looked like he had been up for some time. I wondered where he acquired his energy. He was twice my age and I was exhausted. I packed what I could carry on horseback. The rest would follow by wagon train. It was not as if we had many possessions. We travelled lightly.

As the sun rose in the east the bugler sounded *To Horse*. I mounted Prince and nudged him into line with George, Gottlieb, and Casper. Captain Dutcher ordered the column forward and we turned toward Edward's Ferry on the Potomac; we were heading north. Dutcher assumed command of our company on June 13 after Captain Williams unexpectedly resigned due to medical concerns. Dutcher was a well-respected lieutenant in our company; we could have fared worse.

The entire Army of the Potomac was heading toward Maryland. Supply wagons, light artillery pieces, and ambulances clogged the lane making navigating the road difficult. We worked our way around the wagons until our regiment was in the lead. The 7th Michigan Cavalry followed closely behind us with the 6th Michigan filling in the rear. Whatever the generals had in mind included our entire brigade.

We encountered a light rain, but the Potomac had not yet swollen when we reached Edward's ferry. The river was over a mile wide, and I feared the water would be deep, but Prince waded through without difficulty. Individuals crossing further downstream were not so fortunate. The river reached the tops of their saddles in some spots. At least the weather was warm. Wet clothing quickly chills the rider to the core in colder weather.

The following day we passed Major General John Reynolds' First Army Corps. His foot soldiers appeared exhausted and demoralized, but they pressed on. They must have been marching for several days to cover what we had covered in twenty-four hours on horseback. We were also suffering the consequences of the prolonged forced march. Men were again falling asleep in their saddles. Some men even fell from their horses. At another time and another place it might have provided comic relief. It made me appreciate Prince. He was as exhausted as I was, but he plodded on. Other horses did not share his strength and collapsed in exhaustion. More than one trooper carried his saddle and bridle in hopes of finding a replacement horse.

We reached the village of Frederick by early evening. The clouds had cleared away, allowing the sun to shine on the most beautiful valley. The town squatted in the center of a charming and fertile farming community. Thousands of acres of golden grain waved in the sunlight. Unlike Virginia, this land had not been ravaged by war.

This was also friendly territory. The stars and stripes waved patriotically above many buildings. Men greeted us with cheers, while the women waved handkerchiefs from their porches. That night we camped in the midst of friends. It felt good knowing there were people who appreciated what we were doing. It made our sacrifices more tolerable.

On the Saturday morning of June 27th we awoke feeling much refreshed. We fed and groomed our horses and replenished our haversacks from the supply wagons. A few puffy cumulous clouds tried to obscure the sun, but for the most part were unsuccessful. I feared the day would become too hot. Horses can only tolerate so much heat without frequent stops for water. Three thousand horses can overwhelm any river or watering hole.

The bugler sounded *To Saddle* and Captain Dutcher lead the regiment north toward Emmitsburg. The Sixth Michigan followed behind us; but for some reason that I didn't clearly understand, the Seventh departed our company and traveled north through the Catoctin Valley by another road. I would have preferred keeping our brigade at full strength. Just outside Frederick we passed through infantry camps. There must have been thousands of infantrymen. They were packing up and preparing to travel in the same direction we were going. I was only now beginning to appreciate the size of our army.

"Never seen so many foot soldiers," George said. "I'm getting the feeling something significant is about to happen." We had been traveling in silence. There was only so much one could discuss on a long march. For the most part we were lost in our own thoughts.

"Remember your promise," I said. George gave me a puzzled look. "You promised to look after Mary and the kids."

"Will, don't give me any more of that nonsense." George seemed unusually annoyed by my request. "All four of us are returning home to Salem—as victors."

I wished I shared George's confidence. I had a premonition about this patrol—there were too many foot soldiers. Moving that many people was not a simple task. Generals don't authorize such tasks without suitable justification. They were sending us into battle, and from the number of participants, I assumed it would be one of the larger battles of the war. I wondered how many people would not be marching back to Washington. Perhaps George was right. Maybe I worried too much. The peaceful countryside did not justify my pessimistic mood. We rode through a progression of wheat fields and maple forests. The spacious farm-houses and large barns suggested wealth. The soil was rich and the fields overflowed with abundance. It left me longing for my small farm in Salem.

Men in the fields cheered as we rode past their farms, and women offered freshly baked bread from their outdoor brick ovens. They slathered the bread slices with warm apple butter. I can't remember when I have tasted such excellent apple butter. The women offered fresh milk to drink and oats for our horses. We had to pay for the food, but the price was reasonable and we were hungry. The food was worth every penny.

"They're a friendly bunch," Gottlieb said, "but why are we defending the homes of these wealthy farmers, when they are unwilling to take up a musket to drive the invading army from their soil? And they are unwilling to contribute a cent to the cause."

Gottlieb was right. There were too many young men on these farms. My fields were growing fallow while I dallied here defending these farmers. It didn't make sense.

We camped for the night alongside the 6th Michigan Cavalry near the Pennsylvania border. The weather was warm and dry. I slept in deep grass and enjoyed a pleasant night, while Prince munched on the grass at my feet. I hoped he possessed enough horse sense not to step on me.

On the Sunday morning of June 28, our two regiments resumed our march. We passed through the town of Emmitsburg. It was a small hamlet, with little more than a thousand inhabitants, but it did boast several churches as well as an academy for girls. According to one of the residents they even had a Catholic College northeast of town. I believe he called it Mount St. Mary's College. Most of the inhabitants on the streets were scurrying toward one of the churches. To them it was just another Sunday. Back home Mary would be getting the children ready for my church. By all rights I should be helping her.

We had just crossed into Pennsylvania when a rumor began circulating that Lee had pushed north with his entire army and was now approaching Harrisburg. If the rumor were true his army must have marched up the Cumberland Valley to the west of Hooker's army and was now far to the north of us. We debated whether Hooker would try to cut Lee's communications and supply at the rear of his army. But then Lee would be free to attack Baltimore. The Confederacy had many sympathizers in Baltimore.

Taking the Emmitsburg pike, Colonel Copeland led the Fifth and Sixth Michigan toward Gettysburg. We had now worked our way to the forefront of Hooker's army. That was not a good position to have. I would have felt better if the First and Seventh Michigan regiments were with us. Their whereabouts appeared known only to the generals—gossip was devoid of any suggestions to their location. If we were to encounter even a fraction of Lee's army, I would have felt better knowing we had the support of our entire brigade.

The hearty welcomes we had received in other towns did not prepare us for what we experienced in Gettysburg. Everyone turned out in their Sunday best to welcome the troopers in blue.

Church bells rang a continuous welcome, and people flooded the streets making it difficult for our column of fours to weave through their midst. Men lined both sides of the road with pails of water for our horses and gave us sandwiches as we passed. Gaily dressed women and girls distributed bouquets of flowers. They draped wreaths of flowers around the necks of our horses. Prince had never looked so well attired. The people were overjoyed. Their enthusiasm and infectious hospitality eradicated any lingering traces of depression I still harbored. The throats of the Gettysburg residents grew hoarse from the cheers in honor of the Michigan cavalrymen.

Colonel Copeland turned the column onto a road heading east and then had the bugler sound the call to halt. We set up camp in an open field east of town where the horses were knee deep in clover. Prince must have thought he was in heaven. Despite the apparent paradise, we were still at war. The entire army of Northern Virginia was somewhere in the vicinity, but no one knew where. Copeland sent a squadron to guard each of the roads emanating out of Gettysburg of which there were many. If Lee were to make an appearance we would know about it. An entire squadron to guard one road was a lot of men. Our squadron commander delegated a few men to rotate as pickets, allowing the rest of us to sleep peacefully in the soft clover with our Spencers close at hand in case adversaries were to appear. It proved to be a quiet, peaceful night. No rebels came down our road.

CHAPTER TEN

I awoke well rested.

"Where's Casper?" He was the only member of our eight-man squad not present. None of us had picket duty, so I was surprised by his absence.

"He's at a briefing with the First Sergeant," Gottlieb replied.

That sounded ominous. First Sergeants called meetings to assign work details. We would surely get picket duty tonight. Other than the loss of sleep, picket duty was not bad duty—as long as Johnny Reb didn't show up. Despite all the rumors and needless worry, we had seen nothing of our adversary. Perhaps they were not even in the Gettysburg area.

Casper returned shortly with a sack containing three days' rations for each of us. The supply train must have caught up with us during the night. With the food and sandwiches provided by the local citizens, we were eating well this trip, although extra salt pork in reserve never hurt.

"We got picket duty tonight?" Will asked.

"No, we're returning to Emmitsburg," Casper replied. "General Buford's cavalry division is replacing us."

I wondered if we were heading to Washington. Gettysburg, Pennsylvania was too far north for the Army of Northern Virginia.

It wouldn't surprise me if Lee had us chasing our tails while he marched on Washington.

"Lots of personnel changes," Casper continued. "General Hooker is out and General Meade is in. Meade's the new commander of the Army of the Potomac."

That meant little to me. Washington was constantly changing commanders. It was not as if we would ever meet the commander.

"General Kilpatrick is replacing Stahel as our division commander."

I had heard of Kilpatrick only through gossip, but that was not always reliable. Kilpatrick had a reputation as an aggressive and sometimes impulsive General. If this were true, we could expect more combat—and casualties. That would please the more adventurous men.

"That's interesting," Will said, "but get to the part where you explain who is replacing me?" Casper ignored Will's sarcastic comment.

"We have a new brigade commander. General George Custer is replacing Copeland."

That caught my attention. Copeland had been with us since we enlisted. He was a good man. Someone we could trust. He was also from Michigan. He was one of us. I had never heard of Custer, not even through idle gossip.

"Think he's any good?" Gottlieb asked. Gottlieb shared my concerns.

"The First Sergeant never heard of him. He only knows what was passed down from above. Custer is from Ohio but he did live a few years in Monroe, Michigan."

"I don't give a rat's behind where he was born," Gottlieb replied. "Does he have any military experience?"

Gottlieb must have been reading my mind. I also didn't care where a commanding officer was born as long as he knew what he was doing. Washington had a reputation for filling higher ranks with political appointees who had no military experience. Such individuals could get us killed.

"I have no information concerning Custer's military experience," Casper replied, "but it must be limited. He is only twenty-three years old."

"Twenty-three! Will, he's younger than you are."

George was right. If Custer was twenty-three, he was younger than I was. Casper was not noted for joking or telling wild stories, but he was obviously the recipient of erroneous information. No one in his right mind would place a twenty-three year old in charge of a brigade no matter how influential the man's father was.

After a leisurely breakfast we saddled our horses. We attached what little gear we had to our saddles. Then we waited. Hurry up and wait was an often-repeated event in the military. Our new brigade commander was in no hurry. The bugler finally played "To Mount," and we mounted our horses and headed southwest on the Emmitsburg Pike. The 6th Michigan trailed behind us.

We were half way to Emmitsburg when we received new orders. Both regiments turned east, leaving the Emmitsburg Pike. A rumor passed down the ranks that J.E.B. Stuart's cavalry might be in the area and if they were, it was our job to find them. I was praying we wouldn't find them; Stuart's cavalry was legendry. They were battle hardened. We only read about such battles in newspapers, and that didn't qualify for experience. The carnage Stuart could bestow upon a brigade led by a twenty-three year old boy was beyond my imagination.

We searched the fields and woodlands south and east of Gettysburg throughout the day and into the night. Several times during the night I fell asleep in the saddle. Prince dutifully followed the horse in front of him. Whenever the column came to a halt, I dismounted, ran my arm through the loop of reins, and fell asleep. I am sure Prince slept likewise, but he was careful not to step on me. The breaks were short, and the fifteen or twenty minute catnaps did little to make the remaining night tolerable.

We arrived in Littlestown at daybreak to find mass confusion and chaos. Unlike Gettysburg, there were no garlands of flowers or gratuitous sandwiches. The townsfolk were in panic. I pulled out of rank long enough to hail an elderly man wielding a shotgun.

"What's going on?" I asked. The man, rushing to parts unknown, was reluctant to address my question. He relented only after I maneuvered Prince into his path.

"The entire Reb cavalry is heading toward Hanover," he replied. "They might wander through Littlestown on their way. If they do, we'll be ready for them." The man hurried off on his urgent errand known only to him. I had serious doubt that his shotgun would stop Stuart's troops.

I assumed this was idle talk of an old man, but other men confirmed his story. This was no groundless rumor. J.E.B. Stuart's cavalry was riding toward us, and our division was scattered across the countryside. Last I heard, the 1st and 7th Michigan along with Pennington's horse artillery had passed through Hanover and were scouting the area near Abottstown seven or eight miles north of Hanover. A senior officer sent a courier on a fresh horse to summon them back to Hanover, but it was unclear how long that would take—assuming the courier could find them in a timely fashion. Farnsworth's 1st brigade left Littlestown for Hanover prior to our arrival. Even if they were to arrive in Hanover before the Rebels, one brigade was no match for Stuart's cavalry.

We dismounted and watered our horses in Piney Creek at the southern edge of town. Then we turned them loose to graze on the abundant grass and clover. The current military problems were above our level of expertise. Our future was in the hands of generals, one of which was twenty-three years old. We lay down in the grass beside our horses for some much needed sleep. The sporadic catnaps during the night had done little to diminish our fatigue.

It seemed like I had just fallen asleep when Casper kicked my boot to awaken me. I rubbed the sleep from my eyes and looked around. It took a moment or two before I remembered where we were. Casper was walking around waking the others in our squad.

"Captain Dutcher ordered a formation," he said.

The men gathered around Captain Dutcher. It wasn't an orderly formation like we had been taught back at Bank's Barracks, but we weren't preparing for a parade. Dutcher stood quietly before us until he had everyone's attention.

"Gentlemen, as you have probably heard, yesterday our scouts spotted J.E.B. Stuart's cavalry north of Westminster. That's ten miles south of us. They may be heading for Littlestown, but they are more likely heading for Hanover. General Custer sent Farnsworth's brigade toward Hanover and he is recalling the 1st and 7th. If that is where Stuart is heading, they will provide a warm welcome. The 6th Michigan will remain at Littlestown just in case Stuart comes in this direction."

I counted all the regiments. Each one had an assignment except for the 5th. I knew this was not an oversight. Captain Dutcher was saving the bad news for last.

"I am sure you are wondering about our role in the battle plan," Dutcher continued. "General Custer has asked us to scout the area toward Westminster. He wants to know Stuart's intentions more precisely. We will be taking Troop A of the 6th Michigan with us. Are there any questions?"

That was a lot to digest. We had yet to experience battle and now we were to seek out an entire division of hardened Rebel cavalrymen. I wondered what the boy general expected a regiment to do if we did find Stuart.

"Captain Dutcher, what will we do if we find Stuart?" someone asked. He apparently shared my concerns.

"If we find Stuart, we'll discover how quickly our horses can retreat." This brought some laughter. "We are a scouting force. No one expects us to engage the enemy."

Dutcher ordered the bugler to play *Boots and Saddle,* and we mounted up in column of fours. Gottlieb Miller was on our far left. If we were to dismount and fight, he would hold the reins of our four horses, while we took the fight to the enemy. I was not sure that was good duty. The rest of us could hide behind rocks and trees; he would have to stand and hold the horses. True, he would be in the rear, but bullets often find their way to the rear.

The regiment proceeded down the Westminster Pike at an aggressive trot. Colonel Alger was not a timid man. If he received orders to reconnoiter the area north of Westminster, he would ensure it was done quickly and thoroughly. I expected this patrol would be no exception.

Most of the surrounding countryside was farmland with wheat fields begging for harvest or green pastures filled with grazing milk cows. It would be beautiful land and enjoyable scenery if not for the constant worry of enemy troops. The troop commanders posted pickets to guard our flanks. This was not difficult in farmland where horses encounter few impediments other than an occasional split-rail fence. In theory, the pickets would locate the enemy before they noticed us. Making a hasty retreat was only advantageous when sufficient advance warning was available.

The road occasionally wound through patches of virgin timber where the undergrowth severely limited passage by man and horse. In these areas the troop commanders had to recall their flank pickets, forcing us to proceed unprotected. The thick timber offered numerous ambush sites for dismounted Rebels. They could discharge their muskets at point-blank range and then flee into the woods before we could return fire. In such areas I kept my pistol cocked and ready in my right hand.

I opened my pocket watch and looked into Mary's smiling face. She always made things right. It was almost ten o'clock. We had been riding for nearly two hours. Except for rabbits and an occasional deer, we had seen nothing. If Stuart was in the area our pickets should have run into his pickets. That hadn't happened. Colonel Alger must have arrived at the same conclusion, since he soon had us do an about face. Word filtered down the line that Stuart had slipped past us. We were now heading to Hanover to rejoin the rest of our division.

"Will, do you think there really is a war going on?" George asked. "I mean we been in the cavalry almost a year. We have yet to see any Rebels other than a couple of men on horseback that someone suggested were Rebel scouts. We ride here and we ride there. We're always in a hurry, but we never get anywhere."

"The pay's the same whether they shoot at us or not," I replied. "If I remember right, this was your idea."

Any doubts concerning the war's reality dissipated when we were five miles south of Hanover. Wispy white clouds covered a portion of the sky, but most of the sky was deep blue. The sun was bright and hot.

"Is that thunder?" Gottlieb asked. "It doesn't look like rain."

"Boys, that is the sound of war," Casper said. "That's cannons you hear."

It sounded like rolling thunder, but when I listened closely I could discern individual cannons. Colonel Alger either did not hear the cannons or chose to ignore them; the column of horse soldiers continued toward Hanover.

"How are we going to tell the good guys from the bad guys? The cannons sound the same." It was a rhetorical question. I didn't really expect an answer.

"You'll know when the cannons are shooting at you," Casper replied. "Those cannons are not aimed at us."

As we approached the southern outskirts of Hanover we began hearing small arms fire. It was sporadic and seemed to come from various sections of the town. Since Casper did not appear concerned, I assumed they were also not shooting at us. I wondered if he would ever become concerned. We continued down the road.

"Dismount!" Several officers were yelling simultaneously. I didn't need to ask why. I could hear musket fire—and it was right in front of us. I had no doubt these muskets were shooting at us. A man to our left crumpled over and fell from his horse. I couldn't tell how badly he was hurt. He had the honor of being our first casualty. I dismounted and grabbed my Spencer. Gottlieb grabbed Prince's reins and pulled him along with Casper's and George's horses toward the rear. George and I followed Casper. We assumed he knew what to do. Casper led us to the front of the regiment where men were forming a skirmish line.

This was the first time I had seen Rebels up close. They were firing from a tree line no farther than one hundred yards in front of us. I had thought they would somehow look different but except for the gray uniforms, they looked no different from us.

Casper fell to the ground to reduce his silhouette. That seemed like a prudent idea. George and I did likewise. I saw a puff of smoke from a Rebel's muzzle-loader before I heard the bang. He then rolled on his side to reload his weapon. The woods were full of Rebels, several times our number. The Rebels reloaded and prepared to charge our skirmish line with fixed bayonets.

"Commence Firing." I recognized Captain Dutcher's voice. His voice was firm, but strained. I could tell he was as nervous as the rest of us.

Everyone fired at once causing several Rebels to crumple and fall to the ground. Instead of stopping to reload, we continued firing our Spencers. We had seven rounds at our disposal. The continuous fire took the Rebels by surprise—they assumed we would pause to reload. After a few moments of bewilderment, they retreated into the woods.

"Cease Fire!"

It was our first battle, and we had routed our adversaries. I would be lying if I said it didn't feel good. I didn't see anyone who appeared injured except for the man who fell from his horse. Several of his comrades were attending to him. I took a closer look; it was Captain Dutcher. A bullet had struck him in the arm. He could lose the arm, but at least he was not dead.

I was no longer sure who was in charge, but someone gave the order to mount up. It seemed prudent to rendezvous with the rest of the division before the Rebels had time to regroup. Colonel Alger guided the Regiment around the left flank of the city. We met no further opposition. We entered the town from the west just past noon. The 1st, 6th, and 7th Michigan Cavalry along with Colonel Farnsworth's 1st Brigade were organizing a skirmish line near the train station. They had barricaded the streets with overturned wagons, barrels of produce, and anything else that might shield a trooper from hostile bullets. Our cavalry had pushed the Rebels out of the city, but a counter attack appeared imminent.

"Who's the peacock?" George asked.

I looked where George was pointing. A young man on a commendable mount was dispersing orders to the regiment commanders. He wore a black velvet suit trimmed in gold lace, which conspicuously covered the sleeves of his cavalry jacket. As if that wasn't sufficiently ornate, more gold lace garnished the outer seams of his trousers. A scarlet cravat tied loosely around the neck accented a navy-blue shirt. A wide-brimmed, black hat sported a gilt cord and rosette encircling a silver star. An abundance of gold hair flowed down from beneath the hat and rested on his shoulders. If it hadn't been for his blonde mustache I would have questioned whether he was old enough to shave.

"I do believe that would be your boy general," I replied.

We were given little time to discuss the merits of our boy general. Colonel Alger deployed us on the Forney Farm at the southern edge of town. The 5th and 6th Michigan were to protect the right flank of our skirmish line. In front of us was Brigadier General Fitzhugh Lee's brigade. They were all battle-hardened cavalry. Our only combat experience consisted of the five-minute exchange earlier in the day. That did nothing to prepare us for what happened next. Fitz Lee's men unlimbered four cannons and shelled our position. Lieutenant Alexander Pennington's 2nd and Lieutenant Samuel Elder's 4th U.S. Artillery replied in kind from Bunker Hill, a small rise at the end of Carlisle Street. I looked at my pocket watch; it was ten past three in the afternoon. I looked at Mary's smiling face and wondered if I would see her again.

The artillery barrage lasted over two hours. Many of the shells passed harmlessly over our heads as the Federal and Confederate cannons dueled with each other, but some of the shells exploded above us sending lethal shards of metal down on us. Men screamed in pain as metal found its mark. I felt totally helpless.

General Peacock was not feeling helpless. He led dismounted 6th Michigan troopers to within 300 yards of the Confederate artillery where they opened up with their seven-shot Spencers. Eleven hundred men rapidly firing their Spencers was an awesome sight. It sounded like one continuous roar. It definitely impressed the Confederate gunners, who ran to the rear leaving behind some of their wounded men and all their artillery. Before the 6th Michigan could consolidate their gains, Fitz Lee sent in reinforcements, forcing the Wolverines back to their original line.

I thought the artillery barrage would go on forever, but about dusk the Confederate guns fell silent.

"They're pulling out," Casper said.

I lifted my head to survey the Confederate skirmish line; they were pulling back. Our officers had no desire to pursue the Rebels this late in the day. We had pushed back J.E.B. Stuart, and the officers were satisfied with our victory.

Men began wandering around the battle field, no doubt searching for friends. The 5th Michigan had a few casualties none of whom were close friends, but the 6th Michigan had many injured and a few dead. Some men from the 6th were taken prisoner; at least that was what people were saying.

I meandered around to see if I could be of any help. I found one man from the 6th Michigan on his knees, his head resting on the ground before him in a three-point stance. He was holding his abdomen with both hands. I tapped him on the shoulder to ask if I could be of assistance. He collapsed on his side. Part of his bowel slipped out of a large abdominal wound. He had been holding in his intestines with his hands. I looked into the eyes that stared vacantly back at me. From the dryness of the eyes I assumed he had been dead for several hours. He had died a painful death. No musket was capable of creating such a wound. Only a cannon could produce such carnage. I turned away and vomited.

I was glad no one saw me vomit. When I returned to my squad I found George sitting on a log, his eyes focused somewhere in the distance but seeing nothing. Gottlieb's face was unusually pale. He looked capable of vomiting with the slightest provocation. Only Casper was capable of rational thought.

Perhaps his prior military experience had hardened him to the horrors of war. I didn't think I would ever adapt to such carnage.

"The captain has posted a perimeter guard," Casper said. "Everyone else is to assist the wounded. Several civilian doctors are setting up a make-shift hospital in the center of town."

"What about the dead?" George asked.

"The dead can bury the dead," Casper replied.

We stared at him in disbelief. This was our first taste of war. No training can prepare one for the consequence of armed aggression. When he saw our distraught faces he softened.

"We have nothing to offer the dead. The locals will provide a fitting burial for those we lost. Now we must assist the wounded lest they unite with the dead."

I didn't perceive myself as a coward, but the thought of searching among the dead for wounded troopers filled me with fear. It was not an activity I wished to undertake alone. George harbored similar thoughts. Without discussion we departed together in search of wounded comrades.

I found a sapling that had been severed from its base by a cannon ball. Once I stripped it of its small branches, it made a good probe. I had no desire to physically touch more dead bodies. The first body we came across needed no probing to confirm lack of life. It was a confederate soldier. Blood matted the hair on his left temple. I knew a search of the bloody scalp would confirm the bullet hole that extinguished the man's life. I judged he had not yet achieved the age of twenty-five.

"What's he got pinned to his shirt?" George asked.

"It's an envelope," I replied.

The dead Rebel had conspicuously affixed the envelope to the left side of his jacket for everyone to see. I assumed the name on the envelope belonged to the dead Rebel whose lifeless eyes now stared up at us.

"Do you think we should open it?"

I knew by the way George phrased the question I was the "we" he was referring to. I bent down while avoiding the dead man's gaze and removed the letter. At least there were no blood stains on the envelope. I opened the envelope and extracted a single sheet of paper. I held it up to the diminishing light of the evening. George read over my shoulder.

My name is Samuel Burk of the 13th Virginia. If you are reading this I have likely died in battle. I do not fear death. The All Mighty knows I have led a good life, and I know He has reserved a spot for me in the here-after. What I fear most is expiring on some forgotten battle field with no one to acknowledge my passing. I beseech the reader to notify my wife of my death. Tell her I love her and died doing my best to defend my beloved Virginia. Tell her to find a good man to help raise our son. I have enclosed money for postage.

The envelope contained Confederate money and what had to be the wife's address. Samuel Burk assumed the reader of his letter would be a fellow confederate soldier. The Confederate money was worthless to me. I stuffed the letter in my shirt pocket. I would write a letter to the man's wife, even if I had to pay the postage myself. George said nothing, but his eyes were damp like mine.

Our brief search yielded no wounded. Except for a man sitting on a tree stump, the battlefield was deserted. The man's back was toward us. What little I could see of his face did not look familiar. A Spencer repeating rifle rested on his lap, as he stared at the woods that recently concealed a division of Rebels. We approached to offer conversation; no one should be alone on the battlefield.

"Hello there," I said.

The man ignored my greeting as if he had not heard my salutation.

"Are you okay?" I looked down at his left foot; a lead ball had shattered the bone.

"I would be better off if I were dead," he finally replied.

"The local doctors are setting up a hospital in town. They'll fix you up." I don't know how convincing I sounded. I wasn't sure I could convince myself. He would surely lose his leg and, if infection set in, perhaps his life.

"I'm a farmer. Ever see a farmer on crutches plow a field? How can I support my wife and daughter?"

"I'll get a horse," George said. "We'll need a horse to carry him to the hospital."

For reasons I didn't fully understand I feared being alone with the man, but I couldn't challenge the logic of George's suggestion. The hospital was a better part of a mile from where we stood, too far for us to carry the man. A horse would provide a smoother ride.

George returned with Prince, a wise choice. No horse in the regiment would provide a gentler ride. The man pleaded with us to let him die. I am not sure I would have felt any different. The man was right; a farmer can't plow a field with crutches. I had feared death. Now I knew war offered consequences greater than death. We hoisted the wounded trooper onto Prince against his wishes and delivered him to the makeshift hospital. If he were to die, it would not be at our hands.

CHAPTER ELEVEN

I awoke on July 2nd to the sound of thunder in the distance. It was a low-pitched rumble that rattled the can of coffee I was roasting over a small fire. Clouds obscured the sky suggesting Mother Nature could unleash torrents of rain at a moment's notice, but we were now capable of distinguishing between Mother Nature's thunder and distant cannon fire. What we were hearing was not the work of Mother Nature. Unlike the artillery duel of our recent battle at Hanover, the individual cannon fire blended into a continuous rumble. Hundreds of cannons were exchanging grapeshot, canister, and shell. I pitied anyone caught on the receiving end of such intense cannon fire.

"How far yonder do you recon they are?"

George stirred the coffee brewing over the small fire while he gave my question some thought. He glanced toward the west as if that would provide additional wisdom before he replied to my query.

"At least three or four miles would be my guess," he replied. "Near Gettysburg."

I hoped George was wrong. We passed through Gettysburg four days ago. The people were friendly and the farmland was unscarred by battle. I feared those townsfolk were entangled in the battle raging to our west. I had seen how war can destroy small villages during our forays into Virginia. I would not wish such havoc on any community—friend or foe.

"We'll be part of that battle before the days out." Gottlieb had no independent knowledge to back up his statement, but gossip needed no verification. Gottlieb's logic seemed reasonable. No general would let us remain idle while a large battle was raging. Casper was at a meeting with the First Sergeant and would soon return with more definitive gossip. Until then all we could do was speculate. Some men were hoping for another confrontation with Johnny Reb. They assumed the outcome would be similar to Hanover.

I wouldn't say we were cocky, but the Hanover battle left us feeling we could compete with the best Robert E. Lee had to offer. We pushed J.E.B. Stuart's cavalry out of Hanover. We had forced them to retreat. In our minds, that was a major accomplishment. The Michigan 6th Cavalry Regiment suffered numerous casualties, but we only had one injury. That was Captain Dutcher who was shot in the arm. It wasn't serious, but it was sufficient to relieve him of his command. G. W. Townsend was our new company commander.

Casper returned with a solemn expression on his face. He was a good soldier but had experienced too many battles to find enjoyment in the profession. It did not appear he was the harbinger of good news.

"So, what's up?" George asked. He was always the impatient one. I assumed Casper would tell us in due time.

"The Army of the Potomac is defending a ridge south of Gettysburg against the entire Army of Northern Virginia. That's about sixty thousand Rebels." Casper paused to allow the numbers to sink in. I had never seen sixty thousand men in one place before. That was more than most cities. I didn't see how one or two thousand cavalry men could affect the outcome.

"Where do we fit in?" George asked, sharing my thoughts.

"We have orders to protect the right flank against Stuart's cavalry. Our infantry has enough to worry about without J.E.B.

Stuart attacking their flank. Pack your saddle bags and eat your breakfast. I don't know when we'll eat again."

We finished our breakfast and drank our coffee in silence. There was no further talk of easy victories like Hanover. We were given a significant role in protecting the Union Army. The burden of our assignment felt heavy on our shoulders.

After breakfast the Third Division saddled up and headed down the Abottstown Road in a column of fours with the Michigan Brigade in the lead. Our Boy General rode in front with the 6th Michigan. After the victory at Hanover, most of the men were willing to cut General Custer some slack. He was a West point graduate with professional military training. That was more than many political appointees.

By afternoon we approached Hunterstown, which was a small farming community unravished by the war. Post and rail fences flanked both sides of the road, making it difficult for more than four troopers to ride abreast. The 6th Michigan proceeded down the road until their advance guard encountered a heavy force of confederate cavalry. They quickly returned to obtain further orders.

The Boy General decided to hold the 5th Michigan in reserve, so we dismounted on a ridge overlooking the road and watched the battle unfold. Unless the battle took a turn for the worse, we would be helpless spectators. That did not sit well with many of the men. The 6th Michigan dismounted and waded through a tall wheat field on the right side of the road while the 7th Michigan formed a skirmish line on the opposite side of the road.

"You think the Rebs skedaddled?" George asked. Our troops had yet to meet any resistance.

J.E.B. Stuart's boys don't skedaddle," Casper replied. "They're biding their time."

Lt. Pennington unlimbered his battery of six three-inch rifled artillery pieces and deployed them on the ridge behind us and pointed them down the road. If Johnny Reb was there, we were ready for him. The 6th and 7th Michigan continued their march on either side of the road. Some of the 6th Michigan deployed in a large barn on the right side of the road. I assumed they would be the unit's best sharpshooters.

"What's happening now?" Gottlieb asked. He should have been holding our horses in case we needed to make a hasty retreat. Since we were officially in reserve, he tethered them to a tree; he did not wish to miss any excitement.

"A scouting party spotted some Rebel cavalry at the end of the road," I replied. "The 6th and 7th are flushing them out."

"The boys aren't meeting any resistance," George said. "Perhaps it was a recon patrol and they did skedaddle." What George suggested made sense. Recon patrols avoided confrontations.

Mounted troopers began gathering on the road. There must have been fifty or sixty of them—perhaps an entire company. Riding at the front was our new general. With his long blond hair Custer was difficult to overlook.

"It looks like our general is going to probe their lines to see if the Johnnies are willing to fight," Casper said.

The road was only wide enough for five or six horseman abreast. When the men were in formation, Custer raised his sword and led the unit forward at a canter. We were too far away to hear the commands, but their actions were self-explanatory. After about two hundred yards they began to gallop in a full charge. The men disappeared around a bend in the road. An onslaught of pistol and rifle fire left little doubt they found the Rebels. From our position on the hill, we couldn't tell who was gaining the upper hand. Our troopers could be fighting a small recon force or they could be fighting J.E.B. Stuart's entire division.

The Rebels must have had a superior force. They were able to drive back Custer's gallant charge. Our men came galloping back with a horde of Confederate horsemen nipping at their horses' tails. I didn't know if this was Custer's plan, but it triggered a perfect ambush. Men from the 7th Michigan rose up from the tall wheat field where they had been hiding and turned loose a fusillade from their Spencers. Men of the 6th Michigan opened fire from the other side of the road. Many Confederate soldiers fell from their horses. Once our men made it to safety, Lt. Pennington opened up his artillery. We drove back the Rebels in great confusion.

Even though we were spectators and couldn't claim credit for the victory, shouts of cheer spontaneously erupted from the men of our regiment. The Michigan Brigade now had two victories in three days. The jubilation dissipated almost as quickly as it had erupted.

"Custer's down!"

A stray bullet hit Custer's horse causing the horse to lurch forward and fall to the ground.

"He's pinned under his horse!" George was explaining the obvious. Custer's left leg was pinned beneath the torso of a thousand pound horse. Custer had been our commanding general less than a week and now we were about to watch him die or be taken prisoner. Just when all appeared lost, one of our men rode up to Custer and dismounted. He pulled Custer free of his horse amidst heavy fire and then the two of them mounted the rescuer's horse and rode off to safety. We later learned the man who came to Custer's rescue was his orderly, Norvell F. Churchill.

From captured Rebels we discovered we had battled Hampton's entire brigade. Neither side harbored any desire to renew the skirmish, although Pennington's artillery continued its duel with Wade Hampton's artillery for several more hours. We held our position near Hunterstown until almost midnight when our division commander received orders to relocate to Two Taverns, on the Baltimore turnpike, about five miles southeast of Gettysburg. We arrived at three in the morning according to my pocket watch. We quickly fell asleep.

CHAPTER TWELVE

When I awoke there was still cannon fire in the west, but I could have slept through it had Casper not kicked my foot.

"Everyone up!"

George said something to Casper, which was best not repeated. We arrived at our bivouac at Two Taverns on the short side of four in the morning. I looked at my pocket watch: it was now ten minutes past seven. If my math was correct, that gave us little more than three hours of sleep.

"What's the hurry?" I asked.

"We're covering the army's flank," Casper said. "We'll be riding toward Gettysburg within the hour."

The order came as no surprise. Gettysburg was west of us, where the thunderous roar of cannons never ceased. What we had experienced was little more than minor skirmishes. We were now riding off to the real war. It was highly probable Mary would be a widow before the end of the day. My children could be fatherless by morning. I had been gone almost a year. For all practical purposes, they were already fatherless. I knew I should not harbor such gloomy thoughts, but I could not banish those thoughts from my mind.

"First Brigade is moving out at eight," Casper said. "We are to follow fifteen minutes later. That gives us time for breakfast. Make the most of it."

I warmed up some salt pork and ate it while I waited for my coffee to brew. I had done well in my first two encounters with combat. Perhaps I was lucky. My premonition that I would never return to Salem Township might not come true, but it haunted me just the same. I knew better than to share my feelings with George. I had no doubt he would survive the war. I also knew he would look after Mary and the kids. I opened my pocket watch not to check the time but to see Mary looking back at me. She had advised me to avoid this war, but I wouldn't listen. Now I knew she had been right.

At eight o'clock the First Brigade lined up and headed west. If normal procedures were followed, we would follow fifteen minutes after the last man from the First Brigade trotted down the road. Without some separation the two brigades would converge and lose their integrity.

I led Prince down to a small creek that the locals called Little's Run. The day appeared clear and I assumed it would also be hot. Prince would need the water. I filled my canteen; I would need water as much as Prince would. During the last week we had pushed our horses hard—more than I would have like, but I was not the one in charge. Many horses had gone lame, some even died from exhaustion. I lifted one of Prince's front hooves; his shoe was intact. I didn't need to have Prince throwing a shoe during a cavalry charge. The other hooves were also in good repair.

The bugler played *To Horse* and we all mounted up in a column of fours. As was our custom, Casper, Gottlieb, George, and I lined up together. The other four men in our squad lined up behind us. The summer sun was rising high in the sky, and there was insufficient wind to disperse the dust generated by the hooves of our horses. I tied a cravat around my mouth and nose to filter out the dust, but that did not help Prince. He was audibly wheezing, yet he plodded on. We rode about a mile northwest on the Baltimore Pike. I expected to continue on toward Gettysburg, instead Col. Alger turned north on Low Dutch Road.

"It appears our fearless leader is lost," George suggested.

"I would be careful about expressing such thoughts concerning commanding officers," Casper admonished. "Col. Alger must have received a change of orders. One does not get lost on such a well-traveled road as the Baltimore Pike."

Casper was right. One of these days George would get in trouble with his frank opinions of superior officers, although many troopers shared his views. Rumors abounded whenever there was limited knowledge of our future plans. One rumor suggested we had been ordered to secure the intersection of Hanover Road and Low Dutch Road to prevent Stuart's horsemen from attacking the Army of the Potomac's right flank. That rumor seemed most plausible, since it was passed down from the front of the column where the commanding officer rode. The rumor was confirmed in my mind when we came to a halt at the intersection with Hanover Road.

"Home, sweet home," George said. There was sarcasm in his voice. I looked around and saw only farmland. Large swaths of wheat begging for harvest carpeted the ground, but no sign of Rebels. Other than a wooded area a mile to the north, there was no place for them to hide. I failed to see what our presence had to offer.

Major Ferry had us deploy on the south side of Hanover Road with the 7th Michigan covering our left flank. The 1st Michigan hunkered down at the crossroads while the 6th spread out along a segment of Low Dutch road. If Rebels were in the area we were ready for them.

Our forward scouts returned having found no Confederate activity. Major Ferry gave the order to dismount. It was a welcome respite agreeable to both man and horse. It didn't take long before most of the men fell asleep under whatever shade they could find. I tied Prince to a small sapling and joined them. I could still hear cannon fire in the west, but that was over four miles away. It was not our concern.

Map of E. Cavalry Field

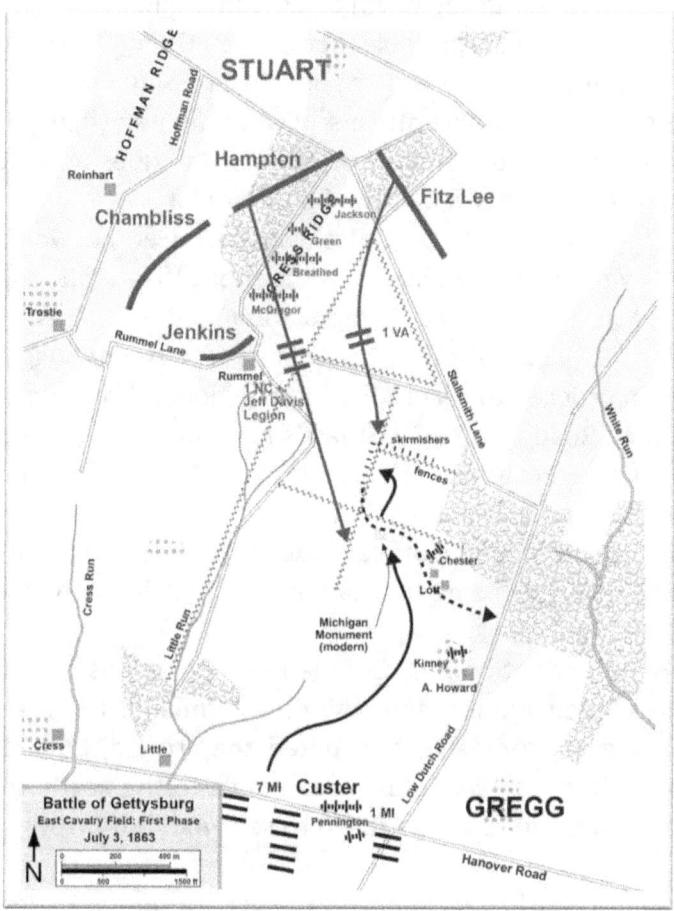

One would think cavalry could ride across fields without the need of roads, but there are obstacles such as fences that need to be breached and rivers that need to be forded. They also have horse artillery and supply wagons. They need roads.

Stuart's cavalry is at the top of the map. They want to ride down Stallsmith Lane to Dutch Road, which leads to Hanover Road. If they reach Hanover Road, they will have a clear path to Gettysburg, where they can attack Union Forces from the rear.

William Goodman is with George Custer and the Michigan 5th on Hanover Road. Pennington's Horse Artillery is also on Hanover Road. They must stop a superior force.

I awoke when Casper kicked the sole of my boot. It took a moment for my mind to clear. I had been dreaming I was back in Salem Township and I had expected to awaken to Mary's smiling face and to be pounced upon by three overly energetic children. Instead I saw men scurrying about. I found George and Gottlieb sitting around the small fire they were using to brew coffee. They were re-checking the contents of their cartridge boxes.

"What's going on?" I asked.

"I don't know if you believe in rumors, but according to the latest rumor, observers on Cemetery Hill reported a large Confederate cavalry force moving east on York Road. Don't ask. I never heard of Cemetery Hill either. I assume it is somewhere south of Gettysburg. It no doubt earned its name over the last several days."

"Is York Road far from here?" Rumors were ubiquitous, but from the way people were behaving, I assumed what George was telling me was fact—or at least people in high places believed it was fact.

"See that stretch of woods over yonder." George pointed to the thick woods a little over a mile away. The land in front of it was divided into cultivated fields by post and rail fences. "York Road is just beyond the woods. Our scouts say the woods are already infested with Rebs. J.E.B. Stuart and 4,800 of his horse troopers will come waltzing down Low Dutch Road any time now. He expects to attack our infantry from the rear, but we'll send him packing before he can create any mischief."

George was right. If Stuart's cavalry could reach Hanover Road via the Low Dutch Road, he would have access to the Army of the Potomac's vulnerable rear. I didn't share George's optimism about repelling such a large force. I drank some of George's coffee hoping it would settle my stomach—it did not.

I felt somewhat better when two brigades from General Gregg's Second Cavalry Division arrived on the scene. The additional troops should make it a fair fight, but for the most part it only added to the confusion. I had just finished a quick lunch when the bugler sounded *Boots and Saddles*. This was quickly followed by *To Horse*.

I mounted Prince and urged him into the column of fours that was forming on Hanover Road. I had yet to participate in a cavalry charge. This would be my first experience if that was what Col. Alger had in mind. I could see no enemy troops worthy of such a charge. The open fields in front of us were empty except for the ubiquitous yellow wheat. If the Rebels were hiding in the yonder woods, they would have all the advantages during such a charge.

I was beginning to believe the warning from cemetery hill was little more than a rumor when an artillery shell fell no more than three hundred yards in front of us. It exploded harmlessly, but it placed my nerves on edge. I don't know why, but I feared cannon fire more than the saber or rifle. It was an irrational fear; they can all kill in an instant. A puff of white smoke at the edge of the distant woods confirmed the source of the explosive round. Several more rounds fell before Lt. Pennington's battery returned the fire. A row of Confederate skirmishers emerged from the distant woods and took cover around a nearby farmhouse and barn.

"Let's get this rodeo on the road." George had his saber drawn ready to slay any dragons that might cross his path. When you are only twenty it was difficult to understand that dragons have sharp teeth and breathed fire. George had no concept of his own demise.

"You can secure your saber," Major Ferry told George. "We are rejoining the rest of our division on the army's southern flank. The Second Division is in charge of securing the crossroad." Ferry continued riding down the ranks to ensure everyone was mounted and ready to move out. Of all the officers of the regiment, Major Noah Ferry was the most respected. It was an honor he had justly earned.

"That don't seem right," Gottlieb said. "Stuart's cavalry is preparing to attack, and we are preparing to skedaddle."

"That is not our decision to make nor is it our job to question why," Casper replied. "General Gregg is a good man. His division can handle the situation."

I was in agreement with Gottlieb. Gregg was a wise leader, but he was short one of his brigades and his remaining two brigades would be no match for Stuart's entire cavalry if that were their adversary. We rearranged our formation, so we were in a column of fours facing west on the Hanover road and waited. And we waited.

"If we aren't going anywhere, why don't they let us dismount," George said. "I'm missing my afternoon nap."

Our horses didn't need us sitting on them just to pass the time of day, but the army seldom considered the welfare of the animals that carried us to war. I would prefer to provide Prince with as much rest as possible.

"Gentlemen, get used to it," Casper said. "Hurry up and wait is an essential element of military tradition."

Although the artillery shells were falling short, they were spooking our horses, making it difficult to keep them in formation. According to my pocket watch we sat sixteen minutes in the saddle before the order was given to dismount and secure the horses. Apparently, during those sixteen minutes the Second Division commander convinced General Custer to ignore General Pleasanton's order to unite with the rest of our division. That sounded like some serious arm twisting had taken place. If I were to ignore an order, I would be court martialed. Being a general officer must convey immunity for such indiscretions. Like it or not we were now unofficially attached to General Gregg's Second Division.

"So what do we do now?" Gottlieb asked. It was a question we were all asking ourselves. Lt. Pennington's battery was silencing the Confederate guns, but more and more dismounted Rebels were emerging from the woods.

"Did I mention the military tradition of hurry up and wait?" Casper replied. That was not the answer we wanted to hear.

General Custer deployed the 7th Michigan to our left and the 1st Michigan on our right. The 6th Michigan was delegated to protect Lt. Pennington's artillery. We formed a formidable obstacle between General Stuart and the rear of the army we were assigned to protect. The 5th and 6th Michigan were the only cavalry regiments in the brigade armed with the seven-shot Spencer rifles. It offered many advantages over conventional rifles. We could fire seven rounds without pausing to reload. It was a formidable weapon, and its remarkable firepower provided some comfort. There were nights when I would awaken from a dream in which hordes of Rebels were charging at me and I had discharged my gun making it useless. I don't know why the dream kept returning when I could fire the Spencer seven times without reloading. I soon discovered that Spencers had disadvantages.

"I think Col. Alger is about to answer your question," Casper said.

Col. Alger mounted on an impressive chestnut gelding, waited patiently in front of the regiment, seemingly oblivious to the artillery shells exploding behind him. He was a man accustomed to being in command. Only when he was assured of our undivided attention did he begin to speak. Like most attorneys, he had an authoritative voice that every trooper in the 5th regiment could hear with minimal effort.

"Gentlemen," he began. "General Custer has given us the task—no make that the honor—of repulsing those treasonous Rebels." Alger pointed to the small figures in the distance. "In a few minutes I will be riding across those wheat fields. When I am finished those backwoods Johnnies will have more respect for the Michigan Brigade. Are you boys coming with me?"

There was much hooting and hollering. I found myself consumed by the excitement. The din created by my fellow soldiers obscured even the noise from the exploding artillery shells. I raised my saber and added my voice to the cacophony.

"Men, if you are with me mount your horses and form up on the road."

Col. Alger road up and down the road until all twelve companies were mounted and eager to take on whatever J.E.B. Stuart had to offer. Alger's optimism was contagious. I don't know about the other men of the regiment, but I was feeling invincible. We were superior to Stuart's troopers. How could we not be victorious?

The bugler gave the signal and we began trotting across the wheat fields in a column of fours. The Rebel troops were still over a mile away, and we had many fields to cross and fences to traverse. It only made sense to proceed in a column through the gaps in the fences created by the lead horsemen.

When we were no farther that a half mile from the enemy, Col. Alger gave the order to form a mounted skirmish line. Once properly dispersed the twelve companies of the 5th regiment provided a formidable half-mile wide front. We were stirrup to stirrup. Our horses slowed from a trot down to a walk, but we continued relentlessly toward our foe. A slight breeze created golden waves that floated effortlessly from one end of the wheat fields to the other. On any other day we would have commented on its beauty—it was a sight any farmer would appreciate. On any other day we would have enjoyed the cooling effects of the gentle breeze, but not today.

Today we were more concerned with sharpshooters hiding among the trees and behind stone walls. We were more concerned with the large puffs of smoke that warned of an artillery shell heading in our direction, but we continued forward. The artillery shells had yet to acquire the proper distance. When we got closer they would change to canister and grape shot. Like a shotgun no aiming was required when shooting grape shot into an approaching mass of people. We continued toward our foe.

Artillery shells from our own battery whistled over our heads and exploded near and among the opposing cannons. Lt. Pennington's guns were more accurate than our opponent's. The puffs of smoke coming from the edge of the woods in front of us ceased. Either Pennington's men had destroyed the Rebel guns or the guns were pulled back to the safety of the woods. We continued forward.

Normally we talk while riding. We talk about the latest news from home. We talk about the wonderful meals our wives prepare. Even if it was only to discuss the weather, we talked. Now there was only silence as we continued forward. More and more Rebels emerged from the woods. We were outnumbered. I no longer felt invincible. I opened my pocket watch and looked into Mary's beautiful eyes. I wondered if she thought of me as often as I thought of her. "I love you," I whispered. It was five minutes to one o'clock.

"Remember your promise," I said to George. He was riding on my right side. He merely nodded. We continued forward.

We would soon be within rifle range. Surely, Col. Alger wasn't considering a cavalry charge. The wheat fields were enclosed in post and rail fences. I was confident Prince could hurdle the fences, but many other horses would falter. A cavalry charge would be a disaster. As I was debating the merits of a cavalry charge, the bugler sounded the call to dismount. Alger must have come to the same assessment that I had.

"Gottlieb, you are in charge of the horses," Casper handed the reins of his horse to Gottlieb. As was our custom, every fourth man held the reins of four horses. That honor had apparently been bestowed on Gottlieb. It wasn't always an easy assignment. The horse handler stayed in the rear, but bullets often find their way to the rear and it was impossible to take cover while trying to calm four nervous horses. I passed Prince's reins to Gottlieb.

"Take good care of Prince," I said. I gave Prince a sugar cube, which he ate with relish. I hoped he appreciated the sacrifice. Sugar cubes were hard to come by. I felt better leaving Prince in the rear. Horses make large targets and even the smallest wound was sufficient justification for sacrificing an animal. I gave Prince a gentle pat on his neck and turned toward our foe. Major Ferry was calmly walking up and down the line of dismounted men.

"Now, Boys, if any of you are unwilling to go forward, you may stay here," he said.

I don't think anyone could have stayed behind even if he wanted to. The Michiganders erupted in cheers and pressed forward through the wheat fields. I crouched low thinking that would provide a smaller target. Only my torso extended above the wheat, but wheat would do little to stop a bullet. Fortunately, the only artillery shells were coming from Pennington's battery. They were hurling them over our heads and exploding in the Rebel held territory. I hoped he would know when to cease his fire. Artillery was not always accurate, and we were approaching the impact area.

"Hold your fire until we get closer," Major Ferry admonished. "You can't hit anyone at this range. You'll waste your ammunition."

There may have been logic to what Major Ferry was suggesting, but Rebel sharpshooters were shooting at us and it was difficult not returning the fire. We maintained our control and pushed forward.

"Yow, I've been shot in the stomach." George was standing next to me. I didn't see any blood on his shirt.

Lift up your shirt," I said.

George lifted up his shirt and examined the area of discomfort. The skin was not broken, but it was red and swollen; he had the beginning of a substantial bruise.

"I think you will survive," I suggested. "But don't try that at a closer range."

We hurried to catch up with the rest of the men. George had been lucky. If he had been shot in the abdomen at closer range the ball would have punctured his gut. No one survived a gut wound. It was a slow and painful death. George lived a charmed life. Luck was on his side. I had no doubt this would be the only injury he would receive during the war. Luck wasn't always on my side.

"What is that?" I asked but I instantly knew the answer. The battle three miles to the west of us had been raging for three days. We heard artillery fire throughout the day and night, but nothing prepared us for the tumult we were now experiencing.

The ground trembled. The rumble echoed from every corner, but no one had any doubts of its origin. It was as if every cannon from both armies had commenced firing. We stopped in our tracks to consider its significance. Even the Rebels in front of us momentarily ceased fire to digest the new development. The battle south of Gettysburg was coming to a climax. Neither army had the resources to maintain this pace. By nightfall it would be over. I wondered who would be the victor. After a few moments of reflection our small war continued. We continued marching toward the enemy with Major Ferry in the lead.

"Fire only if you have a clear target," Major Ferry said.

Everyone must have had a clear target, because we fired in unison. We were much closer and I saw many of the Rebels fall after our volley. One of the officers leading the Rebels pointed his saber toward us.

"Quickly, men, charge them before they have time to reload!" he said.

The Rebels charged toward us. They must have assumed we were easy prey. That was a logical assumption, since they outnumbered us two to one. We fired a second volley and more Rebels fell. Others stopped and stared at us in disbelief. We fired a third volley and they began to fall back. Outnumbering us two to one had little advantage when we could fire four rounds to their single shot. We pressed forward.

Several men collapsed to the ground. I didn't know if they were dead or merely wounded. Some cried out in pain. They were at least alive. For how long, I did not know. A little voice inside me said I should stop and help them, but this was countermanded by a much louder voice.

"Men, we must take that stone wall." It was the voice of Major Ferry. He was pointing toward a stone fence currently defended by a sizeable Rebel force. It provided an excellent defensive position, but stone walls have two sides. If we could drive the Rebels back, it could be our defensive position. The logic was sound. They could fire one shot. We could fire many. If we rushed them, we could be on them before they could reload. The logic was sound, but the emotional part of me wondered how many men would die during the first volley and would I be one of them.

I wasn't given time to debate my choices. Men from all twelve companies gave out a unified yell and charged the wall. The sight of one thousand men repeatedly firing their rifles as they rushed toward the wall must have been unnerving. Many Rebels turned and fled. Others fired their muzzle loaders before taking their leave.

Several more men from our regiment fell. Two paces ahead of me a man grabbed his throat. Blood from a major blood vessel pulsated out from between his fingers and sprayed across my face as I passed. He bled to death before he hit the ground.

"Show those Rebels the courage of the Wolverines!"

Major Ferry was five paces in front of us leading the charge, but had hardly finished his sentence when a ball from a Confederate Enfield rifle-musket tore through his skull. He fell immediately. I slowed as I stepped over him. He lay on his back, his eyes open with that eternal stare. I knew he was already dead. I could do nothing for him. His hair was matted with blood. Somewhere within that blood matted hair was a hole where the rifle ball pierced the skull and lodged in his brain.

"Will, you can do nothing for him. We need to take that wall. That is what the Major wanted us to do."

Sometimes I thought Casper had ice water flowing through his veins. He fought with the Prussian army and served with the U.S. Army during the Mexican war. He had no doubt seen his share of pain and sorrow. Perhaps with time people become immune to the trauma of war and can no longer feel the pain of someone's untimely death. I could not envision that ever happening to me. Life was too precious. I suppressed an urge to vomit and ran toward the stone wall with the others. When we reached the wall only dead Confederates remained to defend the fortification. We pushed them off our wall.

It was an expensive victory. We had lost several men but we could now lay claim to a stone wall. For the price we paid one would expect a more impressive edifice. The wall was little more than a collection of large rocks garnered from the fields in the spring and loosely stacked in a row. There was no mortar to preserve it into eternity, but it kept the milk cows out of the wheat fields, and that made the farmer happy.

"What do we do now?" I asked Casper. I assumed he must have conquered one or more stone walls sometime in his military past.

"We hide behind this wall until some officer suggests otherwise," he replied.

"We pushed the Rebels into that woodlot behind the farmhouse. I say we keep on pushing until they turn tail and skedaddle back to Virginia." George was still feeling invincible even after his abdominal bruising from the spent Rebel bullet.

"We will do as ordered," Casper replied, "but charging toward the woods would be suicidal. They would be shooting from behind trees and we would be walking across the open field. We would be easy targets. They also have artillery hidden in the woods. Once you have been fired upon with grape shot you never forget."

I assumed Casper was speaking of encounters from previous wars. I had no desire to add grapeshot to my inventory of personal experiences. I was happy to hide behind our stone wall until dark. Neither army had a desire to fight at night. I looked at my pocket watch; dusk was a long way off.

"We aren't going to win this battle hiding behind a stone fence." George fired his Spencer toward the woods at some imaginary foe. It was a senseless gesture and a waste of a bullet. The woodlot was too distant and any foe worthy of an adversary was secured behind a log or tree, but when you were only twenty, common sense was not all that common.

"We don't have to win this battle," Casper replied. We all looked at him as if he had lost his sense. Major Ferry and several other good men were dead and Casper was suggesting the outcome of their sacrifice was of little importance.

"Hear those distant cannon?" Casper asked. How could we not hear them? The thunderous roar was unlike anything we had heard before. It had continued non-stop for the better part of an hour.

"The real battle, the one that counts has been raging for three days. What you are now hearing is the grand finale. Both sides are giving their all and paying a far greater price than we could ever pay on this small battlefield. I don't know who is winning, but I do know if J.E.B. Stuart and his four thousand troopers get past us and attack the rear of our army it could just be enough to tip the balance. We don't have to win, but we cannot fail. If we fight the Rebels to a draw and prevent them from joining the big fight, we will have earned an honest day's wages."

What Casper said made sense. Our mission was to block Stuart's advance. We could do that just as well hunkered down behind the safety of a stone wall. The Rebels had possession of the distant woods, but that did little to enhance their cause.

"Do you men have any ammo you can spare? My men are down to one or two rounds apiece."

I didn't know the man's name, but I recognized him as a corporal from our company. We were also low on ammo. After a quick consultation Casper, George, and I decided to each give him two rounds. He would have to beg more from other people. I had just given him my two rounds when I heard a shrill whistling sound. The sound was unlike the sound from any other bullet I had heard. The corporal's face exploded, spraying blood in every direction. Some of the blood must have splattered onto my face, as I could taste the salty blood on my lips. The man was dead before his body hit the ground.

"Jez," George said. "Where did that bullet come from?"

"That was a bullet from a Whitworth rifle," Casper replied. "The hexagonal bullet from a Whitworth has a shrill whistling sound unlike any other bullet. In the hands of a good sharpshooter the Whitworth is accurate to one thousand yards. I've been told some sharpshooters even attach telescopes to their weapons."

Any bullet coming from the woods would have spent its energy and caused little more than a severe headache. The bullet that just hit the corporal had plenty of energy. I looked over the wall, but saw no evidence of Rebel activity.

"Do you think it came from the farmhouse?" I asked.

The farmhouse was five hundred yards away, much closer than the woods. This was within the range of a Rebel sharpshooter with a Whitworth rifle, but too distant for our Spencers to be of any use. The corn crib or the stone and wood barn could also conceal a Rebel sharpshooter.

"Everyone keep your heads down. Stay out of sight. We have a Rebel sharpshooter out there."

The company commander was explaining the obvious. The lifeless man at our feet provided sufficient evidence. Captain Townsend paused long enough to assess the significance of the dead man. I turned my head away. I had no doubt I would be seeing the disfigured face of my comrade many times in future dreams.

"Damn, he's the third one."

It might not be fair, but the captain gave me the impression he was only concerned with numbers. Perhaps such objectivity was mandatory for someone responsible for the survival of the entire company. Emotional attachment could impair his judgment. I thanked the Lord I was only a private.

"Do we know where the sharpshooter is?" George asked before the captain had a chance to move on.

"He's in the barn. We've seen him in the opening to the hayloft."

I extended my head above the stone wall just long enough to better grasp what the captain was explaining. The barn was fifty yards to the left of the farmhouse. The lower portion was constructed of mortar and stone with the upper level of wood beam and plank siding. Midway up on the second level was an opening for filling the loft with hay. Anyone in the hay loft would have a good view of our stone wall. It was the perfect spot for a Rebel sharpshooter.

"If we can see him, why doesn't someone shoot him?" George was making me nervous. Privates do not question the actions of company commanders. Such protocol never occurred to George.

"We had a sharpshooter in the company, but he got himself shot in the leg. We had to send him to the rear. He'll be lucky if he keeps that leg. No one else in the company has his skill with a rifle."

"Will can do it. I've seen him shoot the eye out of a running turkey at twice that distance."

Sometimes George talked too much. That was clearly an exaggeration. No one could hit a moving target at that distance. Our Spencer carbines were good weapons. They could discharge seven rounds in less than a minute, but they lacked range and accuracy. The captain looked at me. I don't know how he knew I was the Will in question. We had never formally conversed.

"Is that true?" he asked.

"I'm a fair shot," I replied, "but no one can hit a draft horse at that distance with a Spencer. Our rifles don't have that kind of range or accuracy."

"We lost our sharpshooter, but we still have his Sharps rifle if you want to give it a try," the captain said. "It has the range. The accuracy would be up to you." Everyone looked at me waiting for an answer. Every rifle had its own personality, and I had never fired a Sharps before. There was no way I could hit a target at that distance, moving or not. It would have been iffy even after weeks of practice, and this was not an appropriate time to begin.

"He'll do it," George said before I had a chance to decline.

"Why did you tell him that?" I asked after the captain left to retrieve the Sharps rifle. I heard another shrill whistling sound, and a trooper twenty feet to my right fell to the ground. That Rebel was good with a rifle. If we did nothing, he would pick us off one by one. If we tried to rush him we would come within range of the Rebels entrenched in the woods. Their artillery would rake us with grapeshot. It was a no win situation. I raised my head to better assess my task. It may have been my imagination, but I thought I saw movement near the right lower corner of the hayloft opening. That could have been the Rebel sharpshooter. If it was, it would be a very small target even with the best rifle. A puff of white smoke emerged from the blackness of the opening. I ducked behind the stone wall. Two seconds later I heard the tell-tale shrill of the Whitworth's hexagonal bullet whiz over my head. It was reassuring knowing I had a two-second warning of such bullets.

"It's a good weapon," The captain said when he returned with the Sharps rifle.

It did look like a good weapon, but its long barrel and heavy weight limited its value to a man on horseback. It was a breach loader. I pulled back on the trigger guard to view the chamber; the gun was already loaded. I set the rear adjustable sight to just above the five-hundred yard mark. That was farther than the distance to the barn, but the shooter was at least ten feet above ground level. I would be shooting uphill and would need to compensate for the additional elevation. I extended my head above the wall for another look at the barn.

"How can I shoot him? I can't even see him." The hayloft opening was a black hole in an otherwise red barn. The shooter could be anywhere in the barn. The captain lifted his binoculars to his eyes.

"He's lying prone in right lower corner."

The captain passed the binoculars to me. I had never used binoculars before. Engraving on a small metal label announced it had six power. I was amazed when I pressed the lenses against my eyes. The barn filled my view. I could discern the individual vertical planks on the sides of the barn. I followed the planks upward until my eyes arrived at the hayloft opening. The barn was still dark inside, but enough light entered the opening to illuminate the prone rifleman who was about a foot from the right edge of the opening. I could even see his rifle. It had a telescope attached to its left side. A puff of white smoke discharged from the gun barrel.

"Everyone down," I said. Two seconds later the bullet sped over our heads. If I hadn't ducked it would have lodged into my head. The rebel was obviously drawn to men with binoculars. I would not have a long time to take aim.

"There is no way I can hit him from here," I said, "but if I can place a couple of bullets in his vicinity, it might spook him." I returned the binoculars to the captain. "Let me know if he moves or if you see any white smoke." I stood to make myself an easy target. I wasn't disappointed.

"White smoke! Everyone down!"

We all hugged the wall and waited for the shrill sound of the hexagonal bullet. The Whitworth was a muzzle-loading gun and took fifteen or twenty seconds to reload. That should provide sufficient time to fire my round. I rested the barrel of the Sharps rifle on the stone wall and lined up the open sights with the right lower corner of the hayloft opening. Then I waited.

"He reloaded his rifle and is back in the prone position," the captain said. "You don't have much time."

I edged the barrel until it was pointing at what I judged was a foot from the right side of the opening. I took a deep breath and then exhaled until my lungs felt relaxed. The discharge from a rifle should always come as a surprise, if it did not the rifleman was pulling on the trigger. I gradually added pressure to the trigger and waited for the discharge.

"White smoke!"

The captain ducked below the stone wall. I continued applying pressure to the trigger until the kick against my shoulder confirmed the gun's discharge. I lowered my head just as the bullet whizzed by. That was too close for comfort.

"He's reloading," the captain said. "You must have missed him."

"It's an impossible shot," I replied in my defense.

"Give it another try. We have more rounds for the Sharps than we do military options. It can't hurt."

I reloaded the rifle and then exposed myself again. It didn't take long for another bullet to seek its target. Fortunately, the target was well below the wall when it arrived. I rested my rifle on the wall and waited for my adversary to reload. This time I would aim a little higher. The distance could be greater than I had estimated. Or the gunman could be farther above the ground.

"He's back," the captain whispered. I don't know why we had to whisper. The 1st New Jersey was skirmishing with Confederates on our far right and Pennington's three-inch guns were hurdling shells overhead. Then there was the constant background noise from the main battle south of Gettysburg. No way was our adversary going to hear our conversation.

I aimed at the black square in the barn, estimating where the gunman would be lying. I assumed he was now placing the crosshairs of his telescopic sight on my forehead. I increased the pressure against the trigger until white smoke belched from the gun barrel and the stock of the gun rammed back against my shoulder. I ducked behind the wall to avoid the bullet I knew would be coming my way.

"Captain, you need to get down."

Captain Townson continued looking through his binoculars. He was either foolishly brave or just foolish. We were pressing our luck. A stiff gust of wind could dissipate the smoke from the sharpshooter's rifle in less than a second. If we failed to notice the smoke, one of us would be dead. Captain Townson just smiled and handed me his field glasses.

I lifted the glasses to my eyes and cautiously examined the black opening to the hayloft. The sharpshooter was lying face down and his chest was convulsing as if trying to inhale air that was mechanically unavailable. My last shot must have pierced his lungs. He would be dead within minutes. I wondered if he had a wife and family. I joined the army to preserve the nation. It had never occurred to me that it might require killing people. I could look no more.

"I told you, Will could do it—shoot the eye out of a running turkey at twice that distance." George borrowed the field glasses to confirm what we already knew.

"You saved a lot of lives today, Private Goodman." Captain Townson gave me a pat on the shoulder and returned to wherever company commanders reside during combat. I didn't know how many lives I saved, but I knew the sharpshooter was not one of them. George and several other troopers in the vicinity were jubilant. Only Casper seemed to understand how I felt.

"I wish I could say combat gets easier with time," he said. "It doesn't. War can be brutal, but right now you need to put that behind you. It appears your sharpshooter's friends are preparing an attack. If it doesn't receive your undivided attention, you'll end up like your sniper."

I cautiously peered over the wall hoping there was only the lone sniper. A line of gray-clad men were forming at the edge of the woods. They outnumbered us, but we had a defensive stone wall and with our Spencers, we had three or four times their firepower. I checked my cartridge pouch; only four shells remained.

"George, I'm low on ammunition."

"Ditto," George replied. I looked at Casper.

"We all are," Casper said. "Make every shot count."

Lt. Pennington must have noticed the men in gray who were emerging from the woods. A volley of three-inch shells hurled over our heads and exploded along the edge of the woods. Perhaps that would make them think twice before leaving the shelter of the woods.

"FALL BACK TO THE HORSES!" Col. Alger must have re-assessed our situation in light of the limited ammunition. I know I could not repulse a major attack with only four rounds. I had a full cartridge case in my saddle bag, but Prince was a quarter mile away. We backed away from the stone fence and then double timed toward our waiting horses.

The Rebel commander sensed our predicament. At his command the entire Confederate horde screamed their Rebel yell and charged toward us. They smelled blood and an easy victory. They quickly closed the distance.

"MEN, STAND AND FIGHT!" Col. Alger must have decided it was preferable to fight a losing battle than be shot in the back running away. "We'll use our sabers if need be." Col. Alger drew his saber from its scabbard and pointed it defiantly toward the advancing Rebels.

"Sabers only work when you can reach the enemy, George pointed out. " Once we run out of ammo, those Rebs can shoot at us all day from the safety of a hundred yards. Even with my long arms that'll be beyond my reach."

George was right. Saber would be of limited value. If we were to charge the Rebels armed with sabers, they could fire three or four rounds before we could get even close to them. I loaded my remaining four bullets into my Spencer and assumed the prone position. The other men in our regiment did likewise. The prone position produced a smaller target. We were well hidden in the tall wheat, but standing Rebels were clearly visible. The prone position would also increase the effectiveness of our limited ammunition supply.

"HOLD YOUR FIRE UNTIL THEY GET CLOSE!" Captain Townson was standing upright and pacing behind us. He presented the perfect target. After a couple of bullets whizzed by his head, he reconsidered his position and decided to join those of us hidden in the wheat.

No one gave the order to commence firing, but once the Rebels were within fifty yards, hundreds of Spencers poured a lethal barrage of bullets into their ranks. Many men in gray fell to the ground. The others paused momentarily while their officers mentally debated if we were truly low on ammunition. They had experienced the firepower of a fully loaded Spencer carbine and did not wish to repeat the experience.

I fired three of my four rounds and three Rebel soldiers fell to the ground. It was much less personal when they fall out of sight in the wheat. Their death was just as painful, but I didn't have to watch it. Perhaps my turn at death would come after I fired my remaining round.

"That was my last bullet," George said. "I'm running back to our horses."

"If the Colonel says we stay and fight with sabers, we stay and fight with sabers," Casper replied.

That seemed to placate George for the moment. I wasn't sure if he really intended to desert his post or was just venting his frustration. I harbored mixed feelings. My instincts suggested the cartridge box in my saddle bag could save my life, but my military training told me the herd offered the best protection. I decided to save my last bullet until the Rebels were upon us and that would not take long. Our withering fire, as more troopers ran short of ammo, gave courage to the advancing Confederates. The volume of their yelling matched the increase of their pace.

I glanced back to see how far we were from our horses. It would be a long run and if we were to outrun the Rebels, they would surely overtake us before we could put the cartridge boxes to good use. More importantly, I noticed a line of horsemen riding into the wheat field. I recognized their banner as that of the 7th Michigan Cavalry Regiment. Company after company filed into the wheat field and lined up next to our horses. There must have been close to a thousand mounted troopers. The advancing Rebels paused momentarily to re-assess their position.

As I watched, a young officer on a lean chestnut gelding rode to the front of the assembled regiment. He was conspicuously dressed in a suit of black velvet over a navy-blue shirt. A scarlet cravat tied loosely about the neck flowed in the gentle breeze. Long blond hair extended down from under a black broad-brimmed hat. Attached to the front of the hat was a gilt cord and rosette encircling a silver brigadier general's star. No one could confuse our brigade commander with any other General. Custer still dressed like a peacock, but he was our peacock, and we were all proud to serve under him.

Custer signaled with raised hand and a line of mounted cavalrymen three horses deep trotted forward through the tall wheat. They had a fair distance to ride before they would reach us, but the spectacle was insufficient to slow the advance of our adversaries. They continued toward us. I felt no further need to save my remaining bullet. I selected a man in the front of the approaching line, no more than fifty yards in front of me. I squeezed the trigger and the man fell among the grains of wheat. Several other men fired their last rounds and then our guns fell silent.

I turned toward George. "Remember your promise," I said. George had his saber drawn and was crouched, ready to spring forward. Either he did not hear me, or he chose to ignore my comment. I opened my pocket watch to see Mary's face and wondered if my watch would become a souvenir for some Rebel soldier. "I'm sorry, Mary," I whispered and returned the watch to my shirt pocket. Then I drew my saber and waited for the command to rush our opponents.

"Advance with sabers—double quick."

Col. Alger's command was echoed by the company commanders and sergeants. With unified yell, eight hundred men of the 5th Michigan Regiment sprang forward and rushed the enemy. At the same time General Custer raised his hat and waved it at the men behind him. "COME ON, YOU WOLVERINES!"

The 7th Michigan covered the remaining one hundred yards at a gallop, reaching the Rebels in unison with our saber charge. Nothing was more terrifying to a foot soldier than a coordinated attack by mounted cavalry. The Confederate line quickly broke and the Rebels fled toward the woods. We stepped aside to allow the 7th to proceed with their attack, raising our clinched fists to offer encouragement. Custer would have chased them clear to the woods if the post and rail fences hadn't limited their advance. The cavalry charge must have broken the Confederate cavalry's will to fight. The regiments skirmishing with the 1st New Jersey and the 3[d] Pennsylvania were withdrawing from the field. We returned to our horses and reloaded our weapons just to be on the safe side.

"Looked like the 7th arrived just in time," Gottlieb suggested.

"Didn't really need them," George replied. "We were finishing them off with our sabers."

Sometimes George needed a dose of humility. This was one of those times. I was tempted to mention he had come close to deserting his post. We mounted our horses and headed back to Hanover Road. We had successfully defended our intersection and prevented Stuart from attacking the rear of Meade's army, but we had too many riderless horses to rejoice in the victory. In the west the guns were eerily quiet.

East Cavalry Field

Visitors to Gettysburg are confronted with an assortment of self-guided tours, placards, park volunteers, and numerous monuments. You will hear nothing about the cavalry battle—unless you ask. The cavalry battle was insignificant only because the Union forces won. If J.E.B. Stuart's Cavalry Corp. had broken through and attacked the Army of the Potomac from the rear, it might have altered the course of the war. That would have made the cavalry battle more historic.

East Cavalry Field is about four miles east of Gettysburg. There is not much to see other than an occasional vintage cannon and lots of corn and wheat fields. This is probably what William Goodman and the Michigan Brigade found when they arrived over 150 years ago.

There were two significant advantages that allowed the Union Cavalry to hold off a superior force. The 5th Michigan Cavalry had Spencer repeating rifles. They could fire three or four rounds in the same time the Confederates fired one round. One Confederate soldier complained that the Union Cavalry loaded their guns in the morning and fired all day. This increased firepower offset the superior numbers of Confederates. The disadvantage is that the Michigan 5th quickly ran low on ammo. Colonel Alger advised the troops to use their sabers. Sabers extend about three or four feet. The Confederates could continue shooting from a distance. All appeared lost.

The second Union advantage was the Michigan Cavalry Brigade. They weren't supposed to be there. General Custer had orders to ride toward Gettysburg, but General Gregg convinced him to stay and help repel Stuart's Cavalry. As the Michigan 5th was about to be overrun, General Custer was lining up the 800 men of the Michigan 7th. The cavalry charge relieved the beleaguered Michigan 5th and chased the Rebels into the woods. They offered no further resistance. The battle was over. A monument to the Michigan

Cavalry Brigade now stands at the point where Custer's charge passed the out-gunned 5th Michigan.

CHAPTER THIRTEEN

I awoke to the pleasant aroma of coffee brewing over a fire. The night had been cold and wet, but my craving for sleep sufficed to overcome physical discomfort. George, Gottlieb, and Casper were awake and stirring. I wasn't sure who was responsible for brewing the coffee, but logic suggested it was Casper. He was normally the first up, and no good German can survive without a morning cup of coffee. Where Casper found dry wood after such a heavy rain was known only to him and God. He took my cup and filled it with the strong brew. The army was eternally short on rations, but they did provide respectable coffee. I thanked Casper for the coffee and then cozied up to the fire to absorb its warmth.

"I have a detail for you and George when you finish breakfast," he said. The coffee was Casper's way of mitigating his guilt over giving us an unpleasant detail, but I didn't care. The coffee was hot and I was cold.

From the relaxed atmosphere I assumed the conflict was over. Gone were the sounds of cannons. The air was cool and damp, but no longer filled with sulfurous fumes from burning gunpowder. Men walked about with neither gun nor saber at their side. Our pickets must have confirmed the withdrawal of the confederate soldiers. Whatever the detail Casper had in mind could not entail much danger.

"What do you have in mind?" I asked. "You need us to ride to the general store for more coffee and maybe donuts? It is Independence Day, you know. We should be celebrating." Casper smiled at my comment. That wouldn't have happened if Rebels were lurking nearby.

"Col. Alger needs forty men to gather up the dead. You and George volunteered."

I felt as if I had been kicked in the gut. I would have preferred a mounted frontal attack against the best troopers J.E.B. Stuart had to offer. We lost too many good men, but they were merely names on some regimental clerk's list. With little effort I could delude myself into believing the missing men were prisoners of war who would miraculously resurrect at the conclusion of this war. With the proposed detail, I could not hide from the dead. I didn't know if I had the inner strength to look into their unresponsive eyes or physically touch their lifeless skin. I considered offering a protest, but could think of no logical reason for evading the assigned duty. Casper said forty men had been assigned to the detail. Perhaps if we dawdled in our labor, we could avoid contact with the more mutilated bodies. Surely others were more capable of performing this duty.

"One of the local farmers loaned us a dray," Casper said. "The ground is flat. One horse should pull it. Rumor has it we'll be chasing the Johnnies back to Virginia, so you need to hustle."

I checked out the dray while I finished my breakfast of hardtack and salt pork. The farmer had recently used the two-wheeled cart to haul manure. It still imparted a faint odor, but not enough to offend an old farm boy. It lacked sides. That would facilitate loading dead bodies. A quality leather harness hung from the two wooden shafts; all it lacked was a good horse.

"Want me get my horse?" George asked.

"No, we'll use Prince. He can be very gentle." I didn't know why I worried about a gentle ride. The dead would not care. For some reason it was important to me. I found Prince eating clover where I had tethered him the night before. Despite the recent combat, Prince appeared well rested. I backed Prince into the space between the two shafts and attached the harness. I wasn't sure if Prince had ever pulled a wagon, but he didn't seem to mind.

"I don't know which I despise more," George said, "yesterday's heat or today's rain."

A steady rain had replaced the drizzle. Water dripped from our clothing, but we still donned our oil skins. If nothing else the oil skin provided a modicum of warmth. One does not expect to be cold on the Fourth of July, but this was no ordinary Fourth of July. We guided Prince onto the Hanover Road where a lieutenant was providing instructions to the assembled men. I didn't know why we needed instructions. How difficult could recovering dead bodies be? There were two other carts, but most of the men had a bareback horse in tow. I assumed they would drape the dead bodies over the horses. I was glad we had a dray. Securing a dead body to a horse would not be an easy task.

The lieutenant assigned a sector to each pair of men. We were given the area near the stone wall. It was an area we knew intimately. I guided Prince into the wheat field. The wind had picked up sending waves across the fields of wheat. It appeared we were in for a donnybrook of a storm.

We passed several dead bodies; they were not in our assigned area. The rain had cleansed the bodies of blood. What previously would have been a gruesome mess was now sanitized and only the small tell-tale bullet holes confirmed the cause of death. If the day were hot and sunny like the previous day, flies would be claiming jurisdiction over the dead. They were blissfully absent. I don't think I could have touched a body filled with maggots.

"George, when my time comes, do you think you could say some words? Maybe read some passages from my Bible? It would mean a lot to Mary."

"Will, you ain't going to die and I don't speak German, so I can't read from your German Bible. I don't want to hear no more of such talk. We're both returning to Salem."

We walked in silence until we found our first body. It was a man from our company. I knew little more than his name. We weren't friends other than to bid each other hello in the morning. He was lying on his back with his eyes staring up at the rain clouds. The Rebels had claimed his shirt and shoes during the night. They probably would have taken his pants if they hadn't been ripped. A small bullet hole over the center of his chest suggested an easy death. I hoped I would be so lucky when my time came.

"I'll get his feet," I said. George grabbed the shoulders and we lifted the body. I expected a limp body that would sag under its own weight. Instead the body was rigid with rigor mortis. The position of the head and outstretched arms did not change. There was no way we could have secured the body to a bareback horse. We eased him onto the dray as if he could still feel pain. I knew he couldn't, but it made me feel better. We continued our search.

"There's another one over there."

I guided Prince toward where George was pointing. I knew who it was before I saw the body. That was where Major Ferry had fallen. Someone had removed his pants and shoes, leaving him naked on the ground. I knew this was part of war but it still infuriated me that someone could be so disrespectful for the dead. Even the buttons on Ferry's shirt were gone. The rain had done little to soften the appearance of Ferry's wound. The bullet had shattered Ferry's forehead, leaving the right eye without a complete socket. The eye stared down at his cheek while the other eye looked toward heaven.

Major Noah Ferry was one of the most respected officers in the regiment. He took good care of his troops. Men like Ferry cannot be replaced. We gently lifted the Major and set him down on the dray. We found one more dead trooper. His face was not familiar—at least in that contorted form. I assumed he was from the 7th Cavalry. I turned Prince around and led him back toward the road. We could have looked further, but there was only room on the dray for three bodies unless we stacked them. That was an option I had no intention of employing.

Someone had lined up the dead bodies with military precision just south of the road. Many were tagged with name and unit. Common decency suggested they should be covered and sheltered from the elements. Sheets of rain inundated their half-naked bodies. Rivulets of water washed around their torsos. We unhitched Prince and left the dray with the dead at the end of the formation. I wished no further contact with the dead.

"Going somewhere?" I asked when we returned to camp. The cooking fire was smoldering and Casper was cinching the saddle on his horse.

"You guys got back just in time," Casper replied. "The division commander thought today would be a fine day for a ride. We're going after Lee's army."

I had been hankering for a day of rest. With the storm blowing rain sideways, constructing a dry shelter was nearly impossible, but I had been willing to try.

"Gottlieb has your rations. We were issued enough for three days. Looks like the General has planned a long ride." Casper checked the contents of his ammo box. He appeared satisfied. "We leave in half an hour."

"Don't suppose there is any chance you are wrong and we are heading back to Washington?" George asked.

Casper ignored George's question. It was senseless. George didn't expect an answer. We were part of the main army. Washington was no longer our home. I only had one home and that was Salem. I wondered what Mary was doing. If there were a storm like this, she would be inside. If she were cold, she would build a fire. I should be home with her. I longed to look at her face, but I feared opening my pocket watch would expose her picture to the rain.

I grabbed my saddle and swung it over Prince's back. "Sorry, old boy," I said. Army life was equally hard on horses. Prince endured the hardship better than most of the horses. I felt a bet of shame asking him to do more. I wished I had an apple to show my appreciation.

The bugler sounded *To Horse* fifteen minutes later—not thirty. Someone was in a hurry. I mounted up and guided Prince onto Hanover Road. We were the only regiment forming up. The 5th Michigan had the honor of leading the pursuit of the Rebels. I assumed the other regiments would follow at appropriate intervals.

We headed west on Hanover Road toward Gettysburg. With all the noise that had emanated from that area over the last several days, it seemed eerily quiet. As we passed north of Culp's Hill we discovered why. There wasn't a tree, bush, or twig that hadn't been slashed almost to the ground by cannon fire or musket ball. Hundreds—perhaps thousands— of dark objects littered the field in the distance.

"You think those are dead bodies?" George asked.

I merely nodded. It seemed almost disrespectful to speak. This should not have come as a surprise. With all that cannon fire, there had to be a price to pay. Still I had not envisioned the magnitude of the carnage. Many widows would be receiving telegrams in the coming days. Can there be a winner in such a battle when so many people die?

We continued through Gettysburg. The cheerful throng of people we had seen the previous Sunday was gone. No one hung bouquets of flowers around the necks of our horses. What townsfolk we did see appeared haggard and wearied. They looked like they had gotten little more sleep than we had.

From the center of Gettysburg we turned south onto the Emmitsburg Road. We were heading into the killing fields. The dark objects we had seen in the distance became larger; details became more distinct. The dead now had faces. Some looked like they had fallen into an eternal sleep; others, with grotesque facial features, were curled into the fetal position. When I looked into the eyes of the men staring forever at nothing in particular, it made little difference which uniform they were wearing. Death was death. We road silently through the battlefield oblivious to the torrential downpour. No one dared say a word lest he break the sanctity of the moment. The memories of those moments were becoming chiseled into our brains. I had no doubt we would relive that ride through the Gettysburg Battlefield for many years to come.

The Emmitsburg Road turned southwest as we left the battlefield behind us. It had rained most of the morning, but now the heavens opened up and sent a downpour such as I had never seen. The ditches on either side of the road transformed into rapidly flowing rivers. Shallow creeks that randomly crossed our road overflowed, causing much mischief for those trying to ford. Rain soaked deep into the ground creating mud that sucked in the hooves with every step our horses took. Prince never complained, but I knew the labor was taking its toll. Our column slowed to half our normal marching pace.

If this was a widespread storm, which it appeared to be, the Potomac would overflow its banks making crossing impossible. Lee and his army would be trapped at Williamsport or wherever they hoped to ford the river. That was of value only if we could muster the forces to profit from Lee's misfortune.

"How far do you think we are behind them?" I asked. As usual Casper, George, Gottlieb, and I were riding abreast. There was no way of knowing the answer to my question. I was seeking speculation. Perhaps I just wanted to talk. Riding in the rain hour after hour produces boredom. It was either strike up meaningless conversation or my mind would wonder to Salem where my wife and children were warm and capable of seeking shelter from any storm. That would only add further melancholy to an already depressing day.

"Their wagon wheels are leaving deep ruts in the mud," Casper replied. "They must have passed this way after the rain soaked into the ground. My guess would be no more than two or three hours."

"We won't catch them before nightfall," George added.

George was probably right. With the storm clouds swirling overhead, estimating the time of day was difficult, but it had to be late in the evening. I was tempted to check my pocket watch. Only the fear of damaging Mary's picture in the rain prevented me. I had wrapped the watch in oilskin to protect it from the rain, but I questioned even if that would be adequate.

"If we can't catch them we should call it a day and find a dry shelter for the night," Gottlieb said.

"I don't think the general is putting his itinerary plans up for a vote," Casper replied. "If it makes you feel any better, the Rebels are enduring the same downpour. The storm actually gives us an advantage."

"How so?" I asked. I was cold, wet, and hungry; Prince couldn't continue indefinitely; and it would soon be dark. I didn't think I could tolerate many more advantages.

"We're riding horses. They're driving wagon trains. You can't see it through all this rain and dark clouds, but we're approaching Monterey Pass. The pass provides a pathway over South Mountain and into the Shenandoah Valley. I hear tell that's a powerful amount of uphill climbing. Our horses can make that climb in the mud better than a wagon. I'm betting the General plans to catch them Rebels with their pants down pushing the wagons up the mountain."

We continued riding in silence. I was miserable and feeling sorry for myself. I was in no mood for further conversation. The rain and wind did not care about my comfort. If anything the weather intensified. Night had definitely fallen upon us, making it difficult to see the tail of the horse in front of us. Only the illumination from the lightning flashes, and there were many, kept us confined to the road. Conducting a battle under these conditions was sheer folly even if we were to catch the Rebels.

It was almost imperceptible at first. I would not have noticed if a flash of lightning hadn't illuminated the rapidly flowing water in the ditch beside our road. We were riding uphill. I thought it might have been a normal variation of topography, but the climb was persistent.

"We're heading uphill," George said. He had reached the same conclusion as I had.

"South Mountain," Casper added. "We're heading toward the Shenandoah Valley."

A steep slope soon replaced our gentle incline, and a sandstone wall bordered the right side of the road where there had been trees only minutes before. It must have taken many men several years to carve the road from the side of the mountain. I was thankful to be the inside man in our column of fours. The left side of the road fell into a large ravine. In the darkness I couldn't appreciate the depth of the abyss, but it would make for a long, painful fall. The road would have been a challenge in the daylight. In darkness it was terrifying. Normally when we ride four abreast one or two feet separate the riders. The other three riders were now pushing me close to the sandstone wall. It made for an uncomfortable ride, but I could understand their anxiety. I wouldn't want to ride close to the edge either—not in this darkness.

I could feel Prince wheezing under the additional burden of climbing the mountain. He was a strong horse, but even strong horses have their limits. I couldn't see any other horses, but I assumed they were suffering under the stress. Sometimes we asked too much from our mounts.

"Our horses can't maintain this pace," I said. "Do you think the generals have enough horse sense to give us a break soon?" I don't normally berate generals—I leave that up to George—but I was feeling Prince's pain.

"I've seen generals ride a horse to its death," Casper replied. "They aren't concerned with the health our horses. If they think we have a chance of catching the rebels, they won't allow the wellbeing of a few horses stand in their way. The road up the mountain is no less steep for the Rebels. Our horses should be thankful they aren't dragging wagons through this mud."

As if to prove a point, we passed a wagon with a broken axle. It blocked most of the road, forcing us to pass single file. A flash of lightning briefly illuminated the wagon sufficiently to gather a glimpse of the inside. Two men were lying on the wagon's wooden floor. I perceived no motion and assumed they were dying or already dead. I hoped for the latter. No one was stopping to offer aid, and death offers an escape from the insufferable pain of a mortal wound.

We were approaching the top of the pass when we heard an explosion. It took me a moment to discern I was not hearing thunder. It was the unmistakable sound of an artillery shell exploding over our heads. Our column of horses momentarily came to a halt. Somewhere ahead of us a general was making a decision. The quality of his decision could determine whether some of us lived or died, but that would not influence the general's judgment. It occurred to me I was becoming as cynical as George. I suppose lack of sleep and the ravages of war can do that. The road was now passing through a saddle that I assumed was what locals called Monterey Pass. We had some room on both sides of the road to maneuver, but not much.

"DISMOUNT AND FORM A SKIRMISH LINE!"

I couldn't see who voiced the order, but whoever it was had the air of authority. I assumed it was one of our officers. I dismounted and passed Prince's reins to Gottlieb. He was the fourth man in our column of fours and had the responsibility of securing our mounts. I crouched down in the mud between Casper and George. They were no more than three feet from me, but I could barely see their dark shadows.

"How do we know where to shoot?" I asked. "I can't see anybody."

"They can't see us either," Casper replied. "Watch for muzzle flashes and after you fire your weapon move three feet to the left or right. They'll be firing at your muzzle flash. You don't want to be there when they return your fire."

The downpour showed no signs it would relent long enough for us to commence a fight. Water swirled around me seeping into a hole I must have had in my right boot. I felt my sock soaking up the water. Someone gave the command to move forward, but it was impossible to walk without tripping over a root or large stone. We waited until a flash of lightning illuminated our way and then quickly marched forward as far as safety permitted.

Fortunately the heavens had no shortage of lightning bolts. One bolt struck a tree no more than one hundred yards to our left, reminding us how close we were to the source of the lightning. Occasionally, we saw lightning in the valley below us. That demonstrated just how far up the mountain we had climbed.

I saw my first muzzle flash when we were no more than two hundred yards in front of our lead elements. I don't know what the Rebel was shooting at, assuming it was a Rebel and not one of our men too far in advance of the main body. There was no way of telling in the dark. Most of our regiment assumed he was foe; at least twenty men returned fire. That could have been the Rebel's intentions. The woods erupted with muzzle flashes as contestants fired at each other's muzzle flash. I fired at several flashes, but I notice no two flashes ever came from the same spot. They must be moving from tree to tree using the same moving-target logic Casper had explained to us.

It occurred to me that this was one of the safest battles. When you can't see your opponent, it was difficult to produce casualties. That was fine with me. Even the artillery was for the most part impotent. The Rebels were unable to lower their cannons sufficiently to aim downhill at us. All their shells flew harmlessly over our heads. Lt. Pennington joined the fray and lobbed shells at the enemy. I didn't know if he was any more effective in his endeavor.

We caught the end of the Rebel wagon train as the generals had hoped, but it felt as rewarding as grabbing a rattlesnake by its tail. In the darkness it was impossible to discern how many riflemen were defending the wagons. We knew the snake could bite; we just didn't know the potency of its venom. No one was eager to test the Rebel's resolve. We traded muzzle flash for muzzle flash with little accomplishment on either side.

"This is a waste of time," George said, stating the obvious. "While we're sitting here in the dark, the wagon train is proceeding down the mountain side. They'll be in the Shenandoah Valley by daybreak."

"We'll cover you if you want to wander over there and ask them to surrender."

Gottlieb's sarcasm did not sit well with George, but his point was well taken. Trying to subdue an invisible enemy was foolhardy. We were as likely to shoot each other as to shoot the enemy, and while we were doing nothing, the wagon train was merrily proceeding unmolested down the far side of Monterey Pass.

I could hear hoof beats behind me. I turned but saw only darkness and sheets of rain. Then a flash of lightning illuminated mounted men forming up on the road. Crazy as it appeared, they were preparing for a mounted charge. At times like this I questioned the sanity of our commanding officers. A mounted charge into the darkness was suicidal at best. At least the land had flattened out. There were no sandstone walls or precipitous drop offs on the sides of the road. From what I saw during the last flash of lightening, the road was free of curves for several hundred yards. If they were to point their horses down the road during a flash of lightning, they might ride though the Rebel ranks and neutralize the lone cannon that had been giving us grief. That was assuming the lightning flashes were frequent enough to make necessary adjustments.

"Are they crazy?" George asked.

"I would assume so," I replied.

"When they charge, we all advance at a fast walk," Casper ordered. "They'll need all the help they can get."

"Yeah, and they will be shooting us sure as roosters crow in the morning."

Gottlieb had a valid point. Even if we had name tags tattooed to our foreheads, the mounted troops could not distinguish us from the Rebels. We looked the same in the dark.

"Use only sabers. I will cut down the first man that fires a shot."

I couldn't see who gave the order, but it had to be one of the mounted officers. It was reassuring. If we kept more than a saber's length from any horse we were safe. A flash of lightning illuminated the regimental colors: The mounted men were from the 1st Ohio. I silently wished them God speed.

At the next flash of lightning the commanding officer yelled, "Charge!" Scores of mounted troopers galloped down the road. It must have been a terrifying experience in the total darkness. I rose from my crouched position and drew my saber; any fighting would have to be hand to hand. Our Spencers were of little use during such face to face fighting. With Gottlieb on my right and George on my left we surged forward as fast as safely possible in the darkness.

The mounted troops gave out a holler as they advanced down the road. We quickly added our voices to the cacophony. It must have been a fearful sound coming out of the darkness. The Johnnies had no way to determine our strength other than our combined voices. We must have sounded like an entire army. The 1st Ohio fought their way past the Rebel skirmishers. I got a brief glimpse of four men pushing the lone Rebel cannon into a ravine where it rolled over several times before coming to a rest.

Our combined charge demoralized the remaining Rebels. We had them surrounded and cut off from their main force. The futility of further resistance was obvious and most of them eagerly surrendered once given the opportunity. A few recalcitrant individuals escaped into the surrounding woods. Trying to apprehend them in the dark proved unproductive. Our reserves, who were arriving at the top of the pass, took charge of the prisoners while we descended upon the unguarded wagon train. The mounted 1st Ohio must have reached the head of the train because all the wagons came to a halt. The drivers either surrendered or escaped into the woods.

"What are we to do now?" I was hoping for a nap in a dry place. Surely there would be room in one of the wagons for a tired horse soldier. Not knowing the answer, Casper set off to find a sergeant or officer who could clarify our orders.

"This wagon is full of hams!" George reached into the wagon and retrieved a large smoked ham. I pulled aside a section of tarp and looked inside the wagon. George was right. More than a dozen hams hung from the inside walls of the wagon. Confederates obviously ate better than we did.

"Are you sure we should take those?" I asked. "It feels like stealing."

"Will, sometimes you worry me," George replied. "These are Rebel hams. Rebels are not nice people. They no doubt stole these hams from Pennsylvania farmers. We are merely returning them to the rightful side of this conflict."

What George was saying made sense. No army carried hams to feed the troops. It had to be stolen merchandise. Any guilt feelings I still harbored disappeared when I remembered Major Ferry's nude body and missing buttons. I grabbed one of the hams and wrapped it in my wet bedroll. We would have hard tack and ham sandwiches for the next several days. Within minutes men had confiscated all the hams. Only a slight smoky smell testified to the contents that had once been in the wagon.

"Listen up, men." Casper had returned with instructions for our squad. I was hoping the new orders included sleep and maybe free time to eat ham. A faint glow of light in the east suggested dawn was approaching; we had gone twenty-four hours without sleep. Given a choice I preferred sleep despite my intense hunger. Ham would keep. Neither option appeared to be on the commanding officer's agenda.

"We demolish all the wagons. What we can't carry on horseback we destroy. Nothing is left behind. Any questions?"

"Some of the wagons contain wounded Johnnies. What'll we do with them?"

"They'll be paroled if they agree to avoid all hostile activities until they are properly exchanged," Casper replied. "We leave them beside the road."

Many of the wounded would be dead before any prisoner exchange returned them to their units. This should disturb me, but it didn't. I felt no compassion. Perhaps it was the sleep deprivation. Maybe it would distress me in the morning when my mind cleared after a few hours of sleep.

We set about destroying the wagons as instructed. I was exhausted, but the wagons offered untold treasures. The rush of excitement flowing through my veins overcame my urge to curl up in the mud for some much-needed sleep. It was Christmas in July and I felt like a school boy as I rummaged through the loot. One wagon had several kegs of molasses. We drank what we could and then filled our canteens. With all the rain, water was not a rare commodity. We poured the remainder of the molasses into a ditch. We found other wagons filled with bacon, sugar, salt, and clothing of every type including women's and children's clothing. The clothing had to have been stolen from the residents of York County. I felt no guilt.

I was rummaging through clothing in one wagon when I discovered what I first thought was an old rag. It had many colors, but lacked the shape of any garment. When I spread it out on the wagon floor I discovered it was a homemade Confederate flag. A blue square with thirteen white stars occupied the left upper corner of the flag. Three wide horizontal stripes, a white stripe with a red stripe above and below, filled the rest of the flag. Neatly embroidered across the center were the words "Liberty or Death." I stuffed the flag inside my shirt; this was a souvenir that I would be sending to Mary. I was sure it would be the talk of Salem.

Once a wagon was void of usable merchandise it was pushed into a ravine. If a ravine were not available, we hacked through the spokes until the wagon was rendered useless. A few wagons were set fire. The floor boards inside the wagons were still dry and quickly surrendered to the fire's appetite. The burning wagons illuminated the pass like giant torches and we were able to see the battlefield for the first time. We were just past the peak of the pass and heading down the far slope. A large building sat at the apex of the pass. It was too large for a residence and had to be a hotel or resort of some sort. Before the wagons were set ablaze, I hadn't even known the building existed. Anyone with reservations for the night surely received quality entertainment at no additional cost; the building appeared undamaged.

We watched the wagons burn, mesmerized by the dancing flames until the bugler sounded Boots and Saddles; the war must continue. We mounted our horses and headed down the pass. I relaxed my grip on the reins and leaned forward against Prince's neck. Within minutes I was asleep. I didn't awake until we had reached the bottom of the pass and had entered the Shenandoah Valley.

Dear Mary,

By the time you receive this letter you will no doubt have heard of the dreadful battle in Pennsylvania near the small town of Gettysburg. The Michigan Brigade is now assigned to the Army of the Potomac and your dear husband played an active role in that battle. On several occasions we went head to head with J.E.B. Stuart's Rebel cavalry but each time we came out victorious. Stuart's cavalry is legendary and I don't think anyone believed we could best them. Rest assured, neither I nor any trooper from Salem was injured, although many families in both the north and south are now without sons or husbands.

We have a new commander of the Michigan Brigade. His name is George Custer, and he is younger than I am. He dresses a bit like a dandy, and some people were referring to him as the peacock or boy general, but no more. He graduated from the West Point Military School and despite his age knows more about military strategy than all those older lawyers and politicians who are leading other brigades. Custer is bold but not reckless. I am convinced he will keep us out of trouble if anyone can.

Our Federal Cavalry Brigades were the only military units that gave chase after the battle. I can't remember when I felt so miserable. It rained constantly. The mud on the roads was so deep that our horses could hardly remove their hooves after each step. Prince did better than most of the horses. I was lucky to have him assigned to me. We had little to eat and no sleep for over twenty-four hours. We couldn't see farther than the tips of our gun barrels in the rain and darkness, but we still managed to capture a Confederate supply train at the top of a mountain pass. I found a

Confederate flag in one of the wagons. I will be sending it to you in a separate package.

This morning a photographer visited our camp. He is taking pictures of soldiers in full dress uniform. I have the picture of you on the inside cover of my pocket watch that I look at any time I feel homesick, which is often. Your picture cheers me up when I am feeling low. The photographer is asking an unreasonable sum for his pictures, but I decided to purchase one anyway. He takes a good picture. I am standing with my right hand resting on my Spencer Rifle. I am holding a pistol in my left hand. A saber is attached to my belt. I think it is a fair likeness of me. The picture will be wrapped inside the Confederate flag. If anything should happen to me I want you to have the picture. You could place it above the fireplace where the children can see it. Perhaps they will then remember who their father was.

Your loving husband,

Will

Monteray Pass

There is an old adage stating that time heals all wounds. Nowhere is it more accurate than the Monterey Pass Battlefield. The casual visitor to Monterey Pass could drive over paved highways, never knowing that two armies clashed at that location during a severe electrical storm more than 150 years earlier. Anyone seeking information about this historic battle must leave the beaten path.

A good place to start is the Monterey Pass Battlefield Park & Museum. The museum is small, but the friendly museum staff can direct the inquisitive visitor toward interpreted trails that further explain this historical battle.

There is a military tradition that to the victor goes the spoils. William Goodman and his fellow troopers ransacked several supply wagons before they burned them. Some of the wagons contained hams. This was not normal far for traveling soldiers, and it is most likely that the Confederates liberated the hams from surrounding farms.

Goodman secured a souvenir flag from one of the wagons. The red, white, and blue Virginia flag has two red strips around one large white stripe. A blue square in the left upper corner holds thirteen stars. Liberty or Death is inscribed in the center of the flag. The black and white image above does not do justice to the flag. A color copy is printed on the back cover.

The flag, along with the Goodman's family photograph album, a 1/6th plate tintype as seen on the cover, Goodman's kerchief and other personal and family effects, were sold to collectors. The author tracked these items to a Don Tharpe who is a private collector. Efforts to contact him have been fruitless.

CHAPTER FOURTEEN

"STUART'S CROSSED THE RAPIDAN!"

I had heard that cry too many times to take it seriously. The Army of Northern Virginia was entrenched along the southern shore of the Rapidan River. With the river providing a virtual moat, their earthworks were formidable, and no one expected the overly timid Meade to take the initiative and attack Lee. But Lee, unlike Meade, was aggressive. Sooner or later Lee would cross the river and strike us—at his convenience and on his schedule. The last two weeks apparently were not convenient. I was hoping today was also not convenient. It was October 11th if I had been counting my days accurately. Six more weeks and winter would be upon us. No one fought during the winter. We had been skirmishing once or twice a week throughout the summer and into fall. We were exhausted. I was looking forward to a winter respite.

"You think Stuart crossed the Rapidan?" I asked Casper. People were scurrying about as if the rumor held substance.

"A courier arrived from the front," Casper replied. "He's briefing the General. Could be some truth to the rumor."

The front was a nebulous designation at best. It could apply to any section between our base camp and the Rapidan River. We had pickets and detachments scattered throughout that region. The courier could be reporting from any one of them. It could be nothing. Our pickets skirmished with Rebel scouts on a daily basis. Those encounters seldom amounted to much.

For the last week George and Gottlieb along with over a hundred other troopers from the 5th Regiment had manned one such post just north of Robertson's River, a tributary of the Rapidan. Casper and I were to relieve them in the morning. I never enjoyed picket duty, but I must admit I was looking forward to seeing George again even if it were just in passing. This was the longest we had been separated since we joined the army. We were a team. I missed him.

"I'm going to wander over by the commander's tent. Some of the men working for the General's staff might know something."

"Suit yourself," Casper replied. "If Stuart crossed the Rapidan we'll know soon enough."

Our base camp hugged the high ground overlooking James City. It was one of our better defensive positions. The six rifled guns of Lt. Pennington's horse artillery commanded the countryside. If Stuart were to attack, we would provide a good account of ourselves.

Several men were loading boxes into a wagon parked near the command tent. They did not appear rushed, but neither were they wasting time. This didn't mean we were moving basecamp, although if we were to move, they would be ready. Another individual was sharpening his saber against a grinding stone. No one was idle.

Unless rain was imminent, the front of the Staff Tent was normally open to take advantage of any breeze. High ranking officers would be sitting at a table covered with maps and regimental reports. Today the tent front was conspicuously closed. It was October, but still a warm day and, with the tent exposed to the sun, it would be unbearably hot inside. Hushed voices seeped through the canvas suggesting the conference participants, whom I assumed were colonels and above, were making critical decisions. Try as I might I could not comprehend the garbled words. Only an occasional word was decipherable, but one of them was J.E.B. Stuart!

Eavesdropping on the conversations of officers was common practice. As long as it didn't become too flagrant it was considered acceptable behavior. Unfortunately I would have to place my ear against the canvas to hear anything of value—that would not be considered acceptable behavior. I decided to try the direct approach.

"You guys know what's going on?" I asked.

"You may want to sharpen your saber." The guy grinding his saber did not look up. "You'll need it before the day is out."

"How so?" The man with the saber obviously wanted to dole out his knowledge piecemeal, a common practice among those who possessed desirable information.

"Stuart crossed the Rapidan. Wiped out an entire detachment of ours. This was no minor skirmish. A courier barely made it out alive. He was covered with blood when he arrived. Even his horse was cut up. The courier is reporting to the General as we speak."

This was more than rumor. If Stuart's division crossed the Rapidan, the Army of Northern Virginia would not be far behind. Details would have to wait until the courier had completed his report and was discharged. The courier's injuries couldn't be too severe or he would be presenting his report from the hospital. I decided to linger near the command tent. I wanted to hear the courier's report first hand after he left the Command Tent. It couldn't be too much longer.

With nothing better to do while I waited, I decided to examine the courier's horse. The man with the saber suggested the horse had been wounded, and I had a compassion for injured animals. Perhaps there was something I could do until the horse's owner returned. A rope attached between two trees behind the Command Tent served as a hitching line for staff horses. Staff horses were easy to identify; they were taller, leaner, and in general better quality than the enlisted men's horses. A bay gelding stood out from the rest. It was covered with sweat. Dry blood surrounded a superficial cut on the right side of the neck. It would definitely leave a large scar when healed. But the wound was not what caught my attention. The gelding had a white star on its forehead. In the center of the star was a small patch of brown. I had seen this horse many times before. It was Toby— Gottlieb's horse!

I looked at my pocket watch; it was ten past nine in the morning. Gottlieb must have ridden most of the night. Robertson's River was half a day's ride from here. I paused to look into Mary's eyes. It had been over a year since I saw her. In the picture she was as beautiful as ever. My children were now a year older. According to Mary's last letter, Mary Elizabeth was walking. She was eight months old when I left her. When I returned I will be a stranger within my own home. What if I didn't return home? Mary Elizabeth will have no memory of her father. The more I stared at Mary's picture, the more saddened I became. The war was to last six months at most, no more. I should have been home by now watching Mary Elizabeth walk. But now it felt as if the war could continue forever. I closed my pocket watch and returned it to my pocket.

I continued lingering near the Command Tent until the tent flap opened and Gottlieb stepped out. His face was covered with blood. Was the information he was bringing from the front so vital it could not wait until after medical treatment? Closer exam revealed a large cut over the forehead extending down to the bone. Gottlieb appeared exhausted.

"Are you okay?" I asked. It was a dumb question considering the blood on his face.

"I haven't had anything to eat for a day and a half. I haven't had any sleep for over twenty-four hours. Did I mention I have a saber cut to the head? Other than that I am doing just dandy." Gottlieb's sarcasm was well justified.

"We need to get you to the aid station. That cut needs stitches. Let me get Toby." I untied Toby's reins and led Gottlieb and Toby toward the aid tent.

"How's Toby?" Gottlieb asked. "I think he has a saber cut."

"He has a nasty cut on the neck but it doesn't look deep," I replied. I wished I believed the lie I was telling Gottlieb, "Casper will fix him up. He's good with animals."

"Toby's a good horse. If it weren't for him, the Department of War would be sending a telegram to my parents."

"What happened?" It was obvious Gottlieb was in no hurry to volunteer information.

"Stuart crossed the Rapidan yesterday morning. I didn't see their colors, but someone said it was Gordon's brigade. They shelled us with cannon fire for several hours but didn't attack. The captain thought that was because they didn't know our strength. He then volunteered me to ride for help."

"Will the General send troops to reinforce them?" I asked.

"It's too late. As I was heading out of camp I discovered why they hadn't attacked. Young's brigade had circled around behind us. We were surrounded. One hundred and fifty men against two full brigades of Stuart's cavalry. There is no way anyone could have survived."

It took a moment for the significance to sink in. I always assumed if one of us did not return to Salem it would be me. George was carefree, sometimes to the point of recklessness, but he was lucky. He always had a guardian angel looking over him. Sometimes the guardian angel worked overtime, but he took good care of George. I found it difficult to accept that George was gone. Other than my family, George was my closest friend. I would have to write to his parents, but at the moment I did not know what I would say.

"How did you escape?" I asked.

"I had Toby saddled and was ready to ride for help when they were preparing to attack. I casually rode north toward Young's brigade at a casual trot, sitting high in the saddle as if I had nothing to fear. They must have assumed I was one of them. At least that was my hope. No one opened fire. When I was twenty-five yards from their skirmish line, I dug my spurs into Toby and galloped toward them. I was within their ranks before anyone could react. If they fired their pistols at me, they were as likely to hit one of their own men. One man managed to get a couple licks in with his saber." Gottlieb pointed to his head wound. "Fortunately, they were dismounted and couldn't give chase. I think they were more interested in the men they had surrounded."

I dropped Gottlieb at the aid tent and then returned to our squad with Toby in tow. I assumed everyone had heard about Gottlieb. Bad news travels fast. Casper cautiously caressed Toby's fur, being careful to avoid the obvious cut.

"Nasty cut," Casper said, "but not serious. Someone find me a needle and thread."

"I have some in my pack," I said. I retrieved the requested items and then held Toby's reins while Casper closed the wound. I think Toby was too exhausted to resist.

"That should do it," Casper said after he tied off his sixteenth stitch. "He needs a good rub down and some oats. " No one rides him for at least ten days."

"I'll take care of him," I said. I filled a feed bag with oats and strapped it to Toby's nose. He dove into the oats as if he were starving. It probably had been more than a day since he had last eaten. I then brushed him down staying clear of his newly sutured cut. Casper had done an excellent job stitching the wound, but it would still leave a nasty scar.

I had almost finished rubbing Toby down when a shell exploded in some trees not far from where I stood. I tied Toby to a rope stretched between two trees for that purpose and grabbed my Spencer—Stuart's cavalry was knocking on our doorstep.

The regiment commander ordered us into a dismounted skirmish line facing James City where several brigades of Stuart's Cavalry were congregating. We waited, but no order to advance was given. We watched for several hours while our artillery dueled with their Confederate counterpart. Our rifled guns had the advantage of high ground, but I am not sure how effective they were. The Confederates continued returning our fire. Fortunately, they were aiming at our artillery, which was some distance from us. We were mere spectators in someone else's battle. It momentarily offered quality entertainment until I realized where those shells were landing, men were dying. Like George, they had close friends. Some of them would have families. They would be grieved.

"Casper, do people ever get used to war?" Casper gave my question some deep thought before he responded.

"I served in the Spanish-American War. People died in that war too. I was younger then. I thought I knew everything there was to know about war. But this war—this war is different. I have never seen so many casualties. People are killed on both sides yet for every person killed two people step in to take his place. Tens of thousands of men have died in this war, but we are no closer to victory than we were when the Rebels fired on Fort Sumter."

I nodded silently. Casper seldom talked about the impact of war or its human toll.

"I have lost many friends in war," Casper continued. "Sometimes I have nightmares. I relive many of those battles. I see my friends die all over again. George Thompson was a close friend of yours. He was a good man. Grieve for him, but eventually you must let him go if you can. You must move on or the memory of his death will consume you."

Casper turned away. It was all he had to say on that subject. It was well that he did so. My eyes were beginning to water as I thought of the many experiences I had with George. I didn't think I would ever be capable of moving on. George and I played together as children. As we grew older we hunted together. We were inseparable. Life would never be the same without George Thompson. I would keep his memory with me forever.

About midafternoon the regimental commander ordered *Boots and Saddles*. Apparently, the artillery duel was creating insufficient progress, at least by the General's standards. I saddled Prince and added extra cartridges to my saddle bag. We were not ordered to pack food. Apparently, the general expected us to soundly whip J.E.B. Stuart's troops and then return to the high ground in time for supper.

Gottlieb had a right to be proud of Toby, but no horse in the army could match Prince for quickness, even temperament, or willingness to please. He had saved my hide more than once. Without Prince's quickness, Mary would have gotten telegrams from the War Department many times over. "You are the best," I whispered into Prince's ear. He seemed to understand.

The bugler sounded *To Horse* and we saddled up. The company commander guided us into a skirmish line at the edge of a clearing facing James City. Some of the men were brandishing sabers, but I preferred my pistol. I liked to keep Johnny more than arm's length from me, and I couldn't do that with a saber.

Once the Michigan Brigade was properly lined up, we began a slow trot toward Stuart's dismounted troopers. We would not advance at a gallop until we were within two-hundred yards of Stuart's men, lest we exhaust our horses prematurely. I hoped we could close the gap before Stuart's artillery could reposition their cannons. Grape shot was particularly deadly to horse and rider.

A case shot exploded off to my left sending dozens of small projectiles into any object living or otherwise that happened to be in the vicinity. More would follow. It was enough to convince General Custer that we had sufficiently closed the distance and had the bugler sound *Charge*.

"This is it, Prince. Don't let me down." I gently nudged his belly with my heels and he leaped forward. I never used spurs. With Prince it was never needed. We closed the distance in less than a minute, rendering their artillery useless. The Rebels were waiting for us behind a hastily made barricade. I nudged Prince and he leaped over the barricade with room to spare. The horsemen beside me did likewise. I began firing at anyone not on horseback. Several men fell to the ground. Any other time I would have been consumed with guilt, but not today. These were the men who killed George Thompson, and I was consumed with hate. Mary would not be proud of me, but I didn't care. I was so consumed with hate I did not notice as my fellow horsemen began to withdraw. I continued shooting. When the cartridges in my pistol were spent I would draw my saber.

I saw a man who appeared to be an officer. I guided Prince toward him, but Prince stumbled and fell. When he hit the ground, he rolled onto his side pinning my right leg to the ground. Red foam gushed from Prince's mouth.

"Drop your gun or you are a dead man, Yankee!"

Four Rebel soldiers quickly surrounded me. I was pinned to the ground and totally helpless. I threw my pistol to the side. I didn't know which was more distressing: being captured or watching Prince gasp for breath. He had been shot in the chest and wounds to the lungs were always fatal. Prince had been a loyal and obedient horse, and now he was dying—all because his master had been consumed with hate. At this point neither Mary nor I had cause to be proud of my actions.

"You won't be needing this," one of the Rebels informed me as he relieved me of my saber. Once they were assured I was harmless, which should have been obvious, they began working toward freeing me. Prince weighed over eight hundred pounds and not easily moved. Without help I would have lain there all day. I found my cap lying beside me just within my reach. I retrieved my cap and while the Rebel soldiers focused their attention on Prince, I slipped my pocket watch under the cap before covering my head. It was customary on both sides to take whatever was desired from dead people. I assumed this practice extended to prisoners of war.

One Rebel grabbed me under the arms while two other men pulled on my trapped leg. I had no doubt the leg would separate at the knee. The leg refused to budge until someone untied the cinch strap on the saddle. I placed my good leg against Prince and gave a shove while everyone else pulled. The leg came free along with saddle and blanket. Prince gave a snort. I assumed what we had done was painful. I felt the point of a bayonet poking at my ribs.

"Move," the man said.

Instead, I knelt beside Prince's head and gently stroked his muzzle. I could see the hair matted with blood on his chest where the bullet entered. Prince was still breathing, but his breaths were erratic and labored. Bubbles of blood streamed from his nostrils and mouth.

"Prince, I'm so sorry," I said. The pressure from the bayonet eased as the fellow horsemen allowed me to cry unmolested. They understood horses. Most of them had brought their own horses to the war.

"We have to end his pain," I said.

One of the Rebels picked up my pistol and removed all the cartridges except one and then handed me the pistol. "Point the pistol anywhere except at the ground or your horse and you are a dead man. Several pistols pointed at my head to emphasize the point. I nodded my thanks.

"I am truly sorry, Prince, but I must do this." I placed the barrel of the pistol against Prince's head, then closed my eyes and pulled the trigger. I could feel his body shutter and when I opened my eyes, Prince was lifeless.

CHAPTER FIFTEEN

We had been walking south for two days and my feet were blistered to the point of bleeding. Cavalrymen were not noted for tough feet. There were twelve prisoners in all, but I knew none of them prior to our capture, not that it made a difference. Yesterday we crossed the Rapidan River, virtually eliminating any hope of rescue by our troops. We were on our own.

Escape was impossible, although I am sure we all thought about it. Our guards were on horseback and armed. If we were to run, they would be upon us before we covered ten paces. Several people tried; they were severely beaten. We were given little to eat, but I noticed our captors also had little to eat. Soldiers on both sides endured many hardships.

We reached Gordonsville on the third day. It was a small railroad hub in Central Virginia. There was little doubt we were now in hostile territory. Local citizens displayed their contempt with derogatory epithets as we marched down the streets. Small children threw stones at us.

Our Rebel guards ushered us into a make-shift corral in the center of town. At one time cattle used the accommodations while they awaited transportation to slaughter houses in Richmond. The enclosure had not changed its purpose. The wooden fence did little to keep prisoners within its confines, but the numerous Confederate guards with bayonets fixed to their rifles got people's attention. There were over a hundred prisoners crowded within the barrier when we arrived. My depression deepened.

I found an empty piece of real estate and sat down. Just getting off my feet was a small pleasure. I assumed this luxury would not last long enough for my blisters to heal. I opened my pocket watch. Time no longer had meaning, but I had to see Mary one more time. It had been three days. She should have received a telegram by now. Would it say I had been killed? Missing in action was almost the same.

"You going to spend all day staring at Mary?"

I instantly recognized the voice from the past. I looked up at George's carefree smile. "George! We thought you were dead!"

"If I didn't stay alive, who would take care of you? When our captain discovered we were surrounded by two brigades, he decided surrendering was the better option. Personally, I think we could have given them a go for their money." George was never one to take life seriously. Being captured by the Army of Northern Virginia did little to alter his outlook.

"What do you think will happen to us?" I asked. George was unfazed by our current situation, which to me appeared desperate. I was hoping there was substance to his exuberance.

"They could parole us on the spot," he replied. "In which case we are on our honor to refrain from further fighting. We return to Salem and wait until someone on their side is paroled. Some free time in Salem wouldn't hurt either of us. The other alternative is they keep us prisoners for a week or two until a direct prisoner exchange can be arranged."

It sounded almost pleasant the way George explained it, but he was not always correct in his facts. What he said made sense. We had many Confederate prisoners. An exchange of some sort seemed appropriate.

"How long have you been in Gordonsville?" I asked. "Have you seen anyone exchanged?" Gordonsville was little more than a hub on the Virginia Central Rail Road where farmers sent their grain and ranchers sent their beef for transport to the bigger cities. I couldn't envision any business of importance occurring here.

"I think the exchange will take place in Richmond. That's where they're sending us." George pointed toward several boxcars lining the tracks next to our confinement area. "They're for us. A trainload left yesterday."

They were nothing more than cattle cars, but after three days of walking I was willing to accept any kind of mechanized transportation. I had nothing to eat and little to drink in the last twenty-four hours. George had nothing to offer in the form of food, but he did show me a livestock watering trough within our confines. On a normal day it would have watered beef cattle on their way to slaughter houses in Richmond. Today thirsty men were cupping their hands for a drink of the warm water. I did likewise. When you are sufficiently thirsty, any water tastes good.

Just past noon they began herding us toward the empty cattle cars. Sharpshooters perched on the roofs of the cars ensured no one got lost in the process. George and I along with forty other men filled the third box car. If everyone crossed their legs, there was barely enough room to sit on the floor. The surrounding men provided a backrest. George and I commandeered a spot next to the wall. The wooden planks on the sides of the boxcar had shrunk as the wood dried leaving narrow cracks, which allowed narrow bands of light inside the cars. It barely provided sufficient light to move about, not that we had any room to maneuver. The knothole in one of the boards proved more valuable. It was waist high, but when on one's knees it provided a limited view of the countryside. When the train lurched forward I looked at my pocket watch; it was one fifteen.

"Don't show your pocket watch when Rebels are watching," George advised, "or you'll lose it for sure."

I would have to be more prudent in the future. I leaned back against the wall and listened to the clickity clack of the train. The sound was soothing and almost poetic. After hearing George's explanation of the parole and exchange system I wondered if capture were a blessing in disguise. As long as I didn't try to escape, I was physically secure, although the quality of life left much to be desired. I closed my eyes and quickly fell asleep.

I awoke with an overflowing bladder. The cattle car was dark—too dark to see the hands on my pocket watch. I had no way of knowing when it would be morning or if we would be provided time to relieve ourselves even if it were morning. I knew from the pressure in my lower abdomen that my bladder would not wait. The smell of stale urine suggested others had similar problems, but I was unwilling to urinate on a floor where I would later sit. I scanned the car for an oak bucket, but no such container was available. Then I remembered the knothole in the side of the cattle car.

The knothole was on the high side, but I was tall and when I was on my tip-toes it became achievable. I would have preferred a larger hole. It was a tight squeeze but I managed. There was no greater pleasure than the sensation of an overly extended bladder as it begins to empty. I savored the moment. It occurred to me that this would not be a good time to look at Mary's picture. Any additional swelling and I would be stuck in the knothole forever. George would soon be dead from hysterical laughter. I finished my business and returned to my small spot on the floor. No one needed to know my nocturnal activity.

The second time I woke up the sun was streaming through the gaps in the boards. George had his right eye pressed against the knothole. I found that amusing.

"See any Federal cavalry?" I asked. It was a meaningless question. We were too far south for that to be a reality. Any hope of relief would come via an exchange.

"No, but the train is slowing down. They probably need to take on water or wood for the boiler." George continued with a detailed description of the outside world. Unless it included Federal troops I was not interested. "If they stop, maybe they will let us out to relieve ourselves," George suggested. "I drank too much water." I was tempted to suggest a solution to his dilemma, but George was shorter than I was. Even on his tip-toes he would be inadequate.

Trains possess a monotonous clickity clack rhythm. Unless you tune out the clickity clacks, they will drive you crazy. But now they were the focus of my attention—the clickities and the clacks were farther apart. George was right. The train was coming to a stop. I looked through the gaps in the boards, but they were too narrow to provide a meaningful view. All I saw was a blur of trees.

"What do you see?"

"Nothing, just a clearing. Perhaps farmland," George replied.

George provided a continuous report to the inquisitive men in our car. Many of them shared George's need for biological relief and were hoping for some free time outside the cattle car. I no longer shared that problem, but I wouldn't mind stretching my legs.

George's prediction proved accurate. The train had stopped for firewood and water for the boiler. While these needs were being fulfilled. They did let us out one cattle car at a time. While most of the men were watering the local bushes I weighed the odds of escaping. The Rebels had sharpshooters perched on the cattle car's roofs. They were called sharpshooters for a reason. There was little chance I would make it to the distant trees before accumulating four or five holes in my torso. I decided to postpone my escape. Waiting for an exchange seemed more prudent.

We were each given four ounces of salt pork and a piece of coarse cornbread as an incentive to re-board our cattle car—it worked; I was hungry. I assumed it was to last all day. George and I were first in line to ensure we retained our reserved seating next to the knothole. When riding in a cattle car, having a personal knothole was equivalent to riding first class.

It took two and a half days to reach our destination. We pulled into a large city late in the afternoon. We assumed it was Richmond. We had been heading east, so it was a logical assumption. I could have gotten to Richmond almost as fast on horseback, although if I had a horse I would have been heading north.

They ordered us out of our cattle cars and into a line, so we could be counted. Once they were assured we were all present and accounted for, they marched us toward Belle Isle. Belle Isle was a rocky piece of real estate in the center of the James River. I estimated the island was more than fifty yards from the southern shore, well within the range of the artillery posted along a ridge overlooking the island. A series of cataracts made any river crossing treacherous. That and the numerous large boulders made escape from Belle Island nearly impossible. I would not proclaim it impossible without further study. I noticed George was also searching for escape routes. I am sure he arrived at a similar conclusion. When and if we left the island would be at the pleasure of our captors. We marched across Long Bridge, which was hardly sturdy enough for foot traffic. I questioned its integrity even for that. The bridge terminated on the eastern corner of the island.

I was unprepared for the horror that awaited us on the far side of Long Bridge. The foot bridge ascended ten feet above the surrounding landscape and provided a panoramic view of our new quarters. What we saw was not comforting. A three-foot deep trench enclosed six acres devoid of any obvious vegetation. Mounds of dirt excavated from the ditches completed the perimeter and formed a barricade. Numerous Rebel guards stood behind the barricade with fixed bayonets, but that was not what stirred my soul.

"There must be four thousand prisoners confined in that small enclosure," I said. George nodded. Some of the prisoners wore little more than rags. Only the most minimal flesh clung to their frames. Their eyes were fixed upon us with a vacant stare that spoke of despair. They had been confined to the camp for weeks if not months. Any thought of an exchange evaporated.

"Can't be room for a hundred more of us," George suggested. "Perhaps they'll permit us to leave. They obviously don't have any vacancy."

George's attempt at levity was lost on me. I counted over three hundred Sibley tents. At ten people per tent, that was insufficient to accommodate the number of prisoners confined to the island; many prisoners were without shelter and exposed to the elements. We would be joining them. I had been looking forward to winter, but not without shelter. We had neither shelter half nor bedroll. It was already late October. Winter would soon be upon us. The guards pushed us forward, forcing us into the enclosure.

"Form a line facing me."

The man issuing orders appeared to be a lieutenant. I was hoping he would assign us to a tent or at least clarify our current situation, but he was only interested in assigning us to groups of one hundred. An older union sergeant who appeared to be in his forties was appointed leader of our group of one hundred. All food would be issued to him for distribution. We were dismissed without mention of shelter. We were on our own.

Belle Isle

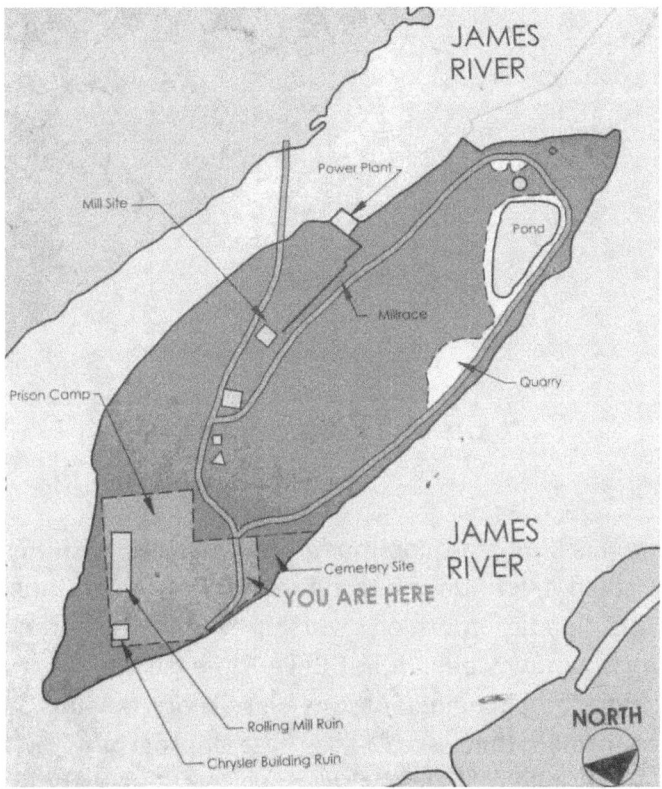

Belle Isle is a 54 acre island in the middle of the James River as it passes through Richmond, Virginia. During the Civil War only the pedestrian Long Bridge connected it to the mainland. The Confederate Army set aside six acres for a Civil War prison camp. They dug a three-foot deep trench around the perimeter of the camp and piled the dirt into a berm. Armed guards with bayonets shot anyone getting close to the trench.

In the beginning the prisoners were given Sibley Tents, but the number of prisoners quickly overwhelmed available resources. Some historians estimate over 1,000 prisoners died of starvation or scurvy. It should be noted that during this same time period, there were food riots in Richmond. The Union Army had destroyed the railroads coming into Richmond. Everyone was short of food.

CHAPTER SIXTEEN

Time was a difficult commodity to measure. With my pocket watch, I could divide days into hours and hours into minutes. In Salem the Sunday morning worship service ushered in the beginning of a new week, but at Belle Isle each day was the same as the next. The changing seasons were more obvious. The cold nights confirmed that winter was fast approaching. Winters in Virginia were milder than Michigan winters, but without shelter they could be just as cruel. If I had counted correctly, George and I had been confined on Belle Island almost three weeks. We heard rumors of an exchange, but nothing came of them. Lt. Bossieux was the prison commander. He was young and appeared in good health. I don't know why he wasn't fighting at the front. Most of the guards were older and unfit for the rigors of combat. Perhaps Bossieux had connections. Bossieux was assisted by Sergeant Hight and Sergeant Marks. They could be cruel when angered. I stayed clear of them. The ditch around the prison perimeter was no-man's land. Anyone approaching it was shot; no questions asked. Two days ago Perry McMichael from Minnesota, nearly naked and burning with fever, deliberately walked up to the ditch. A guard put a ball through his brain as casually as if he were target practicing. I don't know if the fever drove McMichael do this or if he merely wished to end it all. He lay where he fell for several hours before his friends received permission to remove the body.

Our food was insufficient to sustain life. Today we received a half a pint of rice soup, which was mostly river water without flavoring or salt. We also received four ounces of corn bread. The bread was baked in a wooden bake house outside the prison confines. The bread was made of the coarsest cornmeal and had a sour, musty taste. We were starving, so we ate it and wished we had more. When not discussing the likelihood of an exchange the men planned imaginary banquets of the most desirable foods they planned to eat upon discharge. I found myself consumed with thoughts of food during the day and dreamed of food during the night.

It was well into November and the nights were cold even for Richmond. Only half of the prisoners had tents. Unfortunately, George and I were in the other half. We slept on the bare ground with our backs pressed against each other to conserve warmth. Even then there were nights when I wondered if I will see the sun rise. Every morning we found five or six lifeless bodies that failed to make it through the night. They were mostly individuals who had resided at Belle Isle for an extended time and no longer had sufficient body fat to provide warmth. The bodies were wrapped in canvas and buried outside the prison confines. It might not be very Christian of me, but I found myself praying someone would die and provide room for me in a tent.

I hadn't seen George for several hours, which was unusual as we normally hung out together. I decided to hunt him down. I didn't know if I was motivated by idle curiosity or sheer boredom. Either way it provided something to do on a boring day. Even with the large number of prisoners, it was difficult to hide in such a confined area, but I couldn't find George anywhere. He could be a social butterfly, and I assumed he was in one of the tents conversing with a fellow prisoner. If so, I was unlikely to find him until he emerged. Unlike George, I had become despondent over the last several weeks and had little desire to converse with strangers.

I was walking toward the main gate when I saw George heading in my direction. He was wearing that impish grin he reserved for times when he was up to no good or had a secret he was dying to share.

"Where have you been?" My tone was accusatory, not that he had to explain his whereabouts. George looked about to see if anyone was watching. There were many people milling about, but none of them gave us any mind.

"This is for you." George pulled a small piece of salt pork from his pocket. It was little more than one or two ounces, but it was real meat.

"Where did you get this?" I asked. My mouth began to water. It had been almost three weeks since I had seen meat.

"Shut up and eat it before someone notices."

I assumed his reply meant the salt pork was all for me. I placed it in my mouth and began to chew slowly. I had a craving for salt. Not only was it meat but it was also salty. I chewed it thoroughly to saver the saltiness before swallowing.

"Are you going to tell me where you've been and where you found this salt pork?"

"I have a job," he replied.

I looked at him skeptically. The Rebels were paroling anyone willing to build fortifications around Richmond. They received few takers. Those who did were considered traitors. Their lives would be worthless after the war. If George was a part of this, I was willing to regurgitate every bit of the salt pork. It was now leaving an unpleasant aftertaste in my mouth.

"The United States Sanitary Commission sent us a large quantity of new clothes. General Dow from Libby Prison is in charge of doling them out. Some of us are helping him. It's not hard work, and we get extra rations. I signed us up for tomorrow."

I had never heard of General Dow, but I had heard of the United States Sanitary Commission. Despite the imposing name, they were a private organization in the north organized to improve sanitation in military camps and hospitals. The salt pork was beginning to taste better.

"What do we have to do?"

"General Dow lines one hundred men up at a time. He checks out each man and determines if any clothing is needed. If General Dow determines the man is in need of a shirt, we hand the man a shirt. When General Dow isn't looking we give the man pants. There are many boxes and lots of clothing. No sense not issuing all of it."

George was wearing all new clothing, so I assumed there was substance to his story. I couldn't deny the salt pork. George was a loyal friend, but he wouldn't give me salt pork unless he had eaten some himself.

The following morning George and I walked to the gate at sunrise. Sergeant Hight stood guard with his notepad. George provided his name upon request and Sergeant Hight checked him off on the list. I assumed my name would not be on the list, and I was expecting trouble, but when I offered my name Sergeant Hight made a mark on his ledger without looking up.

"Do I take good care of you or what?" George said when he noticed my concern.

"I haven't seen the extra rations yet," I replied. I had no reason to doubt George although the thought of Rebels providing adequate rations did stretch one's imagination. Just getting out of confinement for a brief time was reward in itself.

Sergeant Hight along with several guards with fixed bayonets led our small work detail to a warehouse filled with clothes. There he introduced us to Brigadier General Neal Dow. General Dow was not an imposing figure for a general. His snowy-white beard and hair provided a grandfatherly image, and he was soft spoken and humble, traits not commonly found in generals. I noticed he favored his right arm, which I'm told was due to a recent war injury. He had a reputation as a God-fearing man with Quaker parents. I don't know what compelled him to join the army.

At about fifteen past eight by my pocket watch prisoners began filing in one hundred at a time. Sergeant Hight lined them up in a long row facing the General. It was difficult to believe these men were once hardened soldiers. Their clothes were ripped and torn. Many of them were shirtless. It was a wonder they survived the harsh nights. Individuals who had been confined at Belle Isle the longest had negligible flesh clinging to their bones. Without improved nourishment, they would not survive two weeks.

I was assigned to stacks of shirts. General Dow walked down the row of prisoners, stopping to inspect each man individually. He would announce what items the man needed. We were expected to issue only what was prescribed. George was in charge of issuing pants. After the General moved down the line, George issued a pair of trousers to everyone. It made sense to me. We had ample supplies. We might as well dole them out to the prisoners. I noticed many of the guards were wearing articles of the Yankee uniform. Living conditions were not the best in Richmond, not that I felt sorry for them.

The work was not difficult, but I had yet to see the ample rations George had promised, and we were missing our regular rations. I wondered who would be claiming our share. About midday General Dow called for a break. We had just finished equipping a squad of one hundred. They were now heading back to the confined area with new uniforms, and the next group had yet to arrive.

Moments later two guards arrived with bags of corn bread and salt pork from the kitchen. We were each issued a large piece of bread and a hefty piece of the salt pork. The provisions were twice what we would have received inside the enclosure, and meat was almost nonexistent inside the pen. Half of the guards sat down beside us to eat; we were receiving the same rations as they were. The rest of the guards remained on watch with fixed bayonets.

"Save half of your salt pork," George said.

"Why is that?" I had already eaten half and the other half of the salt pork was begging to be consumed.

"We're sleeping in a Sibley tent tonight."

George's answer did not make sense, but following his lead had provided me with a new uniform and the best meal I've had in months. There were prospects of similar meals in the coming days. I didn't know how long it would take to disperse all the uniforms, but I expected to eat well until they were gone.

It was well into the evening when we headed back to our Belle Island enclosure. I had a large hunk of salt pork in the pocket of my new uniform and several additional shirts under my arm. It had been a prosperous day. We gathered sticks and anything that we could use for firewood on our way. Firewood was always a premium inside our enclosure.

"What's this about a Sibley tent?" I asked once we were separated from the other men in our work detail.

"I saw two men carried out of a Sibley early this morning," George replied.

Sibleys were conical tents that comfortably housed ten people. They were a luxury within our prison confinement. But having two openings meant little when there are several thousand tent-less individuals competing to fill the vacancies.

"Just how long do you think a vacancy sign on the tent will last?" I asked. "It'll surely be filled by now. Even if it wasn't, what makes you think we'll get it?"

"I talked to them this morning. They'll hold it until tonight. Follow me."

George led me to the north side of the compound where the Rebels had lined up several Sibleys. They must have thought the prison camp would hold hundreds, not thousands. We stopped outside a Sibley that had seen better days. It had several tears, which someone had tried to repair. I had no doubt the tent had been retired from the active military.

"Let me do the talking," George said. I nodded. I didn't know what to say if I were to speak. The tent flaps were tied down, but we could hear talking inside.

"Anyone home?" George asked.

Moments later someone untied the tent flaps and a man stepped out. He eyed our kindling wood and the new clothing under our arms. "Come in," he said. Seven men were lying on the ground with their feet toward the center like spokes of a wheel.

They eyed our extra shirts and firewood. They had a small fireplace in the center of the tent, but it had not been recently used.

"Can you use some firewood?" George asked to open the conversation. He laid his firewood near the fire pit and I did likewise. "We have extra shirts." George and I tossed our extra shirts on the ground. There was a mad scramble. We didn't have enough for everyone. "There will be more tomorrow," George promised.

I was pretty sure we had secured a spot in the tent when we offered the new shirts. If there was any lingering doubt, it evaporated when we produced the salt pork. Our two pieces were quickly cut into eight pieces. It wasn't much but contained salt and provided something to chew besides gritty cornbread. While they were eating our salt pork, George and I claimed the two vacant spots. I was pleased to note they were side by side. No vote was taken. With the promise of more food and clothing tomorrow, no vote was needed.

Most of the men were from Ohio and were taken prisoner during the early days of the Gettysburg campaign. When they arrived at Belle Isle, tents were available for everyone. That quickly changed. They explained a few rules of the tent. All food and personal belongings were shared equally. I questioned if that rule had been created on the spot when they discovered we had access to extra rations. Also, two people must remain on guard in the tent at all times. This was to prevent pillaging by Mosby's raiders. They were a gang of camp degenerates known to steal anything not heavily guarded. Previously, we had nothing to steal and I had not given them much thought.

I hadn't realized how vital a tent was to survival. If the night were similar to previous nights, twenty to twenty-five prisoners would succumb to hypothermia before morning. Our Sibley tent trapped body heat from its ten inhabitants. This might not seem significant, but it was enough to make the nights tolerable. With a small fire from the firewood we had gathered, the tent became nice and toasty. I experienced the best night's sleep since my capture. People need food, clothing, and shelter for survival. I had new clothes, tolerable rations, and now shelter. I wasn't overwhelmed with optimism, but I was beginning to believe I might survive until a general exchange or the war was over..

CHAPTER SEVENTEEN

No work today. It was New Year's Day and an official holiday for the Rebels, but for us such holidays did not exist. One day was the same as the next. I would have preferred dispensing clothing. It would have broken up the monotony of the day, and I would have received a substantial meal by prison standards. That meal could never compare to the New Year's feast Mary would have prepared with ham and sweet potatoes and pumpkin pie. My mouth began to water with the thought of Mary's home-cooked meals. I was not fond of queuing up with the other men for a trifling stick of cornbread and a pint of watered-down bean soup.

I spent the morning hunting gray-backs with my tent-mates. This had become a daily ritual. The ground was covered with the blood-sucking lice; and for the most part, it was a losing battle. Gray-backs hid in the seams of clothing, and would eat us alive if we did not devote several hours each day to digging them out of the seams and destroying them. That was another rule imposed by our tent-mates, but it did little to control the infestation.

We still heard rumors of a general exchange, but no one believed them anymore. We had been disappointed too many times in the past. George and I discussed escaping, which I believe was nearly impossible. Several days ago the Johnny Rebs caught five men with Rebel uniforms. The men were bucked and gagged for an hour twice a day. Those of us who witnessed their agony could feel their pain. I could not force the pain on their faces from my mind, making it difficult to sleep. Bucking and gagging was the severest of punishments. A wooden stick was lodged across a man's mouth and then tied behind his ears. It made swallowing saliva nearly impossible. To add further pain, a rod was placed behind the knees and in front of the elbows. The hands were tied in front of the shins. One hour of bucking and gagging had to be the most dreadful experience, and they were bucked and gagged twice a day.

The ringleader was awarded additional punishment. They hung him by his thumbs after the bucking and gagging. If he stood on his tiptoes he could relieve the pressure on his thumbs, but that caused severe pain in the calves. He begged his friends to kill him. I would need an infallible escape plan before I would risk such punishment.

"You picking up your rations?" George asked. It was almost noon when we normally lined up for our meager rations of cornbread and watery soup. George was already searching for his soup container. I assumed he was in a hurry.

"Can you pick up my rations for me?" I asked. "I want to finish this letter to Mary. Someone needs to stay behind and secure the tent."

"Suit yourself," George replied, "but the soup will get cold."

That was a standing joke. The soup was invariably cold. We considered ourselves privileged if the soup was lukewarm. I gave George my soup cup and he headed out the door with the others. Frederick Deitzman volunteered to remain behind with me. We preferred having two individuals guarding our tent. George and I now had possessions worth stealing. Belle Isle possessed a black market economy where anything could be obtained providing you had possessions of value to trade. George and I were able to trade clothing we smuggled into the pen for two well-worn blankets. Even with our tent for shelter there were cold winter nights when we would not have survived without the blankets.

Deitzman was a recent German immigrant and spoke minimal English. Coming from a German settlement, I was as comfortable with German as I was with English. With our shared German heritage and language, we quickly bonded. Other than George, Deitzman was my closest friend at Belle Isle. I wanted to finish writing my letter and was grateful Deitzman was not in a talkative mood as he usually was. He was busy organizing what few personal items he possessed.

Truce boats frequently sailed between Richmond and Washington. They brought the new uniforms from the U. S. Sanitary Commission that George and I were dispersing. In theory, they also brought care packages and letters from home. I have written Mary many times, but I have yet to receive a reply. I knew other people have received letters from home. Those letters provided the only honest news we received from home. Anyone with a fresh letter immediately became the center of focus, the closer to our homes the better. We asked the recipients to read the letters multiple times until we had them almost memorized. Even though they were not addressed to us, it felt like we had contact with our loved ones back home. Although we heard of care packages reaching Richmond, they never made it into the compound. I was sure the Rebels were getting fat eating our food. In fairness to the Rebels, they were also experiencing hard times. Someone smuggled in a recent copy of the Richmond Inquirer. Bread riots was the featured front-page article. An accusatory finger pointed toward us, suggesting we were eating bread that should feed the citizens of Richmond. If they were to see how little bread we were given, they might alter their viewpoint.

Once we received hams from the United States Sanitary Commission, but the hams were infested with worms, making them worthless. If they had been edible I had no doubt the Rebels would have eaten them. Despite my lack of success, I continued to write Mary. I wanted so badly for her to know I was alive. I didn't know why that was important to me, but it was. It will soon be spring and I should be home preparing to plant crops. If I were presumed dead, which is quite possible, the army would cease sending my wages to Mary. Mary and the children could not survive forever on egg money.

"OPEN THE DOOR!"

I didn't recognize the voice, but the nature of the command suggested it could be Rebel guards. They occasionally shook down tents looking for contraband. If it were Rebel guards, ignoring them was not a viable option.

We normally kept the tent flap buttoned down. The fewer outsiders that saw our possessions the more likely we were to keep them. Deitzman unbuttoned the flaps and flung them to the side. Two men I had never seen before carried George into the tent. Each man had a shoulder under one of George's armpits.

"What happened?" I asked.

George's face was covered with blood. A two-inch cut on his forehead gaped wide enough for me to insert a finger and never touch the sides of the wound. The wound extended down to the skull. I questioned if George were still alive. The two men laid George on the ground.

"They took our food." George was almost in tears. "I tried to stop them, but there were two of them. I'm sorry, Will."

"Don't worry about the food," I replied. "We can survive a day without food. We've done it before. We need to fix you up." To be truthful, I had no idea how to fix him up. I wished Casper were here. He would have known what to do.

"Deitzman, can you fetch some water?" I said in German. "We'll need to wash him up."

Washing the blood off made George more presentable, but it did nothing for the gaping wound on his forehead. Exposed bone was never good.

"I'm sorry, Will. I couldn't stop them. They grabbed me from behind. I couldn't stop them. I'm sorry about your food."

"Will you forget the food? We'll survive."

I had no doubt who "they" were. It had to be Mosby's Raiders. They were a group of cut-throats who robbed, cheated, and sometimes killed without remorse. Most of them were bounty jumpers who enlisted in the army for the bonus with the intention of deserting at first chance. Some had enlisted several times under different names. Occasionally they became prisoners before they could desert. They made poor soldiers and even worse fellow prisoners. We nicknamed their leader after the Rebel guerrilla who likewise has no scruples. Like most of the raiders, the ringleader was from New York City. I was not sure if anyone knew his real name. Sometimes one of the Raiders will take a man's food and eat it in front of him. Since they work in gangs, the man was powerless to stop them.

"George, you have a gaping wound on your forehead. I can see the bone. We need to get you to the hospital."

"No hospital," George replied. "No one returns from that hospital."

I had never been to the hospital, but I had walked past it on my way to the clothing distribution point. It was little more than a large tent west of the trenched enclosure. It was not an impressive structure. What was impressive was the silence around the tent. It was unnerving. I have been around many field hospitals. After a battle the hospitals were anything but quiet. I didn't know which was better—the screaming and wailing during amputations or the silence of the lifeless bodies carried into the Belle Isle Hospital tent. By midday most of the morning admissions were stacked outside the tent waiting burial. The cemetery crew was larger than the hospital staff. It took the burial crew the better part of the day to bury the dead. I could understand George's reluctance.

"It's not going heal by itself. It'll need stitches."

"There's a needle in my canvas bag," George replied. "Stitch it."

"I can't do it. I don't know how." I'm sure George saw the fear in my eyes.

"Will, you watched Casper sew up Toby. My hide's as thick as a mule's hide. Can't be much different from sewing up a horse."

"I'll get the needle and thread." Deitzman began searching George's personal items looking for the canvas bag. He produced the needle and thread moments later.

"You do gut job, ja?" Deitzman gave the needle and thread to me. I had little choice.

I unrolled a good segment of thread from the spool and then bit the thread to sever it. Casper made it look easy, but Casper knew what he was doing. He had done it many times before. I wet the end of the thread with my mouth and proceeded to thread the needle with trembling hands.

"Maybe I should thread the needle." I knew George said it in jest, but I had little doubt he could have threaded the needle faster than I could even with his right eye swollen shut. On the third try the thread slithered into the eye of the needle.

"This may hurt," I said.

"Can't hurt any more than it already does. Get on with it or find me a mirror and I'll do it myself." I was sure there was no mirror in the entire prison camp.

Casper had made his first stitch on the midsection of Toby's laceration to divide the wound and then he continued subdividing the wound until all the edges were touching. He made it look easy. I pushed the needle against the skin near middle of the laceration, but it did not pierce the skin; George's hide was tougher than a mule. I pushed harder and the tip of the needle poked through the underside of the skin. I glanced at George as I pulled the thread through the skin, expecting to see him grimacing with pain. His face was drawn and he was biting down hard, but he offered no complaints. He was probably right; the agony from his beating was more formidable than any discomfort I could produce with a simple needle. I attacked the other side of the wound and then cinched up the stitch before tying it off. The wound already looked better with the midsection closed. I added twelve more sutures before proclaiming the repair adequate. It was not as elegant as what Casper would have done, but the edges were at least touching. With luck it would heal without infection. There was little more we could do for his other wounds. They would heal with time—assuming there were no infections. If we were back in Salem, I would have given him whiskey for the pain. It would be a long night. I offered the use of my blanket, but he refused. George can be stubborn at times, even when in pain.

George was sitting up when I awoke in the morning. His right eye was more swollen than the night before. The skin around the eye, which had been red and angry, was now as black as polished boots. He had a cut on his lower lip that I had not seen before. The lower lip was twice the size of his upper lip. If it weren't for the pain George was feeling I would have found his looks comical.

"I'll bring some extra food back with me after work," I said.

"Won't be necessary," George replied. "I'm coming with you." I looked at him as if he had lost his faculties. The work was not difficult, but he could hardly see.

"You are in no shape to work today. Maybe in a couple of days you'll feel better."

"We both know the job will be gone in two days. I need that job. I'll be working today with or without you. Are you coming with me or am I going alone?" George tried to stand to prove his point and would have fallen backward if I had not caught him. Hopefully his balance would improve as the day progressed.

I guided George toward the tent door. His balance was better than I had anticipated, but he still held my elbow for support. Our work detail was already lining up when we arrived at the gate. Everyone examined George's wounds, but no one ventured a comment. Such things were not discussed in public. To acknowledge the wounds suggested concern. Current wisdom advocated detachment from other people's problems. Most individuals had sufficient problems of their own. This viewpoint was not shared by Lt. Bossieux. He looked at George up and down with particular attention to the facial injuries.

"What happened to you?" he demanded.

George spun a yarn about rescuing the honor of a fair maiden from the lecherous hands of six Rebel soldiers. The story was filled with enough humor that Lt. Bossieux and the Rebel guards who were eavesdropping did not take offense. Everyone knew George was lying, but it soothed the tension. Although Lt. Bossieux had a hot temper he was a fair man. He knew better than to interfere with domestic squabbles inside the confinement. He did honor my request to work beside George. It was my intention to work both assignments periodically to give George a rest, but George would not hear of it. He worked continuously, no doubt in considerable pain.

We did have some excitement in the afternoon. A prison inmate informed Lt. Bossieux that one of his prisoners was a woman in disguise. Bossieux was reluctant to believe the story until she was brought before him. The individual in question was young and without facial hair, similar to many young teenagers in our army. Upon confrontation she admitted her real name was Madame Collier from Tennessee. I had probably seen her many times and never suspected she was a woman. Lt. Bossieux was arranging to have her sent north on the next truce ship. According to Collier there was another woman prisoner at Belle Isle. If there was, she will be difficult to find unless someone turns her in.

Lt. Bossieux was in a quandary concerning the disposition of his female prisoner. He couldn't return her to the compound, and it could be several days before the next truce ship arrived. He decided to shorten our work day until he figured it out. We were to return to our prison confines after our afternoon meal. Bossieux sent several men to the kitchen and they returned with the standard cornbread and rice soup. George consumed the soup, but was unable to eat the cornbread. I feared he may have broken his jaw. I wrapped his cornbread in a sock and placed it in my pocket in case he should change his mind.

One of the sergeants lined us up after we finished eating in preparation for marching us back to the compound. The purpose of the formation was to allow a head count and to frisk us for any stolen goods, although they never patted us down or checked for contraband. Surely, they must have known we were bringing in extra clothing and food for our friends.

"Goodman!"

I turned to see who was accosting me. It was Lt Bossieux. I wasn't even aware he knew me by name. I didn't know what I had done, but I feared the worst. Images of bucking and gagging filled my mind. At least it did not appear George was involved in whatever infraction had been violated. He would never survive bucking and gagging in his current condition.

"You missed mail call while you were working. You have a letter." Bossieux handed me a crumpled letter. I recognized Mary's handwriting on the envelope. She knew I was alive! I stuffed the letter in my pocket for reading back in the tent.

December 21, 1863

Dearest Will,

I hope you are receiving my letters. I write every week but I get no reply. Our congressman says you are alive and a prisoner somewhere in the south, but he does not know where. Please write to me if you can.

Mary Elisabeth is walking everywhere now and is constantly finding mischief to get into. She is also talking more. I taught her to say Daddy when I show her the picture you sent me. I don't know if she understands. The boys miss you terribly. They need their father.

The people at church ask about you every week. I wish I had good news to tell them. We hear from Gottlieb and Casper. They are doing fine. Everyone in Salem is praying that this war will soon end, although it seems to go on forever. Christmas will not be the same without you. If you are alive, I hope you still have the Bible I gave you. It will give you strength when you need it.

Love,

Mary

CHAPTER EIGHTEEN

Mary's letter offered hope. I had been writing faithfully to Mary, but I had to admit I had become discouraged. I was beginning to believe Rebels burned such letters. That was one of the prevailing rumors. But one of Mary's letters made it to Belle Isle. That alone made life in Belle Isle tolerable. I now went to mail call every day yearning for another letter from Mary, but there were so few letters and so many prisoners. Every day I returned empty handed and disappointed. At least Mary knew I was alive, and the government was forwarding my military pay to her. My private's pay was meager, but it would help make life tolerable for Mary and the children. I felt guilty that I was not home plowing the fields and planting corn. I was not the husband and father I had vowed to be when Mary agreed to be my wife.

If my calculations were correct, today should be the third of March. Armies will begin their spring offensives if they have not already done so. Such speculation created many rumors, some plausible and others little more than pipe dreams. During the last several days there has been talk of a military rescue. I personally did not give credence to such reports. I have been disappointed too many times in the past. But these rumors had some support. We heard gunfire and cannons in the distance. That was likely little more than target practicing, but we wanted to believe it was a rescue mission. The Rebels doubled the guard around our perimeter, and men scurried about on the mainland as they improved their fortifications. The Rebels seemed to believe the rescue rumors. There was also a report that we had six hundred guns hidden inside our barricade. That claim sounded too ludicrous to be true. Security was too tight for even the cleverest person to smuggle in a handgun.

Our work detail was cancelled for the day. No prisoners were allowed outside the compound. George claimed that confirmed the rescue rumor. He was always the optimist. I'll believe it when I see men in blue uniforms replacing the guards.

George and Frederick Deitzman were out searching for additional gossip or perhaps starting some gossip of their own. It gave them something to do. Sometimes such speculation was all that kept us alive. It provided hope and without hope we would surely die. Although I was not optimistic that the rescue rumors held merit, I believed one of those fairytales would someday bear fruit, either in the form of a general exchange or the termination of hostilities. One can only hope.

Today's rumor was not without its benefits. Privacy in such crowded quarters was a rare luxury that I seldom enjoyed. This morning I had the tent to myself. The Rebels had been transferring six hundred prisoners a day to Georgia. I was not sure if that was good or bad. Georgia was farther south, making a military rescue nearly impossible. Several members from our tent left two days ago, which provided additional room in our tent. In the past we always had two people in the tent for security reasons. The Raiders would quickly strip an unguarded tent. I had the tent flap tightly buttoned down. If anyone other than our normal tent crew should try to enter, I could simulate an entire squad of people. That would dissuade most sane individuals, not that everyone in the compound was sane. Since George was beaten we never venture outside alone. That has deterred further advances by the Raiders. For the most part, they were a cowardly bunch who were reluctant to confront more than one person.

Except for the scar from the wound I stitched together, all of George's injuries had healed. We may not be so fortunate in the future.

I finished my letter to Mary and was about to check the seams of my shirt for those ubiquitous graybacks when I heard someone undoing the straps to our tent door. I was not expecting George and Deitzman back so soon. I grabbed a large stick we reserved for such purposes.

"Who's there?" If it were an intruder seeking an empty tent, I expected him to run. I was prepared to impersonate multiple hostile inhabitants in case he required additional persuasion.

"Abe Lincoln," came the reply. "I have a friend who wants to meet you."

I recognized George's voice and returned my stick to its secure location. George was always making new friends. That was not unusual, but he wouldn't bring them back to the tent unless he desired to share our tent with them. That would not be a problem; we now had extra room. George finished untying the door flap and stepped inside.

"Will, I want you to meet our new tent-mate." George stepped to the side and allowed his friend to enter the tent.

"Gottlieb! Gottlieb Miller!" I rushed over and gave him a hug. His body was solid and muscular. His clothing was free of tears and holes. He was a symbol of everything we no longer were. I momentarily felt shame in my appearance. I had little flesh on my bones and my clothes were torn and the seams were filled with lice. Still, it was good to see Gottlieb again. I only wished it were under better circumstances.

"What happened?" I asked. "What are you doing here?"

"General Kilpatrick thought he could conquer Richmond with four thousand troopers. Wade Hampton's cavalry thought otherwise. We came to rescue you guys and now we need rescuing."

"Tell us about Salem," George asked. "What's happening back home. Do they know we're alive?" We were so eager for news from home that we momentarily forgot Gottlieb's misfortune. We listened for hours as Gottlieb recounted the details of every letter anyone had ever received from Allegan County. The better stories we had him repeat twice. He inserted additional embellishments on the second narration to the pleasure of his audience.

"How's Casper doing?" He was the only one of the Salem Four still enjoying his freedom.

"He's been in and out of the hospital with his rheumatism. Military life is not suitable for a person his age. They now have him driving teams for the supply train," Gottlieb replied. "He was too old for riding with the cavalry, but he knows how to work a team of horses."

"What about a general exchange?" I asked. "When are we getting out of this hell-hole?" Gottlieb became momentarily silent.

"It's not going to happen," he finally said.

"Why not? They have to exchange us. They can't just leave us here." Gottlieb was not providing the answer we wanted to hear. The compound was constantly filled with rumors, but that was all they were—rumors. Gottlieb knew the truth, and the truth he was telling us hurt.

"All negotiations have come to a halt," Gottlieb replied. "There are several free colored units in the Union Army. The Johnnies are forcing them into slavery when they are captured. That isn't setting well with Lincoln. And some generals think prisoner exchanges only replenish Rebel troops. We either escape or we wait for a rescue."

"Escape is almost impossible and we could be dead by the time we're rescued."

Gottlieb became quiet as the reality of his present situation set in. After four months of captivity, we were little more than skin draped over bone. Gottlieb hadn't mentioned our condition, but he must have noticed. One did not have to reside long on Belle Isle before depression set in.

"No one has escaped?" Gottlieb asked.

"We're on an island. Guards can see anyone trying to swim the river, and the water's cold and the current's strong. I haven't heard of anyone escaping, but I know of many who have died trying." I wished I could be more optimistic, but Gottlieb needed to hear the truth.

"They are sending six hundred prisoners a day to Georgia. That might offer a better chance for escape," George said. "It'll be unlikely that we will be confined on an island. I say we mix with the out-going prisoners tomorrow and see what happens. Can't be any worse than Belle Isle, and it looks like we'll have to go sooner or later."

We talked deep into the night. Gottlieb had so much to tell us, and he had unending questions about Belle Isle. By morning we had agreed to cast our fate to the wind and join the next group leaving for Georgia.

Prisoners were assigned to squads of one hundred men for the purpose of feeding and roll call. Six of these squads were selected for transferring to Georgia. No one seemed to notice that one squad consisted of one hundred and three individuals.

The Rebels marched us under heavy guard across Long Bridge and down one of the side roads until we came to several box cars on a railroad spur. They squeezed us into the third car without food or water. Georgia was a long ways off. Surely they would have to provide water and at least some food.

There was insufficient room for everyone to sit at once in the boxcar. Standing all the way to Georgia was not a pleasant thought. I was beginning to wonder if transferring out of Belle Isle was such a good idea. We were hoping security would be more lax, making an escape more achievable. Instead we were locked in a boxcar without windows.

I looked at my pocket watch and also at Mary. It was a minor miracle that I still had the watch. Whenever I got depressed I opened the watch cover and let Mary stare up at me. She always seemed to be saying, "Will, you can do it. I know you can." It was just ten minutes past nine. I closed the watch and returned it to my pocket.

"See anything?" I asked. Gottlieb had commandeered one of the larger cracks and was monitoring activities outside of our car.

"It looks like they are marching in another squad," he replied.

It was just past noon when the final rail car was loaded. A blast from the train's steam-powered horn signaled our departure. For better or worse, we were leaving Belle Isle. I had mixed feelings. As evil as Belle Isle was, it was a known evil. I feared the unknown in Georgia as vehemently as I feared life at Belle Isle. The train momentarily strained with its load but then gradually pulled forward. The slowness of the rhythmic clickity clack suggested we were not in for a fast ride. The Confederates did not enjoy the best train system and repair parts were not as readily available in the rural south as they were in the industrial north. I wondered if they had an alternative plan should the train break down before we arrived in Georgia.

The combined Salem Three had room for two people to stand and one to sit with legs crossed. We aggressively defended our space against all comers, which was not an easy task. It was currently my turn for the floor space, and I sat with my back against the wall. It was not that my feet were tired, but the floor offered a modicum of privacy. I was not face to face with George and Gottlieb or strangers I had no desire to know. At floor level, conversation was not expected. It offered time to meditate, but my mind was condemned to despondent thoughts. I always had been skeptical about my survival chances, but there had been that flicker of hope. George convinced me of our immortality, that eventually we would go home and live out our lives.

I no longer believed that as I leaned against the boxcar wall. I could no longer see that flicker of light at the end of the tunnel. The light had been extinguished by the passing of too many of my comrades. My health was deteriorating. It was only a matter of time before disease or starvation claimed my soul.

I opened my pocket watch and set it on my thigh. Mary stared up at me with her beautiful eyes. Normally that would be all that was necessary to push aside my melancholy. Today even that was insufficient. "What do you want me to do?" I wanted to say, but Mary just stared back at me. My eyes began to water until several tears overflowed onto my checks. I was thankful I was at ground level where no one would notice my weakness.

I retrieved the German Bible Mary gave me from my pocket. I was fortunate that the Bible was written in German. Since few German speaking immigrants settled in the south, no one found the Bible worth stealing. I carried it openly everywhere. The book was beginning to show wear. The edges of the cover were frayed and some of the pages had been inadvertently dog-eared. I turned to the empty page at the back of the Bible where Mary had written numerous Bible references for me to read. Mary knew her Bible better than I. The references were meaningless to me. I randomly selected Joshua 1:9. After some searching I found the verse. *Have not I commanded thee? Be strong and of a good courage; be not afraid, neither be thou dismayed: for the Lord thy God is with thee whithersoever thou goest.* I closed my eyes and had a long chat with Mary. She became real, and I could rake my fingers through her well combed hair. The touch of her soft skin gave me courage. "You can do it," she said. If I told George or Gottlieb about my conversation, they would assume I was demented. Perhaps I am, but I enjoyed the conversation. I leaned back and lapsed into sleep until Gottlieb awakened me—it was his turn for floor space.

The train stopped next to an open field. My pocket watch suggested it would soon be dark. Two Rebel soldiers open the boxcar door and motioned for us to exit. I stepped out the door and fell to my knees; my legs no longer had the strength to stand. Standing upright in the boxcar for most of the day had taken its toll. I rubbed some circulation into my legs and with help from Gottlieb I managed to stand. I surveyed my surroundings to assess the escape potential. We were surrounded by Rebel soldiers with fixed bayonets. If we were all to charge them at once, some of us would escape, but those who led the charge would be dead. That assessment did not encourage potential leaders. I could not run even if the opportunity were to arise. I followed George and Gottlieb to the center of the Rebel circle and sat down.

"George, it's going to take several days to get to Georgia. I don't think I can last another day standing up. My legs are too weak." There was a time when I could walk an entire day behind a horse and plow. But Mary provided great food and my muscles were strong. Now my lower legs were not much bigger than the wooden spokes on my farm wagon.

"You won't have to stand anymore," George replied. "You can stretch out and snooze the rest of the trip if you want."

George was talking in riddles and I didn't have the energy to pursue his thoughts. There was no way we would have room to sleep unless it was from a sitting position, and there was no guarantee we would have that luxury after we loaded up in the morning.

The Rebels passed out some dried-out cornbread and water. Without the water, the cornbread would have been inedible. We still had our blankets; it was one of the few possessions the Rebels did not confiscate. I wrapped up in the blanket and quickly fell asleep.

When I awoke George and Gottlieb were quietly whispering. I assumed they were discussing escape options. Since there were none, I didn't bother entering their conversation. I was more concerned with the pending train ride. When I told George I could not endure another day standing on my weakened legs, I was providing a realistic assessment of my capabilities; I really didn't believe I could survive another day, although I had never heard of death by prolonged standing.

"We need to be one of the first ones in the box car," George said.

I nodded. I assumed he wanted to secure a spot where we could use the wall as a backrest and reserve as much space as we had the day before. If I could sit, I might survive another day, but the ride to Georgia would take many days. Obtaining room to sit would not always be possible. I rolled up my blanket and prepared for the worst.

Our guards provided us with all the water we could drink plus a piece of cornbread. I assumed this was all we would get until we stopped for the night. It was insufficient to sustain life, but we were on a train bound for Georgia. Suppling food for this many people would have been a challenge even for the Union Army. I ate the cornbread and drank all the water my system could hold. It would be a long day.

"Will, hustle up. We have a train to catch."

I couldn't understand George's enthusiasm. We would all arrive at the same time. Gottlieb also had a bounce to his step, but prison life had yet to wear him down. I picked up my blanket and followed George and Gottlieb toward an empty train car. The Johnnies had not yet ordered us into the cars, but didn't seem to mind when Gottlieb climbed into a vacant box car. He helped George and I climb onto the boxcar's elevated platform. I wasn't sure I could have made it without his help. Other prisoners followed our lead. George and Gottlieb faded to the back of the boxcar. I wasn't sure what strategy George and Gottlieb had devised to secure our small personal area until the boxcar was half full.

"Everyone, push up against the door," George said in not much more than a whisper. Gottlieb gently nudged those in front of him toward the door. It took a moment or two before everyone understood George's plan. Once they did we had prisoners bulging into the doorway. With this many apparent men filling our car, Johnny Reb would have difficulty closing the door. Several times a Rebel would bring ten prisoners to our boxcar in hopes of finding space. Five or six layers of inmates filled the doorway. From ground level our car did look overloaded.

"How many men you got in there," one of the Rebel sergeants asked. He was bombarded with insults suggesting he needed glasses if he couldn't see our car was full.

"Let me get a head count." George began counting imaginary heads from the back row. Once he arrived at an appropriately high number the sergeant moved on. We repeated our maneuver for several other sergeants who could not understand why the prisoners no longer fit in all the cars. They finally gave up in despair and slid our door shut. They had to push against several inmates to get the door closed.

There was considerable rejoicing once the padlock was affixed to the door and the sergeant moved on. Several individuals suggested giving George a field promotion to general. We now had room to walk around and everyone could nap on the floor whenever they felt the urge. With nothing to occupy our time many individuals found sleep a welcome respite from reality. Others hoped to achieve their sleep during the day in case an escape opportunity were to present itself during the night when our guards were less observant. Toward the end of the day, George called a meeting—he was now the consensus leader.

"Do you want extra room again tomorrow?" he asked. There were nods of approval. "It will depend on secrecy. If even one man brags about our ruse, we will have standing room only as we had yesterday."

I pity the man who would divulge our secret. His life would be worthless. We all took vows of silence and agreed to be first to board our boxcar. It was a comfortable ride compared to previous standards. No one revealed our secret, and we enjoyed the fruits of our deception for several days.

CHAPTER NINETEEN

(March 1864)

Trains have a hypnotic rhythm. After five days it was difficult perceiving a world without the incessant clickity-clack of train wheels pounding against track. The sound was now firmly imbedded in my soul. For that reason alone I awoke when the train car ceased producing its signature clatter. Unlike the first four days, we had traveled through the night. A faint glimmer of light filtered through the cracks in the boxcar walls; it was early morning.

"George, Gottlieb, wake up. We've arrived." I not so gently nudged my two sleeping companions with the tip my boot. After a few choice expletives from Gottlieb concerning the virtues of my mother, they grudgingly surrendered to the authority of my toe.

"Where do you think we are?" George asked.

"My best guess would be Georgia," I replied. "I think this is our new home."

It didn't take long for the rest of the boxcar's inhabitants to stir. People peered through various gaps in the walls, moving from one hole to the next, seeking views of our home from different vantage points. I saw little more than tall pine trees waving in the gentle morning breeze. My overflowing bladder trumped thoughts of other activities. If any tree needed watering, I was willing to help it survive.

A confederate soldier removed the padlock from our door and slid the door to the side. "Everyone out," he said. A semicircle of soldiers with fixed bayonets greeted us as we disembarked from our train car. That many soldiers had not accompanied us on the train. I assumed they were permanent garrison soldiers attached to our new prison. Their demeanor did not suggest a willingness to tolerate trivial transgressions, but they did allow me to pay my respects to a nearby white oak. We were then given a large allotment of cornbread and a decent size piece of salt pork. It had been a long time since we received livable food portions.

"I'm beginning to like this prison already," George offered.

"I'll reserve judgement until I inspect our furnished bedrooms and sample the room service," I replied. Gottlieb devoured his meal without comment. He had not experienced sufficient confinement to appreciate the uniqueness of our generous portions.

"Line up in column of fours."

George, Gottlieb, and I lined up three abreast, and a man I vaguely knew from Belle Isle filled in the fourth slot. Once everyone was lined up, a Confederate staff sergeant marched us a quarter mile toward a clearing in the woods. It was a slow walk, since many men found even such a short distance over irregular terrain challenging.

The prison we entered was large by Belle Isle standards. Unlike Belle Isle this prison was designed with us in mind. Square-hewed timbers extending upward sixteen to twenty feet formed the wall. They were so closely placed that even sunlight could not penetrate the cracks between the timbers.

"No one will scale those walls," George said. He was right. The posts were shaved flat. There was not a toe hold or hand grip to be seen.

"If you don't like climbing, you walk out that way." Gottlieb pointed to a side of the prison devoid of walls. The stockade was not finished. Instead of a wall six twelve-pounders pointed ominously toward us. I assumed they were loaded with grape shot.

"I think I'll pass," I replied.

The sun was rising in a cloudless sky suggesting a warm day. I assumed July would be a challenge for a farm boy who was used to Michigan's balmy summers. July was still four months away. Perhaps there would be a general exchange or, even better, an end to the war. One can only hope.

With nothing else to do, we explored our new confines. Unlike Belle Isle, the prison yard was spacious with fewer than two thousand prisoners. A single rail on top of three-foot posts eight paces from the stockade wall extended along the prison perimeter. I assumed this was the dead line. I felt no desire to trespass past this line to test my assumption.

A small stream divided the prison into two sections with the southern section half the size of its counterpart. Both partitions gently sloped toward the stream. Not long ago a pine forest covered the prison. Numerous stumps and brush piles testified to this fact. There was little doubt the harvested logs contributed to our stockade wall.

"Where do you think we should set up camp," George asked. "I don't see any tents."

"This spot looks as good as any," I replied. "We can make our own shelter by tying blankets together."

I had a collection of shoe strings taken from the shoes of the dead at my disposal for binding our blankets. There was a time when I would have considered robbing the dead reprehensible if not barbaric. The months at Belle Isle had seriously altered my sense of decency. Sometimes I wondered if I could live with myself if for some fortuitous reason I were to survive my incarceration. I think not.

"We'll need some wooden poles for the frame," I said.

When the Rebels cleared the area they were only interested in the logs. These were hewed square for the stockade walls. They left the ground littered with pine branches of various sizes.

Gottlieb had in his possession a small pocket knife that he had concealed in his sock upon capture. Once we were in the prison system, no one ever re-checked us for contraband—that was too much work for apathetic prison guards. I don't think any of them enjoyed their work. That was to our advantage. We put Gottlieb's pocket knife to good use.

We cut a total of six four-foot poles to form the inside and outside of our "L" shaped tent. We wanted to embed the lower foot of each pole into the ground for stability, but the ground was hard-packed clay and resisted our attempts to penetrate by hand. George fashioned a make-shift shovel blade at the end of a pole which had a side branch for foot leverage. When stepping down on the side branch we were able to break lose the soil sufficiently that we could then scoop it out by hand.

It didn't provide the privacy or spaciousness of a Sibley tent, but it did protect us from the sun. There was no natural shade within the compound. If need be, we could lower the outside wall of our "L" to form a lean-to. This could be advantageous during a rain storm. If the weather were to turn cold, which was unlikely considering we were moving toward spring in the Deep South, we could remove the blankets and use them as they were intended.

"Anyone for a fire?" It was obviously an irrelevant question. George was already arranging kindling wood in a make-shift fire pit he had created in front of our shelter. We had plenty of firewood, but it was all pine and did not create the cleanest smoke. We didn't care. We sat around the fire and savored the modicum of freedom that our tent and fire provided. We lowered the back side of our shelter, forming a lean-to. Just before dark, we gathered pine boughs to "feather" our nest. They provided a welcome relief from the hard ground we slept on at Belle Isle. I spent one of the most blissful nights since our capture.

I awoke to the sound of a train whistle. Steam locomotives produce a whistle that can be heard for several miles if the wind was right, and we were no more than a quarter mile from the track. I assumed it would become a familiar sound. Gottlieb was busy coaxing the remaining embers into a real fire. All that was missing was a pot of coffee. George was nowhere to be seen.

"Where's George?" I asked.

"He went out to water a tree stump."

"I think I'll do likewise," I replied. I always had a full bladder upon waking. Finding a place to relieve my problem was the first order of business for the day. I had learned from experience to find a distant location so strong urine odors did not drift back to camp.

I discovered we had two new neighbors. John Ransom whom I knew by name only had a lean-to no more than thirty paces from our camp. The other fellow with a lean-to was a big Minnesota Indian by the name of Battese. He was all of six feet tall and held his head high with a bit of nobility. He could easily have been a chief among his own people. I have seen several other Indians back at Belle Isle. For the most part they keep to themselves, but they didn't tolerate any nonsense. Battese and Ransom will make good neighbors.

I found a tree stump suitable for the task at hand. As I relieved myself, the north gate to the compound opened and six hundred new inmates entered the confines. We currently had plenty of space but if a train brought in six hundred new prisoners each day, space would soon be at a premium. The abundant firewood would quickly burn up in smoke.

I finished buttoning up my trousers and headed back toward our camp; we needed to stockpile firewood while we still could. I took a circuitous route back to camp and came upon a man sleeping on the ground. He still had significant flesh on his bones consistent with someone new to the prison system. Perhaps he arrived with Gottlieb. I was about to pass the sleeping man when I noticed dry blood about his nose. I stooped to assess if he were in need of help. I rolled the lifeless man on his side. The back of his skull was caved in as if hit with a large rock. His boots were gone and his pockets empty. The man's death could mean only one thing: The Raiders were also in our new prison!

Andersonville

Camp Sumter was the formal name of Andersonville Prison, but the prison commonly took the name of the nearby town. The 15 foot tall wooden stockade originally enclosed 16.5 acres, but it was later expanded to 26.5 acres. During its 14 months of operation it housed 45,000 prisoners of which 28% died of scurvy, starvation, and dysentery.

A small polluted stream running through the prison provided the water for the 45,000 prisoners.

CHAPTER TWENTY

May 1864

"Your turn." George gave me the half-canteen shell we were using to dig our tunnel. I wasn't optimistic about the project, but it was something to do. Since there were twelve of us working on the project, I didn't spend much time underground. I could think of better ways of dying than being buried alive in a cave in. That danger never bothered George. He held one end of a blanket, and I lowered myself into the vertical shaft. The vertical shaft was six feet deep, but it was still over my head. I crawled down the horizontal tunnel toward the stockade wall. After two weeks we had tunneled no more than eight feet. I did the math; at four feet a week I would be gray haired or bald by the time we made good our escape. I waited until my eyes adjusted to the darkened tunnel. Little light found its way into the tunnel even on the brightest day.

I scraped dirt from the end of the tunnel and pushed it backward. All the dirt had to be passed up to a waiting assistant and then carried down to the river, since any fresh dirt around our hole would give us away. I scooped off another canteen container full of dirt. With luck we might be digging in the correct direction, but what did I know about luck. In the darkness I could not be sure. A small section of the tunnel ceiling fell on the back of my neck, reminding me that I could be digging my grave. The soil was hard-packed sand that normally held up well. The odds of survival were in my favor, but I wasn't always lucky.

Part of me feared the darkness of the tunnel and the threat of a life-extinguishing cave in, but another part of me thought it might be a blessing in disguise. There were over nineteen thousand people confined at Andersonville, trying to live on meals that were not sustainable. Ninety people were dying each day from scurvy or starvation. Two additional prisoners replaced every one that died—life was not going to get better. My joints ached with any movement. My arms and legs were swollen, and my gums were bleeding. I assumed these were signs of scurvy. Unless the war ended soon or we had a general exchange, I would be one of the dead. Was dying in a cave-in all that bad? I scooped more dirt and pushed it back until I could barely wiggle back to the vertical shaft.

"George, you ready for some dirt?"

George stuck his head over the opening and I lifted up a canteen-cover full of dirt. A tarp over our shaft concealed our activity, but we couldn't store much dirt without drawing attention to our efforts. Someone had to carry our dirt down to the river in small quantities. That required more energy than I had to offer.

"I'll carry the dirt down to the river."

I didn't argue with George. He knew I was good for no more than one trip. George was holding up better than Gottlieb or I. He always had more energy than we did. I headed toward our shebang. I don't know where the term came from, but that was what everyone called their shelters.

"Will Goodman, you need a haircut."

"I 'spect you're right, Battese." I replied. "But I have nothing to trade at the moment."

My hair was a foot long. Without a comb, it had become matted and filled with vermin. I was in need of a haircut.

"Sit down. You pay Battese when you can."

John Ransom and the Minnesota Indian had a clothes washing and haircut business. They had no overhead or inventory. They also had little profit. Some people paid with personal items that could be traded for food, but for the most part Ransom and Battese never got paid. I sat down and let Battese cut my hair down to the scalp. I watched my hair fall to the ground. Lice and bugs of every description crawled through the locks of hair. It was disgusting knowing those creatures had been inhabiting the top of my head. I thanked Battese and promised to pay him when I had something of value. He waved me off.

Battese was a survivor. If anyone were to make it out of Andersonville, it would be Battese. He dug up edible roots that no one else knew existed. Sometimes he ate them raw. Other times he steeped the roots into a tea. He had survival reduced to a science.

"Wow, who cut your hair?" Gottlieb asked when I returned to our shebang. I knew the quality of my haircut wouldn't be professional, but I was hoping I didn't look foolish. Gottlieb had more recently joined us. His hair wasn't as long, but I could still see vermin creeping through his matted hair.

"Battese, the Minnesota Indian," I replied. "You should have him cut your hair."

"How do I know he won't scalp me?"

I didn't know if Gottlieb was serious or jesting. There were no Indians in Allegan County, making it difficult to judge their race on merit. I had heard many Indian stories, many of which were too preposterous to consider credible. The Indians I met on Belle Isle were decent folks. If truth were told, I think they were holding up better than white people.

"Battese is a decent man," I replied in his defense. "If he scalps you, it's because you deserve it."

Gottlieb considered my reply and then surveyed the rest of me. A film of sweat-smeared mud and sand covered my body. There was no remedy to my condition short of standing in an all-out thunderstorm. Nineteen thousand people had converted our stream into a cesspool of muck and excrement. Bathing in the river added more filth than it removed. That was the same stream where people obtained their drinking water. Several individuals dug wells, and their well water was in great demand. It sold for whatever trinkets men had for trade.

"If any moderately intelligent Johnnies were to see the dirt you and George wear around camp, they would know you were digging a tunnel. You're lucky there are no moderately intelligent Johnnies."

"You know a better way of escaping this hell-hole?" I asked. It was a trivial question. Escape was almost impossible.

"Have you considered dying?"

"That'll come soon enough." If Gottlieb had a point to this conversation, it wasn't obvious.

"No, not all the way dead, only partially dead." That made even less sense.

"The way I hear it," Gottlieb continued. "Yanks are carrying their buddies out on a stretcher and leaving them among the row of dead. The man plays dead until it gets dark and then he gets up and runs for his life. The Rebels discovered several cases of small-pox. They want nothing to do with dead bodies. I hear men have gotten away by pretending they were dead."

Gottlieb's scheme had merit. My arms and legs were swollen, and I had but little flesh on my bones. I could pass for dead without acting. If more convincing were needed I could die with my mouth open to display my bleeding gums. On the downside, I didn't know how fast or how far I could run. I found walking difficult.

"I picked up today's rations while you and George were playing groundhog. I assumed you would be hungry."

That was an understatement. I was always hungry. George and Gottlieb were the only individuals in camp I trusted to collect my rations. Anyone else would have eaten my share.

"What's on the today's menu?" I didn't know why I asked. It was always cornbread made from the coarsest meal.

"See for yourself." Gottlieb gave me a canteen half containing a piece of cornbread, a piece of raw meat, and a black sticky substance.

"Wow! Must be a holiday in the south." The piece of meat was small and raw, but it was meat. "What is the black stuff?"

"Taste it. I'm assuming you still have taste buds."

I dipped my hand-made wooden spoon into the substance and lifted it to my mouth. I would be happy with anything that offered nourishment. During the months of captivity I had learned to like and eat almost anything. Some of the food I now ate I would not have given to hogs back home, but this was sweat and had a pleasant aroma.

"Molasses!"

Gottlieb just smiled.

"What's the occasion?"

"Beats me," Gottlieb replied. "But don't expect meals like this every day. From what I hear, the Rebs can't feed their own people."

I dipped my spoon into the molasses but before I could raise it to my salivating mouth a large hand reached out to grab my canteen-shell plate.

"I'll take that!"

It was one of the Raiders. He was standing and I was sitting on the ground. That gave him the advantage, but I was not giving up my meal willingly. I kicked him in the knee and he fell backward, grimacing in pain. Two other Raiders pounced on me. One kicked me in the ribs while the second Raider fell to his knees and pounded my head and face. After that my thinking became confused. I remembered Gottlieb joining the fight and our shelter collapsing to the ground. I don't remember how many Raiders there were but there were too many for Gottlieb and me to overpower.

When the fog cleared from my mind, George was wiping the blood from my face with a wet rag. I looked over at Gottlieb; his eyes were almost swollen shut. Battese was mopping the blood from his face. I hoped I didn't look as bad as he did, although the pain suggested I might have received the more brutal beating.

"Can't leave you two for a minute without you guys getting into trouble." George had a cut lip, but I could see no other injuries.

"What happened?"

"As far as I could tell, you and Gottlieb were debating the ownership of your daily rations with six Raiders—you lost the debate."

"Did they get my food?" I don't know why I cared. Several of my teeth were loose and I was no longer hungry.

"You still have the cornbread and raw meat as long as you don't mind a bit of grit with your meal. You can thank your neighbors for that. I kicked the guy who was straddling your chest. His ribs may be broken. Battese had two raiders begging for mercy— they didn't get any. That Indian can best any two raiders in a fair fight. Your other neighbors routed the rest of the raiders."

"They'll be back," I said. "And when they do, there won't be six of them." No one ever got the best of the Raiders. Any victories were fleeting. There were many Raiders. In the end, the Raiders were always victorious. Sensible people willingly surrendered their rations. They didn't suffer from swollen eyes.

"Do you think you two can stay out of trouble if I leave you for a few minutes?" George asked. I need to talk to some people." I nodded in the affirmative, although I would be helpless if the Raiders were to return. It might be selfish on my part, but I resented George leaving us at this time.

My knuckles were sore, but I managed to open my watch so I could see Mary's beautiful face with my good eye. She smiled back at me. It had only been a year and a half, but it seemed like forever since I last held Mary in my arms. I didn't know if I passed out or fell asleep. When I awakened my watch said it was three hours later. Gottlieb was sitting with legs crossed. I could tell his pain was equal to mine. George was repairing our shelter as best he could.

"I wouldn't fall asleep with your watch in your hand if you wish to keep it," he said. I closed the case to my watch and returned it to my pocket.

"Doesn't make much difference. Too many people know I have a watch. The Raiders take what they want," I said. "They'll be back, you know." George just smiled. He was never one to take life seriously. The likelihood of the Raiders returning en masse would install fear in a normal man.

"If they return, they will receive an appropriate welcome, and they'll leave in more haste than they arrived."

"George, you must have been smacked on the head harder than I was. You're making no sense."

"While you and Gottlieb were snoozing I was out organizing. We are now defended by a small army. If any Raider tries to take advantage of someone in our neighborhood, we scream 'Raider' and everyone comes to the aid of the victim. The Raiders have free range only because they are organized and we aren't. That has now changed."

What George was saying made sense. In Salem if a barn caught fire, everyone showed up to fight the fire. We were so lost in our own sorrows that we forgot our neighbors. With my swollen legs and scurvy I could offer little in a fair fight, but who says I had to fight fair. I could still swing a stick at an unsuspecting Raider.

"Just how big is this army? Gottlieb and I will be of little help."

"Battese is an army in himself. He can thrash any two Raiders. He organized all his Indian friends. John Ransom is in on the deal. He has a bunch of friends. All told I think we can mobilize a hundred people if the need should arise. The Raiders are cowards. They'll leave us alone once they discover we're organized."

"Find a couple of clubs and Gottlieb and I will help you out, but you'll have to do most of the fighting from our shelter."

"That isn't actually part of my plan." George paused. His smile was gone. He obviously had additional information to disclose, and it wasn't going to be pleasant.

"George, you might as well spit it out. What's the bad news?"

"I'm going to work outside the walls."

I couldn't believe what I was hearing. The Rebels offered paroles to inmates willing to work for the Confederacy. Few Yankees took the offer. Most of us would rather die than help the Rebels build fortifications. George was the last person I would have suspected to accept such an offer.

"It's not what you think." George knew I was irritated. "I will be working in the bakery making cornbread for our own men. I'll get good meals and if it's anything like Belle Isle, I'll be able to smuggle vegetables to you and Gottlieb. Will, look at you. Your arms and legs are swollen and scurvy is causing your teeth to fall out. You can hardly walk. Gottlieb is not much better. If I don't take this offer I'll be dragging your dead bodies to the gate within a month."

George had his mind made up. Nothing I said would change it. George was stubborn like that. Deep inside, I knew he was right. I had less than a month to live. If George had livable rations he might survive this hellhole. It would be nice if one of our three survived.

"George, remember your promise." George looked confused. "You promised to look after Mary."

"Right now I'm looking after Mary's husband."

George didn't say much after that. He packed what few items he possessed and walked toward the gate. He left his blanket behind. He said the nights were warm and he no longer needed it. His blanket was an essential part of our shelter system, which was the real reason for leaving the blanket. He was making a great sacrifice, but that was typical of George.

Except for a few days here and there, we hadn't been separated since we left Salem. As darkness descended upon us I shed some silent tears. In the distance I could hear the guards in their towers.

"Post number one; ten o'clock and all's well." But it was not well. I cried myself to sleep.

CHAPTER TWENTY-ONE

July 1864

"Your friend sent onions."

Battese laid four small onions on the ground before me. The onions were shriveled and appeared close to rotting. Back home we would have considered them unworthy of human consumption and thrown them to the pigs. George sent vegetables whenever he could, but the quantity was never adequate. Scurvy and starvation were too fierce a foe for an occasional onion to defeat. Gottlieb and I lacked the strength to walk to the gate for the extra rations. We relied on Battese for these errands. He was one of the few men I would trust with food. I would not trust myself under similar circumstances. The Minnesota Indians were more noble than many white men.

"Battese, please take one of the onions." It was not mere gesture on my part. I would have shared an onion, but I knew he would decline.

"George sent the onions for you and your friend. Battese will survive." With that Battese took his leave.

"Gottlieb, wake up. We have food."

Gottlieb now slept most of the day. Perhaps it was nature's way of reducing our need for nourishment. Sleep provided an escape from our prison. We needed the escape even if it was imaginary. I no longer felt a need to live. Each day provided another burden. I looked forward to evening when sleep ended the day. I once thought each day drew us closer to a general exchange or an end to this war. I no longer cared. Even Mary's picture failed to lift my spirits.

"Gottlieb, wake up."

It was debatable which one of us would die first. Sometimes I think Gottlieb was the sicker of the two of us; at other times I felt he had more strength than I. Gottlieb opened his eyes, and I held up the onions.

"George sent us onions."

There was a time when I would have eagerly bitten into the onions like an apple. Thanks to scurvy my gums were swollen, and I had few remaining teeth. I lost two teeth several days ago when I bit into some cornbread. The teeth became embedded in the bread. I have since learned to break off small portions and let my saliva turn the bread into mush before swallowing.

I borrowed Gottlieb's pocket knife and cut the onions into small cubes. Saliva would not soften onions. Gottlieb and I picked up the small pieces one by one and swallowed them like pills. There was no joy in eating. We ate because it was good for us. Whether or not it would be sufficient for us to survive remained in doubt. It took us most of the afternoon to consume the onions.

Some men were more aggressive in their fight for survival. For evening entertainment I watched three men catching low-flying swallows. The men used homemade nets on long poles. Seldom were they successful. Swallows fly too quickly. They did catch a few swallows, which they ate raw before the birds had time to cool. They expended more energy in the project than they received in nourishment.

Late in the evening the heavens opened up with a downpour of rain. Our shelter protected us from the sun but within minutes water began dripping through the fabric. July was hot in Georgia, and I found the rain refreshing. Rain provided a cleansing effect and washed away the filth that accumulated in the camp and purified the air. A good downpour caused the river to swell and flushed out the sewage that accumulated along its banks. River water was always purer after a good rain. I fell asleep to the music of the falling droplets.

✳✳✳

"Are you guys going to sleep all day?"

I opened my eyes and found George scurrying about and making minor repairs to our shelter. He looked relatively healthy. Perhaps he had put on weight. Anyone looked healthy compared to Gottlieb and me.

"What are you doing here?"

"That's not a very friendly welcome." We hadn't seen George for almost two months; of course he was welcome.

"What are you doing inside the walls? I thought you were working in the bakery."

"The Johnnies and I had a difference of opinion. They thought I was involved in a plot to escape."

"And were you?"

"Perhaps."

That did not surprise me. If something were happening, George would be in the thick of it. Part of me was sad that he did not make good his escape, but the selfish part of me rejoiced to have him back. Gottlieb and I were almost helpless. The cords in our legs were beginning to tighten making walking almost impossible. We couldn't count on Battese to care for us all the time. We needed George.

"Did you receive punishment? You don't look any worse for the wear."

"Capt. Wirtz had other pressing matters. Surely you heard what happened?"

I had to admit I had not. I spent most of my days reading the Bible Mary gave me or napping. If George was referring to another general exchange rumor, I was not interested. I had heard them all.

"Yesterday three hundred and fifty new men arrived from West Virginia," George said, not waiting for my reply. "They say the war is going well for the Union, and the end isn't far off. The bad news is the Raiders robbed them of their valuables. The way I heard it, a fight broke out involving hundreds of men. The Raiders still whipped the new men, but the fight scared the bejesus out of Capt. Wirtz. He's letting us organize a police force to take on the Raiders. Wirtz gave us clubs. The group that has been protecting our area is now one of many. Each group has a captain. We're making a list of Raiders, and this afternoon we'll make the arrests."

When George used the word we, he was never figuratively speaking. I had no doubt he would be taking on the Raiders come afternoon. A wooden club rested at his side. I still had my doubts. If three hundred and fifty healthy men from West Virginia received a beating from the Raiders, what chance did men like George have who were not in the best health?

"George, you don't have to do this. They beat your face into mush at Belle Isle. They'll do it again in Andersonville."

"Will, that is why I have to do it. I can take a beating from the Johnnies, but I won't take it from some disgusting excuse for a Union soldier. We have clubs, and we're organized into military companies. We are finally behaving like soldiers. We should have done this long ago."

I knew there was no way I could talk George out of it. There was a part of me that wanted to join him. At Belle Isle I could have helped, but not at Andersonville. The best I could do was watch and cheer them on.

Our shebang sat on the north slope of the enclosure where the land sloped down to the creek that bisected the compound. The land then rose upward on the south side of the creek. That was where the Raiders congregated. From high up on the north slope, Gottlieb and I would have a perfect view of the activities.

George left just before noon. I no longer knew the accuracy of my time piece as I had nothing to compare it with. It could be an hour off and I wouldn't know the difference. I had been resetting it to the sentry's hourly chant, but I no longer cared. Time was meaningless in Andersonville.

I lost sight of George when he joined the crowd. Men were gathering into squads. Each squad had a captain and assigned a raider to arrest. A big fellow called Limber Jim was elected head of our newly formed police force. I don't believe I have met the man. He raised his club and motioned the men forward. I should never have doubted the outcome. Thousands of men armed with clubs surged toward the river like an angry swarm of bees. A spirited fight continued throughout the afternoon. The Rebels fought for their lives, but one by one they were arrested and taken outside the compound where they would be held pending their trial. George returned late in the evening. He was bruised and battered, but I can't remember when he appeared happier.

"We got them," he said. His silly smile looked out of place with the cut lip and swollen eye. If he came out best, I shuddered to think what the other guy must look like.

"What will they do with the men you arrested?"

"They'll be given a trial tomorrow. It'll be a fair trial with a jury of their peers—people from within the prison."

"And you think they will give them a fair trial?" I asked. I really didn't care. They were Raiders. They plundered and killed. I felt no pity for them.

"They made their own beds. They can sleep in them. Tomorrow I'll testify against the two Raiders who beat me at Belle Isle. I wouldn't lose any sleep if they hung the lot of them."

That seemed to be the collective sentiment of Andersonville Prison. For the first time people felt secure—as much as anyone could feel secure in such desolation as Andersonville provides. For a few hours into the evening people ignored their empty stomachs and rejoiced. There was much debate on who should be hanged. There were a few individuals who voiced support for one or two of the Raiders, but they were quickly shouted down.

The following morning several black men carried lumber into the compound. They were not planks but heavy timbers. It took little imagination to determine their purpose. The trials had not yet commenced, and they were already building the gallows. That was what civilized people did. They could execute someone with a bullet to the head or crush his skull with a hammer, but refined individuals needed an elegant method of terminating one's life. A formal procedure for taking a life with trap door, blindfold, and sophisticated noose somehow removed all guilt. It was what separates an execution from murder. The horizontal beam possessed sufficient length to hang ten people at a time if the need were to arise. I had no doubt it would be put to use.

George returned shortly after noon. He appeared exhausted after testifying against the two men who beat him at Belle Isle. The euphoria of the previous day had evaporated. George thrived on action. Verbal arguments at a public trial were not to his liking.

"Did the jury convict the men who beat you?" George gave my question some thought. I had assumed a simple yes or no would have sufficed.

"They'll be bucked and gagged like most of the others. Hardly sufficient punishment if you ask me. But six of the ring leaders will be hanged tomorrow morning."

"Are the Rebels going to hang them inside the compound?" It was a hypothetical question, as I had seen them working on the scaffold all day. Still, it was hard to believe. The Rebels would have more control of the situation if the hanging were held outside the prison.

"The Rebels aren't hanging them. We are. Captain Wirtz made that abundantly clear. He is going to do his imitation of Pontius Pilate washing his hands and turn them over to us for the dirty work. I hear people are drawing straws for the honor of releasing the trap door."

Much as I hated the Raiders, that was one honor I did not wish to hold.

CHAPTER TWENTY-TWO

"They are going to wear out that trap door before they put it to good use."

Gottlieb was right. For the past hour men had repeatedly triggered the trap door on the gallows. I assumed this was out of boredom. The men had a perfectly good gallows and as yet no one willing or unwilling was available to fully explore its worthiness. Six nooses hung from an over-head beam. Each noose possessed the requisite thirteen loops to ensure the condemned bad luck.

Our vantage point on the north slope of the compound provided premium seats to the event. Neither Gottlieb nor I had the strength to participate beyond observation, not that I harbored any desire. George was off working crowd control. The Regulators, as our police force called themselves, wanted the execution to proceed in an orderly fashion. An orderly and elaborate termination of life was what differentiated law abiding citizens from common criminals. That made little difference to me. A bullet to the back of the head achieved the same purpose. Perhaps I was too cynical. The value of human life had meaning at one time. It was a vital commodity worth preserving at all costs. But during the last year I had seen how capriciously one's life could be snuffed out. I was now surrounded by death, and it no longer intimidated me. Barring a miracle I would soon join the dead, and I would do so without remorse. Death had become the ultimate escape. There was a part of me that looked forward to it.

"Do you think they will make speeches?" I asked. I had never been to an execution, but I had heard the condemned were allowed to make finale statements. There was not much they could say that would rectify the horrific transgressions they had committed.

"If they do, no one will listen. Wake me up when the action starts." Gottlieb lay back onto his blanket. He slept the greater portion of each day. Even the pending execution failed to change his routine.

I stayed awake out of morbid curiosity. I knew a few of the condemned. William Collins was the real name of the man we called Col. Mosby. He was from Pennsylvania. I had also encountered Charles Curtiss at Belle Isle. He was from Rhode Island. The other four I knew only by name. They were evil men, but perhaps they were only trying to survive. We all wanted to survive. The difference between us and them was we did not force others to perish so that we might live.

Around ten o'clock Capt. Wirtz and a covey of guards ushered in the six condemned men. The men had their hands tied behind their backs, but they stood tall and defiant. They were too distant to see the expressions on their faces, but I doubt if remorse would have been present in their features. Unlike other prisoners, flesh covered their ribs. This extra nourishment no doubt caused the demise of many comrades.

"Wake up, Gottlieb. It's beginning." I gave Gottlieb a poke and he rose to an elbow. "Wirtz is giving a speech."

Wirtz was too far away for us to clearly hear each word, but he was distancing himself from the hangings. They were convicted by their peers. And their peers were conducting the execution. Wirtz concluded his speech and hastily made his exit. The condemned men were left in the hands of 28,000 enraged Union prisoners. The Regulators wasted no time in marching them up the steps to the scaffold. Charles Curtiss of Rhode Island was the last man to start up the steps. He was a big stout fellow who appeared to be in remarkable shape considering the many deprivations of prison camp. As he took his first step his hands came free. After a short scuffle he broke loose. Someone yelled out that he had a knife. The crowd parted; no one was anxious to take on a man with a knife.

"It's starting to get interesting," Gottlieb suggested.

"He won't get far."

A group of Regulators with clubs were already converging on him. Curtiss made it to the river's edge and began wading through the deep mud. He obviously thought he had friends on the far side. His feet sank deeper into the mud with each step, requiring great effort to extract each foot against the mud's suction power. He made it half way across and then collapsed. He offered no further resistance as the Regulators dragged him back to the scaffold.

"Regulators won that round," Gottlieb said.

The men were lined up on the scaffold and allowed to say a few last words. We were unable to hear them accurately amid the jeers and catcalls. There was nothing they could say that would sway the crowd. Many local citizens, looking for quality entertainment sat on the hillside overlooking the prison. To ensure there was no riot during or following the execution, an artillery battalion pointed numerous cannons in the direction of the festivities.

At around eleven o'clock the condemned men were blindfolded and their legs bound. Nooses were tightened. A Catholic priest read from the 23d Psalm. I questioned how much comfort that provided. People who behaved like the Raiders were not devout Christians. At a signal from one of the men on top of the scaffold, the beam holding up the trap door was kicked loose and the condemned men fell until the nooses broke their fall.

"Did you see that!"

It was hard not to see. One of the men fell all the way to the ground, his rope broken. I believe it was the man we called

Mosby. Even from our distance we could see blood spurting from his mouth and nose. There was little life left in him, but the Regulators decided to hang what life remained in him. They dragged him back up the steps. He revived at the top of the platform and begged for mercy. He got none and was soon swinging on a higher quality rope.

Some of the men died quickly; others died slow and painful deaths. John Sarsfield of the 144th New York died a particularly painful death. He pulled his knees almost to his chest. The veins in his neck appeared ready to burst. Gottlieb and I watched without comment. We felt nothing. We had seen too many painful deaths to find compassion now. I wondered if I could ever return to Salem and resume a normal life. I was no longer the man who married Mary. Perhaps it was best I ended it here. I lay down and closed my eyes. I did not have the strength to watch any longer.

✳✳✳

"I have some water for you and Gottlieb." George passed a canteen-half filled with water to Gottlieb and then gave a second canteen-half of water to me. The water was clear, unlike the stagnant water from the stream.

"This is well water," I said. George nodded.

Several prisoners had dug wells. The wells were deep and the water good, but still in short supply. It takes a lot of water to quench the thirst of twenty-eight thousand prisoners in the heat of July. Water came at a price.

"What did you give for the water?"

"Don't worry about it," George replied.

It had been a rhetorical question on my part. I knew what he had done. Neither Gottlieb nor I could eat our cornbread. Our gums were too swollen and sore from scurvy. We had given the cornbread to George to supplement his insufficient rations. Someone needed to survive Andersonville and return to Salem. The guardian of some well was munching on our cornbread.

George helped me sit up so I could drink the water. I no longer had the strength to do so on my own. My joints were swollen and no longer worked on command. The water tasted good but did little to quench my thirst. The recent weather had been hot and dry. The Georgia sun scorched the land. No sun in Michigan could compete with its wretchedness. I tried to remember when it last rained, but my thoughts of late have been jumbled.

Life at Andersonville was more relaxed since the hangings. The Regulators now patrolled the compound. There was still minor thievery, but seldom any violence. The thieves when caught were tried and provided with appropriate punishment such as bucking and gagging. I no longer feared people would steal my rations, not that I could eat anything less than soup.

"That was good water." I looked toward Gottlieb for confirmation, but he had already drifted off to sleep.

I opened my German Bible and turned to the last page were Mary had penciled in suggested readings. There was no category for pending death, only Fear. But I no longer feared death. Death no longer possessed a sting. Several scriptures were listed with the 23d Psalm at the top where I knew it would be. It was the same passage the Priest had read to the condemned men. My future was no less bleak. I turned to the Psalm.

The Lord is my shepherd; I shall not want. He maketh me to lie down in green pastures; he leadeth me beside the still waters.

I closed my eyes and tried to imagine the green pastures and still waters. I was lying in knee-deep grass with Mary at my side. We were near the edge of a small lake with crystal-blue water. The water was clean and pure, unlike the filth-laden water in our stream. I wanted to drink a beaker of the fresh water, but I knew it was an illusion. I opened my eyes.

He restoreth my soul; he leadeth me in the paths of righteousness for his name's sake.

I knew I had faults, but I tried to live a righteous life.

Yea, though I walk through the valley of the shadow of death, I will fear no evil; for thou art with me; thy rod and thy staff they comfort me.

The Lord could create no greater valley of the shadow of death than what now lay before me. Andersonville had to be created by the devil himself.

Thou preparest a table before me in the presence of mine enemies.

Lord if you prepared the table you could have increased the quantity and variety of the food. I found the last passage depressing and closed the Bible. I closed my eyes and let my mind wander. I relived memories of Mary and the kids and the delicious meals Mary cooked. There was always plenty of food.

"George, remember hunting turkeys before we enlisted? I bagged a turkey and you saw another old tom. We both fired at the turkey. I said I missed and it was your ball that brought the turkey down. I lied. You missed the tom turkey by several feet." I don't know why it was important to I tell George that.

"I always knew that, Will. I never could hit a running turkey. You were the marksman."

"We had some good times together. George, you were the best friend a man could have. It has been an honor knowing you."

"A good friend would not have talked you into enlisting. Will, I am sorry for the mess I got you in."

"George, please don't talk that way. I enlisted of my own free will. You made life in Andersonville bearable. I could not have made it this far without you. I owe you for that. I have one favor to ask."

"What is it? Will, you know I'll do anything for you."

"George, you are a survivor. I don't know how you will do it, but I know you'll survive Andersonville. Will you keep your promise? Will you look after Mary?"

"You know I will."

I took out my pocket watch and looked at Mary for the last time. She smiled back at me as if to say it was okay. I removed the picture from the pocket watch and placed it in my breast pocket, Mary's face against my heart.

"When they bury me, I want to take Mary's picture with me. Don't let them take my shirt."

"You know someone will steal your shirt," George replied.

"Not if you tell people I died of small pox. Scurvy has left blotches on my face. They'll believe it."

George nodded. I knew he was uncomfortable discussing my death. We both knew the time had come.

"Give this Bible to my eldest son. He reads German." The cover was soiled and scratched, hardly a worthy gift to an eldest son. "Tell John the Bible has served me well." I gave the Bible to George using both hands. Even such a small exertion was tiresome. I looked at the watch Mary had given me. It was my sole remaining possession. If the watch was correct, it was two thirty-five in the afternoon. I no longer reset the time to the chorus of evening guards singing out the hour. It could be morning for as far as I knew.

"George, this is for you. I won't need a watch where I am going." I closed the cover to the pocket watch and gave it to George. "Thank you for sticking by me. I know I have been a burden." I could see George's eyes were getting misty. I had never seen him cry before.

I lay back down. I felt no pain. Even the perpetual hunger was held in abeyance. I was at peace with the world. I was ready to accept the next step. My last thoughts were of Mary and the kids romping in the grass. They were smiling and waving at me. Mary was saying it was okay. She understood. Then I closed my eyes.

William E. Goodman, 1838–1864, Grave Number 3863.

Gottlieb Miller, 1844–1864, Grave Number 4144

Headstones

William Goodman's headstone

The bodies of the executed Raiders were buried separately from the main cemetery.

During the night of August 15, 1864 lightning struck the north hillside during a major thunderstorm, causing a bountiful supply of fresh water to gush forth and flow down the hillside. The prisoners declared this marvel a miracle from God and named the fountain Providence Spring. Goodman and Miller died three weeks prior to the thunderstorm and were unable to reap the benefits of this miracle. Providence Spring continues to flow to this day.

State of Michigan

ss

County of Allegan

On this 21st day of November A.D. 1865, personally appeared before me, a Notary Public in and for said County, George W. Thompson who being by me duly sworn doth depose and say that he was well acquainted with William Goodman who was a private in Company I Commanded by Capt. Townsend in the 5th Michigan Regt. Of Cavalry Volunteers. That deponent was a member of the same cavalry and was well acquainted with him in the service up to the time of his death. That this deponent and the said William Goodman were captured by the Rebels at Robinson River, Culpeper County, Virginia on the 10th day of October A.D. 1863 together with others of the same company and were sent as prisoners of war to Andersonville, Georgia on the 4th of March A.D. 1864. That the said Goodman was well at the time of his capture and remained so until about the first of June 1864 at which time he was taken sick with scurvy and diarrhea and was removed to the hospital on the 28th or 30th of June. That at the time of his removal to the hospital he was much reduced in flesh and could not walk or stand up and was carried out by his comrades. That deponent never saw him afterwards but was informed that he died about the 11th of July in the hospital at Andersonville. That there was no commissioned officers belonging to our forces that deponent is aware of that could have been acquainted with the said Goodman. That from his situation when he was carried out of the stockade, deponent has no reason to doubt, but that the report as to his death is true, as he could have lived but a short time.

And deponent further says that he has no interest in any claim for pension in behalf of the Widow of said deceased soldier or in any other claim which she may have against the United States.

George W. Thompson

Sworn to and subscribed before me and I certify that I am not interested in said claim nor concerned in its prosecution. That I believe the affiant to be a credible witness and the person he represents himself to be.

S. ------

Notary Public

Allegan Co, Mich.

EPILOGUE

Prison records reveal William Goodman and Gottlieb Miller (author's great, grand uncle) died from dysentery complicated by starvation and scurvy. The small stream flowing through the compound proved insufficient for 30,000 prisoners, and human waste from the upstream Confederate guard camp polluted the water prior to flowing into the compound. Between rains the water became so stagnant that a stench was noticeable over a mile away. It is little wonder that dysentery was the norm for those confined within the stockade walls.

During the night of August 15, 1864 a miracle occurred. According to reports from eye witnesses, lightning struck the north hillside during a major thunderstorm, causing a bountiful supply of fresh water to gush forth and flow down the hillside. The prisoners declared this marvel a miracle from God and named the fountain Providence Spring. Unfortunately, Goodman and Miller died three weeks prior to the thunderstorm and were unable to reap the benefits of this miracle. Providence Spring continues to flow to this day.

Many Andersonville historians will question the inclusion of John Ransom and Battese in this novel. It is unlikely Goodman knew either one of these men. They were included because the

Native American contribution to the Civil War needs to be told. Native Americans fought on both sides of the conflict with North and South each producing a Native American general. Company K composed of Native Americans from various Michigan tribes obtained notable fame as sharpshooters, and it is claimed members of the unit could hit a five-inch circle at 220 yards.

Battese was an Ojibway Indian from Minnesota who took a particular liking to John Ransom. While white men were starving, Battese was digging up roots to eat. Ransom penned one of the most comprehensive diaries of life at Andersonville, and without the assistance of Battese, Ransom would have died and his diaries would have been lost. *Andersonville Diary* by John Ransom is highly recommended for the more inquisitive reader. From Ransom's diary, it appears Battese survived the war. Unfortunately, Battese must have been a nickname, as there is no civil war or Andersonville record of a Native American named Battese.

George Thompson was the sole survivor of the three incarcerated at Andersonville. Thompson was released on November 20, 1864 and given several months' leave to recover his health. He rejoined his unit on May 19, 1865. The entire 5th Michigan Cavalry Regiment was mustered out at Fort Leavenworth, Kansas on June 23, 1865, but were offered no provisions for returning to Michigan. Many individuals were stranded in Kansas. The Michigan Legislature hastily passed appropriations for their return. Thompson returned to Allegan County where he was instrumental in helping Mary Goodman obtain survivor's benefits. He left Allegan County soon after his return, as he is not listed on any subsequent Allegan County census records.

Mary Slagle Goodman was twenty-four and a mother of three children when William left for the war. Mary Elisabeth who would become the author's Great Grandmother was a mere six-month-old infant. It remains unclear why Goodman left his wife and children to serve in the military. Perhaps he believed the war would be short or maybe he capitulated to patriotic peer pressure. Either way, Mary was as much a victim of the war as William. Life is never easy for a single parent, and farming is not a suitable occupation for a woman. The 1870 census finds Mary Goodman still living on the small farm valued at $24,000 in today's money. She received a widow's pension of eight dollars per month, which was equivalent to $122 in current dollars.

The farm finally proved too much for Mary. In later years she supplemented her pension as a domestic servant. Mary married Gabriel Cole in 1901, but the marriage was not pleasant and ended in divorce four years later. Mary died on May 31, 1915, three days after her 77th birthday. She was buried in the Salem Cemetery in Allegan County, Michigan.

Casper Raab (author's great, great, grand Uncle) was the only one of the foursome who had prior military experience. He served nine years in the Prussian army before migrating to America. He then served in the Mexican American war. Unlike Gottlieb Miller, William Goodman, and George Thompson, Raab was not a young man. Records reveal he was a fifty-one year old widower when he enlisted in 1862. German was Raab's preferred language, which would have drawn him to William Goodman and Gottlieb Miller both of whom spoke German better than English.

Raab listed tailor as his occupation upon enlisting for the Mexican-American War. According to the journal written by Corporal James Avery, Raab put those skills to good use during the Civil War. Uniform pants were cheap and came without pockets. Raab earned extra spending money sewing pockets into regulation trousers.

The cavalry corps was a very demanding branch of the military and better suited for younger men. According to military medical records, Raab was in and out of military hospitals due to severe (rheumatoid?) arthritis. He was eventually re-assigned to the supply train supporting the 5th Michigan Cavalry. Coming from a farming community, Raab would have been good with horses, and driving a supply wagon better suited a man of his age.

Raab was discharged in Washington D.C. on July 11, 1865 and returned to his farm in Salem Township. Raab had six children, most of whom died at an early age. Mary, his oldest daughter, married John Smith while Raab was serving in the Civil war. After the war, Mary and her husband moved in with Raab to keep house and help manage the farm. Mary faithfully cared for her father until his death on February 1, 1893. He is buried in the Salem Township Cemetery.

From this novel and other historical records it would appear southerners were particularly brutal in their treatment of prisoners, and they were. After one hundred and fifty years it is difficult to appreciate the hatred and bitterness that existed between the north and south. Members of both armies plundered and ransacked homes in the towns and cities they conquered, often with the tacit consent of its officers. Prisoners provided the perfect target for venting anger.

In defense of the South it should be noted that many southerners were also starving. While Goodman and Thompson were complaining about rations at Belle Isle, food riots were breaking out in downtown Richmond. Union cavalry destroyed so many bridges and tracks that farmers could not transport produce to the cities.

In the beginning of the war, prisoners were quickly exchanged and long-term incarceration was not needed. This changed when General Grant decided that exchanges were no longer in the North's best interest. Henry Wirtz, the only Confederate executed for war crimes, sent several prisoners to Washington in hopes of resuming prisoner exchanges. The North ignored their pleas.

Prisons in the north were not much better, and they were capable of providing food and shelter. Some historians estimate that between 17 and 23 percent of the prisoners at Camp Douglas near Chicago died from scurvy, hypothermia, and disease. The exact number of deaths was never properly recorded. Fort Douglas encountered the same problem as Andersonville—too many prisoners for the size of the prison camp.

The Civil War has produced deep emotional scars that many people still find painful after multiple generations have lived and died. As the author was wrapping up the first draft of this novel, a "cultural revolution" was running rampant in the country. Self-proclaimed activists were demanding that all Confederate flags, statues, and other remnants of the war be banned or removed. Someday the countryside may be totally "sanitized" and all reminders of the war banished. We will then have lost a vital segment of our heritage. On April 9th, 1865 General Robert E. Lee surrendered to General Ulysses S. Grant at Appomattox. The following day President Lincoln asked the band to play Dixie. It was time to move on.

ABOUT THE AUTHOR

Larry Buege is a retired physician assistant who lives with his wife along the southern shore of Lake Superior. His literary work has won both regional and international awards. He writes in a variety of genres although his Chogan Native American Series is most popular. The Native American Series follows an Ojibway family in the year 100 B.C. (Before Columbus).

LSBuege@aol.com